The Servant of God
Mother M. Angeline Teresa, O.Carm.
(1893-1984)

(Brigid Teresa Mc Crory)
1893-1984)

Daughter of Carmel
Mother to the Aged

*A Critical/Historical Biography
by Jude Mead, C.P.*

**St. Bede's Publications
Petersham, Massachusetts**

St. Bede's Publications
P.O. Box 545
Petersham, MA 01366-0545

97 96 95 94 93 92 91 90   5 4 3 2 1

Imprimatur:
Most Reverend Howard J. Hubbard, D.D.
Bishop of Albany
September 29, 1989
Feast of St. Michael the Archangel

Imprimi Potest:
Very Reverend Columkille Regan, C.P.
Provincial, St. Paul of the Cross Province
October 19, 1989
Feast of St. Paul of the Cross

Cover design: Bruce Crilly

LIBRARY OF CONGRESS CATALOGING-IN-PUBLICATION DATA

Mead, Jude.
    Mother M. Angeline Teresa, O. Carm., 1893-1984 : daughter
of Carmel, mother to the aged : a critical-historical biography /
by Jude Mead.
        p.   cm.
    Includes bibliographical references.
    ISBN 0-932506-79-8
    1. M. Angeline Teresa, (Marie Angeline Teresa), Mother, O.
Carm., 1893-1984. 2. Nuns—United States—Biography. 3. Little
Sisters of the Poor—History. 4. Carmelite Sisters for the Aged
and Infirm—History. I. Title.
BX4315.Z8M43 1990 BX4705.M32 N42 1990
271' .97102—dc20
    [B]
                                                90-32360
                                                CIP

Carmelite Seal

The official Carmelite Shield displays a mountain, three stars, a fiery sword over a crown, and the motto:

With zeal I have been zealous
for the Lord God of Hosts.

This device symbolically expresses both the spirit and history of the Carmelite order. The mountain denotes Mount Carmel, the birthplace of the Order, and for many centuries its home. The mountain also recalls the spirit of contemplation and prayer, proper to Carmel. The fiery sword of Elijah, over Mary's diadem, Carmel's crowning glory, signifies the spirit of zeal for God, and for Our Lady. Prayer and zeal are the double spirit of Elijah, which is the spirit of Carmel. The three stars represent the three human "stars" in the Carmelite firmament: the Blessed Virgin Mary, Elijah, and Elisha.

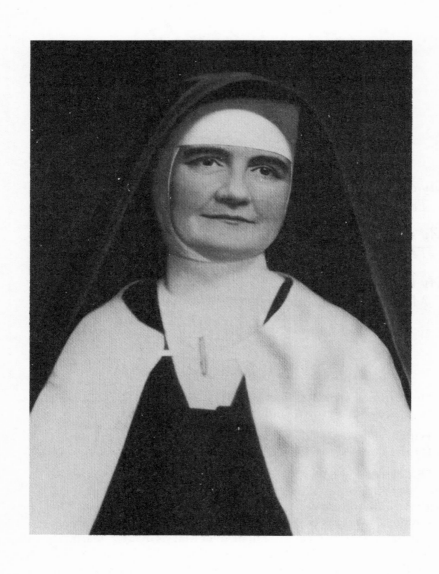

DEDICATION
TO THREE TERESAS

My own mother:
  Teresa Lawless Mead (1893-1966)

My spiritual mother:
  Teresa of Avila (1515-1582)

My beloved mother:
  Mother M. Angeline Teresa, O.Carm. (1893-1984)

Contents

Preface

Bishop Howard J. Hubbard

At a time in which the elderly constitute a large part of our national population, it is indeed fitting that *The Servant of God Mother M. Angeline Teresa. O. Carm. (1893–1984) Daughter of Carmel, Mother to the Aged: A Critical/Historical Biography* authored by Father Jude Mead, C.P., should memorialize and celebrate the extraordinary ministry to the elderly of this foundress of the Carmelite Sisters for the Aged and Infirm. The First Foundation of this congregation was made on September 3, 1929 at St. Elizabeth's Rectory, 4381 Broadway, New York City, which served as their temporary residence.

As Father Mead points out, Mother Angeline's congregation was established during the Great Depression and at a time when many elderly Americans faced especially difficult human and financial crises. The Irish-born foundress, initially a Little Sister of the Poor, was also greatly influenced by the Carmelites. As this biography reveals, her personal charism and spirit combined, in the congregation which she founded, the wonderful heritage of service to the aged exercised by the Little Sisters of the Poor with the contemplative spirit of the Carmelites.

Father Mead's work examines in detail the direction and the effects of Mother Angeline's vision of her community's service to the aged and infirm. From the beginning of this ministry, her vision precluded those aspects of "institutionalization which were depersonalizing and regimentalized," as the biographer notes. What she sought was the provision of a "true home that would respect personal dignity with an emphasis on interested concern for each resident (her term) individually."

This vision of service persists throughout the decades of Mother Angeline's leadership and of her foundation of the many homes for the aged and infirm. The young congregation had its first permanent location at 66 Van Cortlandt Park South in the Bronx where they began their residence on September 29. 1931. Along the decades that followed. Mother Angeline established fifty-nine foundations for the care of the elderly.

The paths of the Carmelite Sisters for the Aged and Infirm and of the Diocese of Albany crossed in a significant way when Bishop Edmund F. Gibbons expressed his approval of acquisition of property by the Carmelite Sisters in the Village of Tivoli, Town of Clermont, Germantown, in Columbia County. The community had moved into this new home by January 13, 1947 and before long it was known as Avila on Hudson.

This biography delineates a living portrait of a remarkable woman who in our twentieth century exercised vigorous faith and leadership and unfailing reverence for the human dignity and individual needs of the elderly in the numerous foundations that grew from her initial vision and charism.

In a homily delivered at the Golden Jubilee Celebration for Mother Angeline Teresa, the then Msgr. Terence Cooke observed: "Mother Angeline was decades before her time in the dreams she had of ways and means to preserve the spirit of independence of the elderly who need care." Her insistence upon this key dimension of service to the aged and infirm presents a vigorous challenge to us on the threshold of the closing decade of the twentieth century as we confront the plight of those elderly in our country who suffer from loneliness, neglect, dehumanization, and fear.

Aeschylus, one of the major creators of Greek tragedy, believed that "Pain begets wisdom." Mother Angeline's biographer gives appropriate attention to the many trials, misunderstandings, accusations, and formidable hurdles that confronted this undaunted and wise woman during the productive and memorable decades of her leadership and service on behalf of the elderly and infirm.

The Most Reverend Edward D. Head, Bishop of Buffalo, at a Memorial Mass for Mother Angeline at St. Patrick's Cathedral in New York City, spoke of the "special American insight and lively spirit" of the congregation founded by her and observed that "its special genius was the manner in which it challenged men and women to live their later years in dignity and in independence." He viewed Mother Angeline and her sisters "as trail-blazing pioneers in the field of modern geriatrics."

Father Mead's biography concludes with a chapter devoted to Mother Angeline's "Reputation for Sanctity" and to continuing efforts since her death toward a Cause for Canonization for this foundress who now bears the title of Servant of God. The Appendices and Bibliography reflect the careful and significant research of Father Jude Mead that underlies the text of his *Critical/Historical Biography*.

I commend Father Mead for his contribution to the life and the mission of the Church through this biography of the foundress of the Carmelite Sisters for the Aged and Infirm and through the light that this work throws on the quality of care and support needed for many aged persons as we draw near the last decade of our twentieth century.

Howard J. Hubbard, D.D.
Bishop of Albany

Feast of Nativity of Mary
September 8, 1989

ACKNOWLEDGMENTS

After three years and three months, I have laid down my pen. Actually I have returned my portable Smith-Corona Classic 12 manual typewriter to its gun metal case. It was a personal gift to me from herself, Mother M. Angeline Teresa, O.Carm., in 1976 when I returned from the doctoral program in Spiritual Theology I undertook at the *Teresianum*, Rome, where I had gone for post Vatican II recycling. I made the mistake of telling Mother Angeline that I had left my own typewriter behind for one of my brethren who needed it more than I. Within days I had this one.

I shared my Passionist preaching apostolate for the first time with the Carmelite Sisters for the Aged and Infirm in preparation for the feast of the Immaculate Conception, December 8, 1950 at Mount Carmel Home, Manchester, New Hampshire where Mother M. Colette, O.Carm., one of Mother Angeline Teresa's first companions, was the Superior. After preaching in other homes I met Mother M. Angeline Teresa, O.Carm. some twelve years later. On my return to our Boston Monastery I told my brethren that I had met the first person in my life whom I thought would be canonized. From this meeting there arose a unique relationship of mutual respect, intuitive understanding and complete trust which matured throughout the next quarter century.

Less than a month before her death I visited Mother Angeline at the Avila Motherhouse before departing for Peru. To my delight she spontaneously recognized me and called me by name.

The writing of this book was a labor of love. It was not without its own excitments as when the hotel in Glasgow caught fire in the wee hours of the morning. With klaxsons keening we were forced to evacuate. I left both my wallet and passport to possible conflagration but crushed to my chest the notes for this book as I came down the fire escape.

Now I have at hand the most rewarding chore of authorship, i.e., to acknowledge so much support and assistance from so many. In the first place, those who gave me the commission to author this critical historical biography of the Servant of God, Mother M. Angeline Teresa (McCrory), O.Carm. on June 6, 1984, and who subsequently supplied me with credentials duly presented at home from the Atlantic to the Pacific and abroad in Ireland, Scotland, France, Italy and the Vatican City State: Mother M. Michael Rosarie, O.Carm. and the General Council of the Carmelite Sisters for the Aged and Infirm, urged on by the late Father Eugene Robitaille, SS.CC.; to the Most Reverend Howard J. Hubbard, D.D., Bishop of Albany, New York; the Very Reverend Columkille Regan, C.P., my Provincial Superior; the Most Reverend John Malley, O.Carm., Prior General of the Carmelites of the Ancient Observance at Rome, and the Very Reverend Redemptus M. Valabek, the Postulator General of the same Order.

I also express my deep gratitude to the Carmelite Sisters, especially those at Avila Motherhouse viz. Sister M. Bernadette de Lourdes, O.Carm., Mother Angeline's first biographer, who, with Sister M. Elias, O.Carm. are the unique survivors of the second novitiate group and living witnesses of events from the outset; Sister Mary Gabriel, O.Carm., Treasurer General of the Carmelite Sisters and close associate of Mother Angeline whose devotion and love toward the Foundress in her declining years is legendary; Sister M. Adelaide Therese, O.Carm., General Archivist; Sister Jacinta Mary, O.Carm., General Councilor and Director of the Teresian Library, who made available to me both Carmelite and Gerontological resources; the indefatigable Sister Mary Suzanne, O.Carm., Secretary General and Sister M. Veronica Robert, O.Carm., who together typed and retyped this manuscript over and over again and finally transferred the text to computer disks; also Sister Matthew James, O.Carm., who chauffeured me literally hundreds of miles for research throughout New York State and New England often at sizeable personal sacrifice.

I am likewise indebted to the twenty-nine Sisters who graciously responded to my request early on for their personal *Recollections of the First Decade* (1929–1939) and scores of other Sisters who by personal interviews, phone calls and letters came to my assistance as requested when precise information was solicited.

The author further expresses a debt of sincere gratitude for documentary data obtained through personal visits to the following archives and chanceries: The Congregation for Institutes of Consecrated Life and for Societies of Apostolic Life at Rome through the kind cooperation of Most Reverend Archbishop Vincenzo Fagiolo, Secretary; Msgr. Joseph A. Galante, Undersecretary; and Sister Basilisa, A.C.I., archivist; the Archdioceses of Baltimore, Boston, Chicago, Cincinnati, where the Reverend Jerry Hiland and his archives staff continued to research after my visit and repeatedly sent me their findings; Dublin (Ireland), Miami, New York, where the gracious archivist Sister Marguerita Smith, O.P., of the Archdiocesan Archives at the Dunwoodie Seminary showed such courtesy at the time of my visit and her multiple competent and efficient follow-up mailings; Philadelphia, Seattle and Washington, D.C.; to the Dioceses of Albany, Altoona, Argyll and the Isles (Scotland), Bridgeport, Brooklyn, Columbus, Covington, Davenport, Fall River, Harrisburg, Joliet, Manchester, Palm Beach, Providence, St. Augustine, St. Petersburg and St. Leo's Abbey, Scranton, Syracuse, Trenton, Wheeling-Charlotte and Youngstown. Moreover, I was received with exquisite charity by Mother Marie Antoinette, L.S.P. and the Little Sisters of the Poor at their Motherhouse, La Tour St. Joseph, Pern, France.

Nor could I omit the gracious librarians who assisted me at the Library of Congress, the Catholic University of America, St. Joseph Seminary, Queensborough Public Library, the Passionist Monastic Seminary Library and the Teresian Library. Across the seas at Trinity College Library, Dublin, Ireland; the National Library of Scotland at Edinburgh; and at Rome, the Pontifical Scots College Library, the Pontifical Irish College Library, and the Library of the International Carmelite College of St. Albert.

I am also in debt for the valued guidance received from Monsignor Robert J. Sarno, J.C.D. of the Congregation for Sainthood Causes; Reverend Peter Gumpel, S.J. of the Office of the General Postulation of the Society of Jesus, Rome, and Brother James Johnson, C.P., M.L.I.S., for his scholarly research in newspapers.

Finally, I make my thanks to countless priests, Sisters and laity who supported me by their concerned and loving prayers during the past triennium in "my journeyings often, perils in the city, toil and hardship, through many a sleepless night" (cf.II Cor.11,26) as we sought to spread the Glory of God through the knowledge of the life and virtues of His servant, Mother M. Angeline Teresa (McCrory) O.Carm . . . Daughter of Carmel and Mother to the Aged.

Father Jude Mead, C.P.
Triumph of the Cross
September 14, 1989.

IRELAND

It has been said before that there are really two Irelands. There is the actual geographical place with its mind-boggling contradictions. Here is its physical beauty at once verdant and watered with crystal lakes and streams elsewhere seaswept, craggy and barren. A land of wealth and shocking poverty. A chair of soaring scholarship and demeaning ignorance. A haven of peace sundered by internal strife. A cradle for lofty saints and arrogant sinners. Mountains and meadow. Light and shadow. All this is Ireland.

Then there is that other Ireland. It lives in the minds and hearts not only of those who have loved and left her but their children's children who have never seen her. This is the Ireland of figment and fancy, of legend and illusion. In truth, it has become a lover's memory. It has forgotten all the harsh and galling things and places and people. It conjures up only the softness of yielding mists, of gentle rains, of subtle lights, of gracious living and of tender loving. It purges violence from its history and recalls only the good and the beautiful. Few would return to the real Ireland while myriads live with the mystical Ireland in their hearts.

The Black Water River tumbling down green hills and spreading out through the brown bogs finally spills into the lower basin of Lough Neagh, Ireland's largest inland lake. It has become the boundary between County Armagh to the south and County Tyrone to the north although both counties are in Northern Ireland. Here among the lower reaches of the lake in a tranquil rural setting lies the village of Mountjoy. For centuries Catholics driven down from their ancestral homes on the hills and fertile uplands have laboriously earned their livelihood in this region from their sparse littoral fields and fishing skills. Even today, the daily parish Mass is set for nine in the morning so that these fishermen, out on the lake hours before dawn to net their fish, may have the opportunity to attend.

Into this contrasting culture and great natural beauty Brigid Teresa McCrory was born on January 21, 1893. The future Mother M. Angeline Teresa, O.Carm. was a perfectly formed child, with large brown eyes and a flawless complexion. According to the ecclesiasti-

1

cal records of St. Brigid's Chapel, as Catholic Churches were then designated, little Brigid was baptized on January 22nd, 1893 the very day after she was born.[1] This was the common practice of the time. Oddly enough the date of her birth was omitted. The civil record erroneously gives her birth date as January 19.[2] The McCrory family always celebrated Brigid's birthday on January 21st. Throughout her life, Mother Angeline Teresa, O.Carm. delighted to tell that she was born on the feast of St. Agnes, the Roman virgin and martyr, God's own little lamb.

The sponsors at the christening were Sarah O'Neill, the O'Neills were relatives, and singularly enough a priest, Father John Keenan, C.C.[3] This designation, Catholic Curate, is still in use today. It is more than a coincidence, that one who through the rest of her life had such an outstanding reverence, love and appreciation for the priesthood, including the formation of a crusade of prayer for priests, would have at her side along with the priest administering the sacrament of baptism, yet another priest as her godfather. And ninety-one years later when she would give back her soul to God, full of years and full of virtue, she would have at her side three priests.

Although the little parish church of St. Brigid had been remodelled in 1939 and again,to conform to the liturgical requirements coming out of Vatican II, the original baptismal font still stands in the back of the church as a mute witness to the salvific event of Brigid McCrory's baptism.

The McCrory family was long part of the local history of the area. Solid landowners and staunch Catholics they peopled this region of Northern Ireland in the Province of Ulster, in the district of Dungannon, especially in the vicinity of Coalisland and Mountjoy (Brockagh). A relic of their once extensive holdings remains in the name of a rolling knoll called McCrory's Hill. About 1600 this homestead was taken over by the British. The family was forced down to the less arable area by the lake. Sir Charles Blount, the eighth Baron Mountjoy, had been granted a large tract of Dungannon land for his estate. When he arrived from England he erected Mountjoy Castle in 1603. Its ruins still stand and it has been marked officially as a national monument.

Brigid McCrory's both parents came from farming families in the neighborhood. Her father, Thomas McCrory, lived in Upper Back where he had a house and farm in which Brigid was later born. Her mother, Brigid Taggart, came from Magheralamfield further up the shore of Lough Neagh. They married Februrary 5, 1890 in St. Brigid's Chapel. Besides the church records the civil register of the district of

Coalisland notes that the witnesses were Patrick O'Neill and Mary Hughes.

Over the years this faithful Catholic couple were blessed with five children. Again the records of St. Brigid's church detail their baptisms and sponsors:

> July 7, 1891. Elizabeth, daughter of Thomas McCrory and Brigid Taggart McCrory, godparents Authur McCrory and Elizabeth Hughes. January 22, 1893. Brigid, daughter of Thomas McCrory and Brigid Taggart McCrory, godparents Rev. John Keenan, Catholic Curate, and Sarah O'Neill. December 14, 1895, Owen, son of Thomas McCrory and Brigid Taggart McCrory, godparents John and Annie Conaghy. March 5, 1898, Anna, daughter of Thomas McCrory and Brigid Taggart McCrory, godparents James McGuirk and Johanna (Jane) McGuirk.[4] The last child, James, son of Thomas McCrory and Brigid Taggart McCrory was baptized December 4, 1900 in St. Francis Xavier Church in Scotland with Peter Flood and Mary Flood as godparents.

The little parish church of St. Brigid at Mountjoy was the center for the devotional and sacramental life of the McCrory family. In Ireland, not infrequently, a parish embraces a large territory. As a result the pastor and the curates do not always live in the same house, as is the American practice, but have a residence close to one of the several churches in the parish. St. Brigid's is one of these. It is part of the larger parish of St. Patrick in Clonoe where official records are kept but has its own priest and rectory. St. Brigid's is in the Archdiocese of Armagh which includes both sides of the Black Water River with the counties of Armagh and Tyrone.

The well kept parish cemetery which surrounds St. Brigid's Church is the resting place of Brigid's paternal grandparents, Eliza McCrory who died in 1889 and Owen McCrory who died in 1901.

Brigid was born in the family homestead surrounded by its sizeable farm in Upper Back where she spent the early years of her childhood. This house somewhat modernized still stands today near the shores of Lough Neagh and a cousin, Eugene "Des" McConnaghy, the last of the McCrory family in Mountjoy, makes his home there.

In November 1897 Brigid was enrolled in the little parish school in Mountjoy adjacent to the church.[5] It had been built and in use since 1840. It was a white-washed masonry building consisting of two rooms and was taught by one lay teacher. The curriculum was basic and elementary, the three R's plus the most important subject of all, religion called then Christian Doctrine. The text used at this time was a children's abridgement of *"The Catechism of Christian Doctrine"*, by Reverend Andrew Dunleavy, LL.D. It was commonly called the *Maynooth Catechism* or *Dunleavy's Irish Catechism*. Its twofold purpose of keeping alive both the Faith and the Irish language clearly manifested itself in the printing, the left side page in Irish, the right hand page in English. The quintessence of its method and content is revealed in the following entry:

Q. What are the principle articles of the Christian Doctrine which we are obliged to know punctually?

A. The mysteries of faith, which are contained in the Creed of the Apostles; the Commandments of God and the Church; the things which regard the Sacraments that we are bound to receive, together with the dispositions for receiving them; the Lord's Prayer, and the particular duties of our profession, trade or calling.[6]

In the year 1901 there were 636,777 pupils in the primary grade school system in Ireland of whom 471,910 were in Catholic sponsored education facilities.[7]

Little Brigid, now Bridget, loved school and demonstrated both a keen mind and a retentive memory. The long walk to school along narrow country roads, made most often on foot, never seemed to be a burden to her as she reached out for knowledge. Beyond her registration, there are no surviving records from her school days but her never to be forgotten recollections of that happy time have been recorded in her personal notes of later years and some treasured conversations.

One such retrospect of her childhood was made in an interview with Kay Leen, a feature writer for the then *Catholic News* of New York, at the time of the Silver Jubilee of the Congregation of the Carmelite Sisters for the Aged and Infirm in 1954. Mother Angeline Teresa was questioned about her special vocation for the care of the elderly. She responded: "I guess that first of all it was my close association with my 82 year old grandfather in County Tyrone on Lough Neagh's banks in Northern Ireland where I was born."[8] This, of course, would have been her maternal grandfather Taggert.

As recently as 1987 the indestructible old schoolhouse was extended with a new wing. This has become the parish center for the youth of the area. Thus modernized it houses sports equipment, meeting and shower rooms, and an attractive snack bar. Meanwhile an entirely new and modern parish school has been built on a pleasant site with ample playing fields some distance from the original parish plant.

The untroubled years of this happy childhood underwent an abrupt change when Thomas McCrory faced with grave financial difficulties bravely decided to follow the example of so many of his closest friends and emigrate to Scotland with his wife Brigid and their then four children.

These were the days, both sad and bad, when the Catholic populace was still persecuted for their religious beliefs and discriminated against in employment practices and even in the prices given them for their agricultural products and marketing their freshly caught fish. All this despite the repeal of the so-called Penal Laws in 1829. The statistics of the period give mute and devastating witness to the despoliation of Ireland and her people at the time. In the fifty years between 1851 and 1901 nearly three and a half million (3,486,393) persons emigrated from their homeland.[9] Most of these went to the United States, Great Britain, Canada and Australia. Eighty-two percent of these were between the ages of 15 to 35 years old.[10] The core of Ireland's able bodied work force took her and their own futures with them. Another appalling statistic was that the great majority of these emigrants were Catholics. The little McCrory family was caught up in this second diaspora.

The following excerpt written by a priest, who was taken from Ireland as a boy, was discovered almost as this book went to press and adds a personal perspective to soulless statistics.

Homes in Ireland

The secluded cottage, set in its wealth of green fields and flowering hedges, is now distinctly before the eye of the soul, with the calm little lake near at hand, and the hills rising beyond and sloping away to where one gigantic form towered in mid-air, its top crowned with some ruin of far-off ages, and at its foot a cluster of villages nestling, as if the generations which once peopled them had found protection in now ruined stronghold. There was, just where the lake ended, and a young brook ran wildly out, and ancient mill, which still did service to farmers for many a mile around; while at the opposite end the ivy covered wall of the ancient abbey or parish church lifted itself above the silver mirror of the lake, and around the ruin slept untold generations of men and women who had 'kept the faith', and whose descendants still wished to rest by the side of their parents till the final wakening.[11]

We know not what change the hand of time has made in this scene thus indelibly stamped on heart and memory. Famine has been busy there also with fever always following in the train of famine; and many a ship like that which bore away the writer well-nigh fifty years ago, has sailed from the glorious neighboring bay crowded with the sorrowing but hopeful men and women who followed across the deep in the track of the westering sun![12]

What is the purpose of this narration? This: to show that famiies who boast,—albeit only the families of the laboring poor,—their descent from this ancient stock of believers, must not allow the most precious and venerable traditions of their former home, the home of their fathers, to be lost in the homes they create for their dear ones in another land.[13]

This, then, is what we would impress on the minds and hearts of our readers, that the new home in America, in Australia, in Africa, in Asia, wherever the dividing wave may have cast the exiles,—should be more Christian, more supernatural, more lovely, than the homes on the banks of the Shannon or the Moy, on the shores of Loch Corrib or Loch [sic] Neagh."[14]

Against this troubled background Thomas McCrory opted for Scotland. It was close at hand both physically and culturally. It was not so expensive for his limited finances. Some of his neighbors and relatives had preceded him and had settled in quite readily. It was also possible for him to send his children back to the lakeside farm during the summer holidays. Towards the end of summer 1901 after a tearful but hopeful farewell Thomas McCrory, his valiant wife Bridget, with their children, Elizabeth, Bridget, Owen, and Anna barely a toddler, left Ireland to begin a new life in Scotland. Their future was uncertain but their faith was deeply rooted. Through this faith they placed themselves in the hands of God, accepting His Will whatever it entailed.

NOTES

[1] *Certificate of Baptism.* Brigid McCrory. January 22, 1893. Official Transfer. St. Patrick's Church, Clonoe, Co. Tyrone. Extract from *Register of Baptism* of above Church. Signed and sealed by Rev. Patrick J. Collins, P.P. 25 September 1948.

[2] January 19, 1894. NB incorrect day and year! William M. Griffin, Superintendent Registrar of Births, Deaths and Marriages. District of Dungannon, copy 3 February 1912. Excerpt Entry No. 103. Coalisland, County of Tyrone. Bridget (not Brigid) Indication her father could not write—*His mark* over signature. Based on this official record all Mother Angeline's future documents, passport, entrance into Little Sisters, etc. give her name as Bridget and her date of birth as January 19 with year 1893.

[3] Certificate of Baptism, Cf.note (1) ut supra.

[4] cf. *Register of Baptisms*, St. Patrick's Church, Clonoe, Co. Tyrone. 1893–1898.

[5] *Record Book Mountjoy School.* "November, 1987. Registration No. 421 Bridget McCrory. Last birthday 3 years old. Roman Catholic. (RC) Residence, Mountjoy. Occupation of parents. Farmer." (She was actually 4 but the erroneous civil record only was accepted.) From this point onward she was taught to write her name as Bridget.

[6] Dunleavy, Rev. Andrew, LL.D. *The Catechism of Christian Doctrine,* published for the Royal Catholic College of St. Patrick,Maynooth. James Duffy, 10 Wellington Quay, 1848. Abridgements suitable for children p.xx. Citation p. 37. Library, Pontifical Irish College, Rome.

[7] Catholic Encyclopedia, Robert Appleton Co., N.Y., N.Y. 1910 Vol. VIII. art. *Ireland*, E.A. Dalton, Athenry, Ireland. p. 114.

[8] Leen, Kay. *Interview with Mother Angeline Teresa.* Catholic News, N.Y. October 27, 1954. On occasion of 25th Anniversary of Foundation of Carmelite Sisters for the Aged and Infirm.

[9] E.A. Dalton, *op. cit.* p. 114.

[10] *Ibid.*

[11] O'Reilly, Rev. Bernard, L.D. (Laval) *The Mirror of True Womanhood.* 17th Ed. P.J. Kenedy, 5 Barclay St., N.Y. 1892. p. 172.

[12] O'Reilly, *op. cit.* p. 173.

[13] O'Reilly, *op. cit.* p. 176.

[14] *Ibid.*

SCOTLAND

Perhaps the most compelling reason for the McCrory family's immigrating to Scotland was Thomas McCrory's need for employment seeking as he was in the hope of work and a just day's pay. His lodestar was the Clydesdale Steel Works which employed a great number of Irish emigres who had already arrived and were settled in before him. This spreading plant had mushroomed just outside the city of Glasgow along the Clyde River. The transported family was able to take up residence in one of the stone row houses originally built for miners in Carfin village, Motherwell.[1]

Just after their arrival that autumn all four children were brought down in a measles' epidemic. Little Anna, aged three, did not recover but went into pneumonia and died.[2] All were devastated by such a dreadful tragedy at the very outset of this drastic move undertaken to improve the young family's condition. Bridget and her sister Elizabeth recovered in time to attend the newly erected parochial school of St. Francis Xavier completed in 1897. (At this time both mother and daughter changed from the Irish way of spelling Brigid to Bridget. This new spelling appears on school records and legal documents hereafter.) Miss Mary Jane Meechant was the Head Mistress.[3] Still in use was the old Chapel School built in 1863. This later became Little Flower Hall and is still standing. Miss Mary Rodgers and her sister Miss Elizabeth Rodgers were assistant teachers in the school.[4] There were 400 children enrolled in the school at that time.[5]

Just before the ceremony of confirmation was to take place a competition was held among the confirmation class. A prize was offered for the first student who would be able to recite from memory what was then called "The Last Gospel", the Prologue to St. John's Gospel verses 1 through 12. It was expected that one ginger headed lad would be the champion but instead the chestnut haired Bridget McCrory aged ten first recited the piece perfectly from memory at a rapid fire pace and won the medal. The actual text which she committed to memory was that found in the Douay Version approved in 1901 for use in Scotland:

In the beginning was the Word, and the Word was with God and the Word was God.

The same was in the beginning with God.

All things were made by him; and without him was made nothing that was made.

In him was life, and the life was the light of men.

And the light shineth in darkness, and the darkness did not comprehend it.

There was a man sent by God, whose name was John.

This man came for a witness to give testimony of the light, that all men might believe through him.

He was not the light, but was to give testimony of the light.

That was the true light, which enlighteneth every man that cometh into this world.

He was in the world and the world was made by him, and the world knew him not.

He came unto his own and his own received him not.

But as many as received him, he gave them the power to be made the sons of God to them that believe in his name.

Who are born, not of blood, nor of the will of the flesh, nor of the will of man, but of God.

AND THE WORD WAS MADE FLESH, [*here she devoutly genuflected*] and dwelt among us; and we saw his glory as it were of the only-begotten Son of the Father, full of grace and truth.[6]

Even in her latter years Mother Angeline Teresa could still recite this Gospel passage from St. John and impishly smile when she related the incident.

The parish church of St. Francis Xavier was outstanding for its time. It had been designed by the famous architectural firm of Pugin and Pugin of Westminster of Early Gothic Style. It rose 62 feet to the top of its tower cross and measured 88 feet by 34 feet. It boasted windows of tinted cathedral glass. The altars were a blend of Sicilian, Galway and Cork marbles. It was dedicated July 2, 1882.[7] It was here Bridget made her first communion and the McCrory girls were confirmed on October 5, 1901 by His Grace, Archbishop John A. Maguire of Glasgow.[8] The parish record book notes that Bridget McCrory had as her sponsor Mary Jane Meechant the headmistress of the school[9] and took as her patron in confirmation St. Teresa of Jesus, the great Carmelite of Avila.[10] No one could have dreamed that golden autumn day what tremendous grace and inspiration this Foundress had in reserve for her newly confirmed little soldier of Christ.

Not long after this, the family circumstances having improved, Thomas and Bridget McCrory moved with their family away from the company row houses of Carfin to a house at 480 Main Street in

Mossend, Bellshill, another Glasgow suburb. The backyard of the house was separated only by a fence from the parish property of Holy Family Church which was located at the corner of Caldron and Hope streets just off Main. The McCrory children could enter the school grounds without walking around the entire block. This easy access was a delight for Bridget Teresa and when not around the family home she could be found in the parish church. Besides her devout visits to Jesus in the Blessed Sacrament she very often helped the pastor, Father Francis Cronin, in arranging flowers for the altar and appropriate shrines for Our Lady in May and October, as well as the Sacred Heart of Jesus in June.

Holy Family Church constructed of yellow sandstone was built by Father Michael Fox in 1884. *The Scottish Catholic Directory of 1885* noted: "On 16th November (1884) there was opened at Mossend a very beautiful church designed by Messrs. Pugin and Pugin of Westminster . . . one of the neatest, most chaste and elegant in this part of the country." The rectory is set behind the church. The parish school had opened in 1868. It was enlarged by the same Father Fox in 1886. The present two-storey building of red sandstone was erected in 1907. No religious Sisters ever taught in these schools which were always under the direction of competent and deeply religious lay staff and headmistresses.

The McCrory home was two storied. One morning as her mother was doing house work at the rear of the second floor she was shocked to look out the window and see Bridget looking in at her almost eye to eye. With a tilt of the head and her disarming smile the vision disappeared. It was discovered that the three inseparable children, Elizabeth, Owen and Bridget had borrowed stilts from a neighbor and wanted their mother to see them at play. However, unannounced and unexpected, the performance shocked the mother and after all were returned safely to *terra firma* there was a very clear caution not to try that again.[11]

Bridget was always the leader. Liz was two years older and Owen two years younger but for good or bad Bridget had them in the palm of her hand. Whether it was giggling or gaggling these three were united with Bridget in the middle but always at the head. Another family story which has come down the years from the McCrory Main Street home was the comic tragedy of the "good" plate. On a dark and dread mid-winter's day all the usual fun things to do had been exhausted or found wanting. To cheer up the others Bridget suggested making taffy. A splendid idea thought all. The mixings were assembled, carefully blended, duly cooked and becomingly hardened. Then came the real pleasure of six busy hands pulling and stretching the viscous lump. It took on a life of its own and grew in length and solidity. There was a quick problem-solving meeting as to what to do with it. The solution was to lay it out on their mother's "good" plate, the largest in the house. This done the three confectioners awaited results. Results there were, but tragic indeed. The taffy attached itself together as the intended separate strips became an inseparable jumble. Worse still it was also found to be so firmly attached to the plate as to be irremovable. Another quick consultation. Yes. A well-tempered blow of the hammer would take care of everything promptly. It did just that, except it also broke the plate. When the ill-fated candy making experiment was finished the plate was glued together and returned to its place in the cupboard. (To use one of Mother Angeline's later expressions,if you came in the dark you'd never have noticed.) But when the mother returned in time for tea, a chastened absolutely honest ring-leader tearfully told the whole truth. A loving mother,certain that a hard lesson had been learned, wisely mended hearts and overlooked the ill fate of the "good" plate.[12]

School days continued apace. In the parish centenary brochure, *Holy Family Church, Mossend* 1884 to 1984, among the vocations from Holy Family parish, Bridget Teresa McCrory is fondly listed as "Mother Angeline (B. McCrory) Foundress of Order of Carmel for the Care of the Aged and Infirm."[13]

It was now time for Bridget to move onwards and upwards to high school. In September of 1906, when Bridget was then thirteen years old, she entered the Elmwood Convent School in Bothwell taught by the Franciscan Sisters under the patronage of the Immaculate Conception of the Blessed Virgin Mary.[14] Bridget excelled in all her courses but especially French. She spent some six years at the convent school graduating in 1912.

Not all the days in the McCrory home were idyllic, however. The first shattering blow came when the beloved father, Thomas McCrory was fatally wounded in an industrial accident at the Clydesdale steel works. In the accident her father's body was traumatically burned by white hot molten metal, only his face being spared. He survived twenty-nine agonizing days in the Royal Infirmary at Glasgow where he had been rushed from the steel plant. Both Bridget and her sister Elizabeth remembered the extraordinary response of this shocking news brought to their mother by co-workers of their father. Stunned, she lifted her eyes and hands to heaven saying, "Welcome be the Holy Will of God."[15] And this from such a loving wife and tender mother. Small wonder her children had such a deep spirit of Faith. After his death in the hospital Thomas

McCrory's body was laid to rest in St. Joseph's cemetery at Aidrie, Scotland following a funeral Mass at Holy Family. He was only forty years old. He left behind his wife and four children ranging from eleven to twenty years old. Although consoled by their love of God and supported by their lively Faith this was a shocking experience for them all. Bridget, the loving daughter, was so affected by the untimely death of her father, and the memories of that time so painful, that in later life she could say no more than "my father died of an accident."[16]

Over the grave of this good man the following headstone was raised:

ERECTED BY BRIDGET McCRORY
IN AFFECTIONATE REMEMBRANCE OF HER BELOVED
HUSBAND THOMAS McCRORY WHO DIED IN GLASGOW
ROYAL INFIRMARY 20TH JANUARY 1911
THE RESULT OF A BURNING ACCIDENT RECEIVED
IN CLYDESDALE STEEL WORKS
AGED 40 YEARS

The continuing saga of the McCrory Family was added subsequently:

ALSO THEIR BELOVED SON JAMES
DIED 8TH AUGUST 1919
AGED 18–1/2 YEARS

ALSO THE ABOVE BRIDGET McCRORY
DIED 27TH FEBRUARY 1942 AGED 80 YEARS

PARENTS OF MOTHER M. ANGELINE TERESA
FOUNDRESS OF THE CARMELITE SISTERS
FOR THE AGED AND INFIRM IN THE
UNITED STATES OF AMERICA

And the final inscription:

ALSO THEIR DAUGHTER ELIZABETH[17]
DIED 4TH JANUARY 1985 AGED 93 YEARS

Bridget Teresa McCrory stood by her valiant mother as her father's remains were consigned in consecrated soil. From this day forward she continued to work hard at her high school studies of English, History, Mathematics, Composition, Religion and Music Appreciation. The elegant French language continued to be her favorite subject however. Bridget was now a charming young lady: tall, slim and straight; chestnut brown hair and sparkling brown eyes; exquisite skin and remarkably expressive hands. Although fun-loving she was modest and at times serious. Her constant smile added to her physical charm and spontaneous wit. Truly she had all the makings of a success story but inspired by the Holy Spirit she was now thinking seriously of a religious vocation. There was the thought of leaving her wonderful mother and being separated from her close-knit circle of brothers and sister. Still there was also the ever growing thought of what she could attain in the service of Christ and His Church, God Himself. Would this not be the most perfect success story?

NOTES

[1] *St. Francis Xavier's Parish Carfin 1862–1962* Centenary Book—John S. Burns & Sons (September 23) Glasgow-1962. p. 8. One of rare remaining copies given author by Rev. Brian Logue, assistant parish priest June 12, 1987 occasion of personal visit.

[2] Personal Testimony of Katherine McCrory, author's visit, December 3, 1987.

[3] Carfin Centenary Book p. 95.

[4] *Op. cit.* p. 9.

[5] *Ibid.*

[6] *The Holy Bible*, Douay Version, London Catholic Truth Society, Old and New Testament. Revised 1885–1901. Approved by Gordon Joseph, Archbishop of St. Andrews and Edinburgh. (Library Pontifical Scots College, Rome).

[7] Carfin Centenary Book p. 11.

[8] Extract: *Liber Confirmatorum*, in *Ecclesia Sti. Francisi Xavierii*, Carfin, Motherwell, Scotland. Signed and sealed, Die 21 mensis Januarii, anno 1912. Dyonsius McBrearty, Rector Missionis. Actual entry in book seen by author June 12, 1987.

[9] *Ibid.*

[10] *Ibid.*

[11] Personal testimony: Sister M. Gabriel (Reis) O.Carm. Author's interview, Avila Motherhouse, May 24, 1987. Also cf. *Teresian Society* (publication) Vol. I, num. 1, page 1.

[12] *Ibid.*

[13] *Holy Family Church, Mossend, 1884–1984.* Centenary Program. Solemn Dedication of Church, 16 November 1984. John S. Burns & Sons, 25 Finlas Street, Glasgow, G22 5DS, page 14.

[14] Mother Gonzaga Sim, Abbess, *Franciscan Convent of Our Lady of the Immaculate Conception*, Elmwood, Bothwell, 2 August 1878. (Descriptive Brochure).

[15] Personal testimony: Sister M. Gabriel (Reis) O.Carm. *ut supra* note num. 11.

[16] Mother M. Bernadette de Lourdes (Wisely) O.Carm. *Woman of Faith, Mother M. Angeline Teresa, O.Carm. Foundress*. Published privately. Carmelite Sisters for the Aged and Infirm. St. Teresa's Motherhouse, Avila on Hudson, Box 218, Rte 1, Germantown, N.Y.1984, p. 11.

[17] Verified, occasion of author's personal visit, June 12, 1987, Aidrie, Scotland.

FRANCE

The Little Sisters of the Poor came to Glasgow from France in 1862.[1] Glaswegians, then as now, did not readily accept outsiders and strangers into their midst. However, when they saw the tremendous work done by the Little Sisters among the poorest of the poor in the city's aged sector, as well as their unlimited generosity and frugality, they adopted this group of dedicated religious women as their very own. It is amazing to recall that this religious institute had been founded just twenty-three years earlier in France. Yet here in Scotland its particular apostolate, namely the loving care of aged men and women, its unique identity, its charismatic ministry and deep spirituality had been effectively transposed by Little Sisters themselves as young as the Community.

Their work progressed and the capacity of their home for the aged had been improved and expanded surrounded by the arms of its great sheltering wall. The consuming charity of the busy Little Sisters at home was daily manifested by those Little Sisters who witnessed to their own charity and the charity of God by seeking to have this charity participated in by others. The familiar horse-drawn black wagon, driven by one of the old men, with its hardly visible seat for two Little Sisters who were collecting in the name of the Sisters themselves for the means to support the elderly inmates of their home, became a daily commonplace and witness along the cobbled streets of Glasgow. In this manner small and large businesses were solicited for whatever they could spare for the aged poor. Meat, vegetables, flour and grain as well as already baked bread and goods were gratefully accepted. No gift was too small or none too large to be hoisted into the back of the collecting wagon. From time to time people of wealth were approached for money to maintain the work. Not infrequently good hearted people far poorer would press their offerings into the gentle hands of these ever smiling young French women, whose beauty was hidden by their starched white-bowed bonnet and their enveloping black cloak with its capacious hood so reminiscent of early beginnings in the French Province of Brittany.

To Bridget and the McCrory family living at 480 Main Street in Bellshill, a Glasgow suburb, the weekly visit of the Little Sisters of the Poor and their collecting visits were a part of ordinary Catholic life.

At this time the girl-into-woman, Bridget, after her father's untimely death became the spiritual daughter of the Reverend Francis Cronin, pastor of Holy Family Church. It was he who had encouraged her to go to high school with the Franciscan Sisters at the Elmwood Convent School.[2] As already remarked they shared the decorating of the parish church in flower arranging. Dean Cronin was her spiritual director also. At this time when Bridget was deeply reflecting on her vocation to the religious life he was a kindly guide. As Mother M. Angeline Teresa, O.Carm. in later life she often spoke with gratitude and affection of this zealous parish priest.[3] After much prayer and long talks with her mother, Bridget Teresa visited the Little Sisters of the Poor and much moved by their sacrificial life in the service of the aged poor she asked to enter the Community. The fact that many of their devotions and exercises of piety were still in French was no problem to the young aspirant because of her own love of and fluency in that language.

After due consideration she was accepted as a candidate. The date for her entrance was set for the Feast of the Purification of the Blessed Virgin Mary as it was then celebrated in the liturgy on February 2, 1912.[4] Father Cronin supported this choice by Bridget. On the evening of February 1, 1912 when she went to say goodbye before leaving for the convent Father Cronin extended his open hand toward his personal collection of books in his study offering to his spiritual daughter anyone she might wish to choose. Bridget Teresa's eyes travelled along the tiers of shelves and then her hands reached out for the Life of St. Teresa of Avila.[5] This book was written in 1562. It was a long letter to her confessor Father Garcia de Toledo, O.P. The original text was lost and she rewrote the work again about 1565. This book is more than an autobiography, more than even a spiritual diary since it includes not only biographical data but more importantly her experience of the interior life with its supernatural favors and graces bestowed on her by God. Amazingly, also in this book St. Teresa so appropriately wrote of her own feelings at leaving her family for Carmel:

> When I left my father's house I felt that separation so keenly that the feeling will not be greater, I think, when I die. For it seemed that every bone in my body was being sundered.[6]

Again we see the almost prophetic intrusion of the great St. Teresa of Avila in the ongoing pilgrimage of Bridget Teresa McCrory towards the eventual fulfillment of God's plan for this young woman.

The next day, February 2, 1912 Bridget McCrory with her book under her arm, left her beloved mother, two brothers and her sister and her family home. It was understood that soon she would leave for France with no assurance of returning home again. The farewells were brief, poignant and evinced restrained loving emotions. In the absence of Dean Cronin the curate Father Kellegher accompanied Bridget to the convent. She was welcomed with open arms by her new family of religious Sisters.

The days of preparation sped by quickly. In early August she received her obedience to come down to London overnight and in company of some other young women to report together August 11, 1912 to the home of the Little Sisters in Paris under the patronage of St. Lawrence.

The long train trip from Queen's Station, Glasgow to London's Euston station, in those days practically eight hours, was an ordeal. The rain came down in torrents. The coach was unbearably hot. The windows so steamed up that little could be seen as the train wended its way south through Crewe, Preston and Carlisle. It was crowded with holiday travellers at the height of the season. Bridget McCrory felt all the more alone in the press of these joyous vacationers.

Years later she would narrate this doleful trek to her postulants and novices to let them know that she empathized with their own difficulties of leaving home to join the Congregation she had founded.

Her mother had given her an outsize box of chocolates to be shared with her new companions when they met up. Crowded into a corner against a murkey and unopening window she decided to seek the comfort at hand and opened the box of candy. The longer the journey the worse she felt. The worse she felt the more candy she consumed. By the time she reached London she was deathly sick and had to go to bed at once.[7] The Little Sisters even feared that she would not be well enough to join the other postulants en route to Paris the next day. With a great effort she overcame her physical distress and joined the group when they left the following day. The stay at St. Lawrence's was designed to increase their knowledge and fluency in the French language. During this period Bridget's own knowledge of French was perfected and she was able to help some of the others who did not have the same lingual preparation as she had.

From a resume in Mother Angeline Teresa's own hand, actually prepared for presentation to the Congregation for Religious in Rome, the following description of events follows:

> Sent to Paris to St. Lawrence home to study French, August 11, 1912
> Went to Novitiate February 14, 1913
> Received Habit September 8, 1913
> Professed March 19, 1915 at La Tour St. Joseph, St. Pern, France.
> Remained at Motherhouse until October 15, 1915.[8]

At this point a brief note should be made concerning the Congregation of the Little Sisters of the Poor. This pontifical religious Institute, international in its work and mission, was founded in 1839 at St. Servan along the North coast of France in Brittany. They were called "The Servants of the Poor" until 1844 when their special designation as "Little Sisters of the Poor" became universally adopted. Their mission in the Church since the foundation has been the care of the indigent elderly both men and women. Their special approach to their dedicated apostolate has always been evangelical simplicity of life and total dependence on the Divine Providence. From the beginning they have considered begging or collecting as a means which brought God's blessing on themselves and their work and shared these blessings with those who contributed to the support of the work. Their Constitutions were approved once again by Pope St. Pius X on May 7, 1907. At the time Bridget McCrory entered the Congregation had remarkably increased to 307 houses and over 5,400 Little Sisters.

Blessed Jeanne Jugan (1792–1879) Foundress of the Little Sisters of the Poor was born in Brittany at the small seaport town of Cancale. Until she was forty-seven she led an unobtrusive life of domestic service and nursing. Impelled by the Spirit of God, the Father of the Poor, she began her life-long work of caring for the aged poor. In 1839 she brought home her first guest, Anne Chauvin, old, blind and abandoned. Jeanne carried her on her own back and gave up her own bed for her. For the next twelve years she was indefatigable in opening new houses, in recruiting companions and in collecting throughout the area to support her growing "family." The last years of her life were spent in the Motherhouse at La Tour in humility, prayer and an undeserved retirement. To the end she served her blessed poor to the best of her ability. She died in 1879. *Humble So As To Love More* is the most recent biography of Blessed Jeanne Jugan, in religion, Sister Marie de la Croix.[9]

Blessed Jeanne Jugan's spirituality was as intense as her loving apostolate. She was a member of the Third Order of the Heart of

Mary. A Tertiary group promoted by the Eudist Fathers, sons of St. John Eudes with a special emphasis on the Amiable Heart of Mary. Thus her spirituality and that of her Little Sisters was Marian. Later on, as the appreciation of her charism of hospitality deepened in her soul,as an expression also, of interior spirituality the assistance of the Hospitaler Brothers of St. John of God ,who like the Little Sisters had a fourth vow of hospitality, affirmed her vocation. Father Felix Massot, O.H. helped her in formulating the chapter of the constitutions of the Little Sisters on hospitality in 1846. Now the burning spiritual charity of St. John of God seconded her own divine call. This twofold affirmation certainly expanded and interiorized her own unique call to share in the open hospitality of Christ toward the poor and the homeless.

When Bridget McCrory arrived at the Motherhouse on Valentine's Day 1913, she became immersed in a spirituality of both place and heart. The Breton people were men of the sea and men of the land. Their fishing livelihood and their agricultural labors, expecially the herding of sheep brought her back to the days of her childhood. The tremendous Motherhouse encompassing the general administration, the formation program of postulants, novices, temporary vow Sisters, and Little Sisters from all over the world, the aged poor and the Little Sisters deputed to care for them was a microcosm of the whole Congregation. Its splendid architecture with the dominating tower of the great gothic chapel had earned it the title of *La Tour*, the Tower of St. Joseph. Her own soul and spirituality grew in this blessed atmosphere. She received the Holy Habit of the Little Sisters on September 8, 1913. According to the practice of the Little Sisters at this time she also received her religious name Little Sister Marie Angeline de Ste. Agathe. The spiritual direction given by so many holy priests as well as the conferences by the Novice-Mistress opened up for her new dimensions of the love of God and in Him the love for his poor and needy aged. These long days of work and prayer made an unforgettable and memorable impression on both her mind and soul.

Once many years later on the eve of Corpus Christi she reflected on the wonderful ceremonies at La Tour for this feast. She recalled the outdoor altars prepared for the triple Benediction and the Procession of the Blessed Sacrament. Great displays of flowers in the form of a heart were a memory as clear as the original event.[10] Even the beaming countenance with which she spoke was love remembered.

These were grace-filled days. A time of planting. A time of growth. Even the troubled days of World War I could not interrupt the peace of heart and the spirit of sacrifice. La Tour became a hospital stop for so many youthful French soldiers returning from nearby battle fields. The more mature Sisters looked after their valiant countrymen while the added work for the aged, increased by refugees from the other houses, fell to the loving care of the younger Sisters. Sister M. Angeline experienced the special grace of her vocation at this time as spiritual instruction became selfless charity expressed in God's service.

Bridget McCrory, Sister M. Angeline de Ste. Agathe professed her first vows of religion here at La Tour St. Joseph March 19, 1915. She remained in France until October, the war delaying her first assignment. She again returned to the Motherhouse for her final profession April 21, 1925.[11]

The days and years of her sojourn in France were a lasting memory for her. She loved to read French spiritual writers and never forgot the devotional hymns in French in honor of Our Lady. She taught some of these from memory to her later novices and postulants.[12]

Years after she publicly attested to her esteem for the Little Sisters of the Poor and all that she cherished from her sojourn in France.

> I have always loved my former Congregation and value the spiritual foundation that was mine and the reverence and respect for the aging that I learned in the Congregation.[13]

NOTES

[1] The Scottish Catholic Directory. 1987.

[2] Mother M. Bernadette de Lourdes (Wisely) O.Carm., *op. cit.* p. 14.

[3] *Op cit.* p. 13.

[4] *Extract*: Archives Little Sisters of the Poor. Maison Mere, La Tour St. Joseph. Document October 7, 1987.

[5] Personal Testimony: Sister M. Gabriel (Reis) O.Carm. Author's Interview Avila Motherhouse, May 24, 1987. Also cf. *Teresian Society* (publication) Vol. I, num. 1, page 1. Mother M. Bernadette de Lourdes (Wisely) O.Carm. *op. cit.* p. 15.

[6] Collected Works of St. Teresa of Avila, Volume One. Translation by Kieran Kavanaugh, O.C.D. and Otilio Rodriguez, O.C.D., I.C.S. Publications, Institute of Carmelite Studies, Washington, D.C. 1976—*Life*, Chapter 4, n. 1, p. 41.

[7] Personal Testimony: Sister M. Gabriel (Reis) O.Carm. cf. n.5.

[8] Autograph Manuscript A. Undated. Conserved General Archives O.Carm. Motherhouse, Avila-on-Hudson, Germantown, N.Y.

[9] Milcent, Paul. *Humble So As To Love More*, trans. Alan Neame. Darton, Longman and Todd, London, 1980.

[10] Personal Testimony: Sister M. Gabriel (Reis) O.Carm. Author's Interview Avila Motherhouse, December 16, 1987.

[11] *Extract*: Archives Little Sisters of the Poor. up supra n. 4. Vow Formula in French—autographed—preserved at the Motherhouse, Avila, Germantown, N.Y. (Archives).

[12] Personal Testimony: Sister M. Gabriel (Reis) O.Carm. cf. n. 10.

[13] Mother M. Angeline Teresa, O.Carm. Cited in an Interview with Brian Baker, Staff Writer, *The Evangelist*, Albany, N.Y., October 18, 1979.

AMERICA

When Mother M. Angeline Teresa, O.Carm. wrote in her precious *Resume* that as Little Sister M. Angeline de Ste. Agathe she left the Motherhouse at St. Pern on October 15, 1915 and arrived in America October 31, 1915, she certainly gave no indication of the circumstances of the times.[1]

The Great War of 1914 to 1918 which had cast its grim shadow on the Motherhouse in Brittany had spread over all of France. August 1, 1914 Germany began hostilities with Russia. Three days later she invaded Belgium and declared war on France. Great Britain declared war on Germany August 4, 1914. For the next three years the German and Allied Forces were bogged down in a mortal stalemate along a 380 mile front. The United States entered the fray April 6, 1917. World War I, a designation arrived at after the United States engaged in a second global war, ended at 11 a.m. on the 11th day of the 11th month 1918. It had lasted four years. Eight million men in uniform had been killed. Twelve million civilians had been slain during this period and in its sequela of epidemic, famine and revolution, three vast empires had fallen and faltering new nations had been created.[2]

On February 18, 1915 Germany had declared all British waters to be a war zone and ordered its naval forces to sink on sight any ship.[3] In retaliation the British Admiralty on March 11, 1915 ordered a blockade against any ship bound for Germany.[4] The war at sea escalated May 7, 1915 when the luxury liner *Lusitania* of British registry was torpedoed by a German U boat and sank with some 1200 passengers and crew including 128 United States citizens.[5] To the consternation of all it was later discovered that the ship was in fact carrying 173 tons of ammunition in her hold.[6] It was against this background that Mother M. Angeline Teresa awaited a passage by sea from France to the United States.

She did not avert to the fact that October 15 was the feast of St. Teresa of Jesus, she of Avila, called "the Great" whose life and mission had such an effect on her own life and mission.

She did not even mention the name of the ship which despite war zones and blockades courageously ventured to set out from France crossing to America. Checking the shipping and arrivals section of the New York Times for Sunday, October 31, 1915[7] three ships docked that day: The *Vitalia* which had embarked from Rotterdam in the Netherlands; the *Francisco* which left Hull on the River Humber in the British Midlands; and the *King Bleddyn* which had sailed from the port of St. Nazaire on October 15, 1915. The port of St. Nazaire is just about sixty miles south of St. Pern. There can be no doubt that this was the ship which carried Mother M. Angeline Teresa to the United States to begin her work of love and zeal for the aged poor.

Her first assignment was Brooklyn where Mother Marie Claire and seven Little Sisters of the Poor had arrived from St. Pern on September 18, 1868 at the request of Most Reverend John Loughlin, D.D. (1817–1891), first Bishop of Brooklyn.[8]

Although her original mission to America was given March 15, 1915[9] the anxious delays were forgotten when the then Sister M. Angeline de Ste. Agathe took up her residence at St. Augustine's Home.[10] Full of vitality and anxious to serve the aged poor committed to her care she was a welcome addition to both the religious Community and the residents of the home. Here also began her love affair with America and the American people. Although many of the elderly in residence were from different ethnic backgrounds, mostly Irish and Germans, she saw that they all had adapted to an American life style. All these had suffered for their faith and as a result were strong and devout Catholics who resonated to the many prayers and devotions provided for them by the Sisters. In spite of the adversities which had rendered them alone and poor they manifested a sense of humor about themselves and their circumstances. Living so close together they still treasured their little privacies and few possessions. Their gratitude toward the Little Sisters and their benefactors was touching. The chapel was hardly ever without worshippers. For those up and about there was also a pride in their persons and abilities. While the old men worked as cobblers, gardners, handymen and porters, the women plied their skills as seamstresses, or crocheting and knitting. There were few idle hands and each one was keenly aware of the contributions they made toward the upkeep and well-being of the home.

Besides her occupations in the home and in the various departments given to her charge another assignment brought her face to face with the American scene. During her nine-year assignment in Brooklyn, she became one of the Sisters who went out begging. It was her duty to collect alms from the general public. This work of piety meant going out in the ancient black articulated wagon, horse drawn in those days, driven by one of the men inmates. It had obscured seats for two collecting Sisters and a copious storage space for the goods collected. They passed along busy streets, over which elevated trains rattled. There were certain stores where open-hearted naturalized American business people gave them a share in God's goodness to them—groceries, meat, fish, staples and bakery goods—also, a little tobacco for the old men. Even hawkers from the ubiquitous handcarts, poor themselves, offered their bit for the poor at home, represented by the Little Sisters of the Poor on the quest.

Another aspect of the collecting was obtaining money instead of goods. This meant approaching households both rich and poor to seek donations. In either case not every one approached was gracious or even courteous. Rebuffs were part of everyday collecting.

Sister M. Angeline became an expert in this specialized apostolate for the aged and poor. She was a striking image, tall, smiling, sensitive to those with whom she came in contact. She listened to the needs of those who helped her poor. She made them feel their generosity was even greater by her warm gratitude and her sincere promise of her prayers and those of the elderly she served. People actually began to look forward to her collecting days and visits.

This well-attested image of Sister Angeline would conjure up the vision of one well-suited to a humble task, and enjoying this apostolate. The truth of the matter was quite to the contrary. She was really a very shy person. It was an effort of both heart and soul for her to face the public in this way. An effort joyously endured for Christ and for His poor. Of herself she later wrote:

> The reason why I sympathize so much with the timid is because I myself have suffered from timidity from earliest childhood and my sufferings came from my imagination. If I ever get to heaven I will feel great pity for cowards and will do my best to help them; in fact I would be quite willing to become their patroness, though the title would not do me much honor.[11]

This revelation of natural shyness, or timidity, from one who faced monumental difficulties with such equanimity could only come from her own admission and never from the peaceful fortitude she manifested in her own life and mission in reaching out to alleviate the sufferings of others whether spiritual or physical.

It was a surprise to none that in September 1919 at the early age of twenty-six she was appointed by the Superiors in France to be a Councillor to assist the Mother Superior in the operation of the Brooklyn Home both in administration and internal Community affairs.[12]

Her own spiritual life matured along with the development of her natural gifts. So in August 1924 Sister M. Angeline was recalled to the Motherhouse at La Tour St. Joseph in France to prepare for making her Perpetual vows.[13] Following the Community custom she had previously made temporary triennial Vows December 8, 1917, December 8, 1920 and December 8, 1923.[14]

This return to the gracious and spacious ambience of the General Motherhouse was a time of renewal at the very font of her vocation. Now, however, having broadened her appreciation of this vocation of serving the destitute elderly by personal and practical experience of both ideals and charism of the Institute, the reality of the grace of her vocation was deepened within herself.

It was a great privilege and joy for her to make her perpetual vows on April 21, 1925.[15] At that time she inscribed the official document of her Profession as follows:

Jesus! Mary! Joseph!

I, Sister Angeline de St. Agathe, in the presence of Monsieur the Abbe Potier, Almoner, holding the office and place of His Eminence Cardinal Charost, the Archbishop of Rennes, Dol and St. Malo, make my profession and promise God to observe faithfully the vows of Poverty, Chastity, Obedience and Hospitality forever under the authority of the Reverend Mother Marie Esther of St. Pacificus, Superior General of this Congregation of the Little Sisters of the Poor and to those who will succeed her in the same office, according to the Rule of St. Augustine, Bishop and Doctor, and according the Constitutions of the Congregation that have been approved by the Holy and Apostolic See.

At our Motherhouse of La Tour Saint Joseph, 21 April, 1925.

(autographed signature) *Sr. Angeline de Ste. Agathe, p.s.d.p.*[16]

Sometime after her vows it was decided that Sister Angeline after nine years in Brooklyn would return to the United States but this time to Pittsburgh in May, 1925.[17] Shortly thereafter she was named Assistant Superior in August, 1925.[18]

Here in Pittsburgh Sister Angline was introduced into another slice of American life. The Diocese of Pittsburgh was erected by the Holy See on August 11, 1843. It was at first vaguely designated as Western Pennsylvania. The first Bishop was Rt. Rev. Dr. Michael O'Connor, S.T.D. He was born in Ireland on September 29, 1810 and ordained a priest in Rome on June 1, 1833. He came to the United States in 1839 and moved to the Pittsburgh area June 17, 1841. He was consecrated a Bishop while in Rome on August 15, 1843. At the time there were thirty-three churches, sixteen priests and less than 25,000 souls. He was a dynamo of a man. Within a year he had begun the diocesan newspaper, the Pittsburgh Catholic, still functioning; started the first parochial school, held a diocesan synod, opened a chapel for Negroes and founded a seminary. He introduced many religious orders of both men and women. This ecclesiastical giant resigned his episcopate in 1860 and entered the Society of Jesus. He died at Woodstock, Maryland on October 18, 1872.

With such a tremendous start the Diocese of Pittsburgh flourished. There are now almost 900 priests, over 300 parishes and a Catholic population of over 870,000. At the time of Sister Angeline's arrival the whole area was booming after a period of war time prosperity. Peoples from many nationalities had immigrated in large numbers to the Pittsburgh area and sought employment in the rapidly developing iron, steel and coal industries as well as the Pennsylvania mines. Certainly such people, immigrants and hard working steel laborers won her heart as she recalled her own family's immigrant days in Scotland working at the Clydesdale Steel Works.

The future Mother M. Angeline Teresa's agreeable efforts in the Pittsburgh area came to an early end when she was informed by the authorities in France that she had been named Mother Superior of Our Lady's Home in the Bronx in September 1926.[19] She was only thirty-three years old. For the first time as "Mother" Angeline, she assumed her new office on October 7, 1926.[20] She carefully noted down the census of the Home when she arrived: 18 Little Sisters and 230 old people.[21] The fatigue from the long train ride from Pittsburgh to New York City evaporated after going from the old Pennsylvania Station in Manhattan to her new home in the Bronx. She was received with marked affection by the Sisters and her elderly charges. She prayed her heart out in the chapel that she might indeed be "the Good Mother" and also "the good Servant" whom the Lord had placed over His household to give them food at the opportune time.[22] It was her earnest desire to feed them not only with food for their tables, but also food for their souls.

Gradually and with great prudence she sought out ways to improve the lot of her elderly children. Loving and dedicated service by each Sister had given them the basic necessities for their old age and infirmity. In every way their spiritual needs had been well attended by the generous priests who carried out the work of chaplains and the Sisters themselves were always on the alert for the spiritual welfare of their charges. But the Good Mother Angeline endeavored to supply for other needs as well. She was aware of loneliness as a great Cross to the elderly who were institutionalized. She knew the fear of older persons not only for the future, but even for the present. She empathized with the needs of individuals who for the first time in their lives must adjust to corporate dwelling and institutional behavior. Convinced that she was acting according to both the letter and the spirit of the Rule and Constitutions regarding the care of the aged, Good Mother Angeline introduced small adaptations in the diet plan, some areas were brightened up with new paint, religious colored prints and statues were added, and simple new furniture acquired. All these niceties showed her special sensitivity to the needs of the elderly in America. The results were tangible. The old folks felt more at home and grew more contented as well as grateful. The dedicated Little Sisters acquiesced in these modifications as they saw in them a reflection of their Blessed Foundress' own words:

> We are blessed to be a *little sister of the poor*. Making the poor happy is everything . . . never cause suffering to anyone old or poor. We must *spoil* them all we can.[23]

At this time there were three Homes of the Little Sisters in the New York Archdiocese. One at East 70th Street, another at West 160th Street and 660 East 183rd Street in the Bronx section where Mother M. Angeline was the superior.

In a report sent to His Eminence, Patrick Cardinal Hayes, under date of April 15, 1929 Robert F. Keegan of the Office of Catholic Charities wrote:

> Undoubtedly the Little Sisters of the Poor care for aged poor who have no haven anywhere else. Their charges are kept clean, warm and well fed: the Sisters make every personal sacrifice even to depriving themselves of food in order to give the old people the best they have. The Sisters are kind and gentle with the aged, some of whom prove very difficult to handle.

> We find that the atmosphere in the various homes reflects the attitude of the Superior in Charge.[24]

Little wonder then that under the benign and expansive direction of Mother Angeline de Ste. Agathe Our Lady's Home in the Bronx fostered both spiritual peace and earthly contentment.

NOTES

[1] *Resume, op. cit.,* 1st page.

[2] *World War I,* (1914–1918) in *Great Events of the 20th Century,* Ed. Richard Marshall. Reader's Digest Association, Pleasantville, N.Y. 1977 pp. 100–131. *Statistics* p. 101.

[3] *Op. cit.* p. 124.

[4] *Op. cit.* p. 141.

[5] *Op. cit.* p.125.

[6] *Ibid.*

[7] *New York Times*, October 31, 1915. Vol. X:V, No. 21, 099, p.19 N.B. Cost of Sunday Edition was then five cents.

[8] Sharp, Rev. John K., *History of the Diocese of Brooklyn* (1853–1953) II vols. Fordham University Press, New York 1954. Vol. I., p. 221.

[9] *Extracts*: LSGA re Sister M. Angeline de Ste. Agathe, Oct. 7, 1987.

[10] *Ibid.*

[11] EXHIBIT "D"., *PERPETUAL YEARBOOK: A Perennial Diary*. Type-written Transcript. page 7c.

[12] *Extracts: op. cit.*

[13] *Resume, ibid.*

[14] *Extracts: op. cit.*

[15] *Resume, ibid.*

[16] AVGA (General Archives Avila.) autograph certificate. author's translation.

[17] *Resume: ibid.*

[18] *Extracts: op. cit.*

[19] *Ibid.*

[20] *Resume: op. cit.*

[21] *Ibid.*

[22] cf. Psalm 144:15

[23] Cited: Milcent, Paul. *Jeanne Jugan, Humble So as to Love More*. Trans. Alan Neame, Darton, Longman and Todd, London, 1980. p. 178.

[24] AANY Box P-4, Folder 7B.

NEW YORK

In song and story New York is often considered to be the cross-roads of the world. It has been the port of entry for countless immigrants. It has been in turn the port of departure for numerous young Americans leaving home and country to go off to the wars. Many of these never returned. In the caverns of its financial district fortunes are made and lost.

New York in the late 1920s became indeed the scene of the greatest crossroads of decision for Mother M. Angeline. The decision thrust upon her at that time affected her own life, the life of hundreds of young women who would follow after her, and the lives of thousands of aged and infirm Americans whose lives would be radically changed because of her efforts to serve them.

At this time, the time of her courageous decision, she was in her mid-thirties. A vivid word picture of herself and her personality has come down through the personal recollections of so many of her early Sister companions.[1]

She is remembered as being tall, stately, calm and composed with an air of serenity about her countenance and bearing. So many attest to the fact that she had exquisite and expressive hands. In her prayer which was frequent she was completely recollected. In her actions she was gentle, kind and joyous. She radiated a magnanimous wholeness. Moreover, there is an almost unanimous testimony that in spite of her many gifts she was actually shy in the natural order and truly humble in the supernatural order. She was straightforward by nature yet always reserved in her manner. Her personality was dynamic. Her large dark eyes sometimes appeared to look through one. She possessed drive and determination. Once she was convinced that she was doing God's Will she quietly yet inexorably surmounted every obstacle that stood in the way. None could forget the strong sense she had of her own commitment. It was this personal integrity which culminated in her eventual confrontation and ultimate separation.

Were the chain of events that follow to have taken place fifty years later they probably would have been taken as a matter of course and their solution equally so. But in those days when political, social and economic changes were coalescing to inspire heady risk on one hand and paralyzing apprehension on the other, even Church leaders were divided on their perception of the signs of the times. Bold optimism and constraining suspicion were pitted against one another in almost every phase of progress and development. Against this background Mother Angeline's dreams, hopes, and designs for the care and well-being of the aged were to be assailed, rejected, tried and proven at a great cost to herself and to others. Eventually her loving spark would ignite a conflagration.

The Great American Society was an accident waiting to happen.[2] Unwittingly and unsuspectingly so was the fulfillment of Mother M. Angeline's projected enterprise for advancing theory and technique in the care of the elderly.[3]

History is the sad witness that so many confrontations ending in division take place among very good people. Each one totally convinced of the merit of their own opinion, practice and certitude. Mutually understood ideals and the possibility of honorable compromise are often prevented by a strong emotionalism. More often than not it is precisely the goodness of both parties that creates such situations so painful, so soul-searching and subsequently so hard to heal.

To understand the confrontation to follow certain elements must be kept in mind. There is the matter of the obligation of vows. On one side the emphasis on Obedience and the acceptance of conformity. On the other the vow of Hospitality toward the aged poor, their care, their comfort and their contentment. Then there was a subtle nationalism the French ambience of uniformity and the American temperament for pluriformity. There was also the interpretation of poverty, absolute, in the sense of destitution, and attenuated, among the aged who had some or even more worldly goods but had social indigences with no one to look after them in their desolate loneliness. In a correlative development there was the relationship between the local hierarchy and internal religious autonomy.[4] In this way the stage was set.

Baring her own soul at this precise period Mother M. Angeline could write in her own hand:

> Our present Community of Seven, were all very happy as Little Sisters of the Poor.[5]

What the Community at Our Lady's Home in the Bronx honestly felt was both peace and progress came to an abrupt halt with the

arrival of the Mother General from France. This was the Reverend
Mother Esther de St. Pacifique who governed the Little Sisters of
the Poor from 1919 to 1931. She was a remarkable woman whose
task was laid out for her, namely to restore the Congregation after
the effects of World War I. The war had cut off communications to
and from the Motherhouse. Some houses had been abandoned and
others occupied. She felt a firm hand was needed to restore regular
life and tranquility. The modifications inaugurated by Mother M.
Angeline at Our Lady's Home were cancelled. The time for restoration was not the time for innovation. The ensuing confrontation
arose from selective prioritization. The Mother General looked for a
prompt response flowing from the vow of Obedience. The custom-
ary procedures universally practiced were the only norm. No thought
was given to the fact that these had a French character and might
not be totally acceptable to the American mentality. This actual
situation would be alluded to in an otherwise very positive report
of the Archdiocesan Catholic Charities regarding the Little Sisters in
April 1929.[6] Accommodation to the American life style would be
divisive and disrupt a unity predicated on a global uniformity.

The reaction to this direction on the part of Mother Angeline and
the Sisters who had freely accepted her more benign approach was
disbelief and hurt. She expressed both herself and her associates
when she wrote down her reflections on this period shortly afterwards under obedience.

> The consciences of many of the Sisters became troubled, they had four
> Vows, each equally binding. If they kept their Vow of Obedience, as the
> Superior General demanded they were failing in their Vow of Hospitality,
> and if they were observing this Vow as the Rule required they were
> failing in Obedience to the General of the Congregation. For instance the
> Rule said regarding Hospitality: 'They, (meaning the Sisters) shall receive
> the old people according to their means, in order to lodge them, feed
> them, etc. with the same happiness, as if they were serving Our Lord.'
> Now the means the Sisters have in the city of New York differ a great
> deal from the means of the poor Country homes in France.[7]

Mother Angeline's well-intentioned desire to serve the old people
with an American approach and practice was looked upon as being
against unity in the Congregation and as an expression of nationalism. Although criticized at this time for being too Americanized,
Mother Angeline did not become a naturalized United States citizen
until April 3, 1933 at the age of thirty-nine.[8]

In truth Mother Angeline was ahead of her times. She would
embrace inculturation taught and prized by Pope John Paul II. This
is a dimension of evangelization by which the Church does not

bring peoples the culture of another race but Christ. She recognizes what is good and communicates the divine message through the culture of each people.[9]

This process of inculturization, sometimes also called acculturization, has its roots in two distinct documents of the Vatican II Council.[10] The Council Fathers urged the evangelizing ministers of the Church to share in the cultural and social life of the peoples by becoming familiar with the national and religious traditions and illumine these treasures in the light of the Gospel.[11] According to the doctrine of the Council such inculturization is a means to heal, preserve, permeate and transform local culture in such a way that the Christian life may be accommodated to the genius and dispositions of each culture.[12] Both by nature and by grace Mother Angeline truly intued this principle. Yet she was directed to cancel her already prepared Thanksgiving Day celebration for her beloved old folks because it was not among the feast days to be observed.[13] She lived, however, to see the Church give the dioceses of the United States a special Mass, appropriate liturgical readings, and a proper preface for this uniquely American observance.[14] This was just another example of the genius of Mother M. Angeline Teresa reaching out to the aged and infirm of the United States by acknowledging their own traditions thus making them feel loved and cared for as they had been accustomed in their own homes.

Collaterally another point surfaced regarding poverty. The Blessed Jeanne Jugan when she founded the Little Sisters of the Poor with evangelical exigence restricted their apostolate to the care of the indigent aged. God has always blessed this service for a specific element of the People of God often so helpless and unhelped. Yet there are others perhaps not poor in the sense of destitute but with meagre funds or even middle class who are socially poor for they have no one to care for them. Mother Angeline's maternal heart felt their need also. Again the American ideal resisted institutionalism and sought the maintenance of a modicum of financial security. This also was placed in the scale of social justice. Much later Mother Angeline could recall in a *New York Times* interview that she: " . . . came to dislike the institutional aspect of homes for the aged, and decided to establish ones where people would be able to keep the freedom they had for their first seventy or eighty years. So many widows came to me for help and I thought that if only they had a bit of a corner of their own where they could hang their husband's picture, things would be better."[15]

These problems have been dissipated today by social security and legislation in the field of social services but in the 1920s they became the basis for antithetical objectives.

Meanwhile the Superior General had returned to France. The Superior Provincial, Mother M. Josephine de la Croix was delegated to implement the directives left behind. Again, as good people convinced of their rightness stood fast, differences magnified and created a rift which could not be bridged.

Of Mother M. Angeline Teresa it must be said that once she was convinced of the rectitude of a decision or action she was resolute in carrying it out. At a later date, the Most Reverend Kilian Lynch, O.Carm., Prior General of the Carmelite Friars, and longtime friend of Mother Angeline Teresa observed, "If one did not know the depth of Mother Angeline's spirituality she might be regarded as just a stubborn woman."[16]

When it became evident that there was no hope of the life style which she and her companions envisioned for the care and freedom of the elderly in accord with the American standard of living being accepted in the Homes of the Little Sisters she looked about for help. The first one approached, typical of Mother Angeline's sensitivity for due process, was the confessor, Father Edwin T. Sinnott. Having heard the problem he advised her to go directly to Cardinal Hayes, the Shepherd of the Diocese and explain to him exactly how things were. Mother was overcome with timidity as she considered this course of action. Rising to the occasion Father Sinnott went himself to the Cardinal preparing the way for Mother and filling him in on the subject of the proposed visit. In a few days, it was about the end of December 1928, Mother Angeline was given an appointment with the Cardinal. Her anxiety was calmed when Father Sinnott encouraged her that since the Cardinal represented the Supreme Authority in New York she should approach him with the certain conviction that whatever he would tell them to do would be the Will of God.[17]

The Cardinal received them most kindly. He promised to do all in his power to assist Mother Angeline even if he would be obliged to take the matter to Rome. He assured the Sisters that they had done perfectly right, in coming forward and explaining conditions. He said it was their duty to do so.

As a result of this interview with Cardinal Hayes, Most Reverend John J. Dunn, his auxiliary Bishop was sent to make a canonical visitation of Our Lady's Home as soon as he returned from Europe. This canonical visitation was held January 15, 1929. He then visited the other two homes. The Bishop submitted a lengthy report to the

Cardinal on January 23, 1929, in which he carefully balanced all of the goodness of the Little Sisters but acknowledged some problems in administration.[18]

In the interim conditions worsened between the Mother Provincial and the Sisters at Our Lady's Home in the Bronx. As they did, the kind services of Father Sinnott, Bishop Dunn and Monsignor Patrick Breslin continued. Mother enlisted further help from the noted Passionist preacher, Father Casimir McNulty, C.P., who had preached a retreat to the Community some time before, making a tremendous impression on the Community. Under date of May 5, 1929 she asked him to intercede for them with the Cardinal.[19] As soon as Father Casimir received Mother's plea he forwarded it to Cardinal Hayes from St. Benedict's Rectory in Somerville, Massachusetts where he was preaching a Mission. He described Mother and her companions as "genuine religious, so devoted to their God and their work."[20]

Bishop John Dunn made a second visitation to the Home in the Bronx June 19, 1929. At this time the Assistant to the Mother General was staying at the house. The seven Sisters in her presence spoke to the Bishop. This was arranged so that Mother Gertrude would understand what was said and speak for the Mother General whom she represented. The Bishop was informed that their minds were made up to remain no longer among the Little Sisters. The Bishop then advised them to ask for their dispensations from vows, this time through the Mother General of the Congregation, directly to Rome. The requests were sent June 21, 1929. The documents arrived August 5th and were personally signed on August 9th. The little group left the Little Sisters on August 11, 1929.[21]

The Mother General in France felt that this action was at least an embarrassment if not a rejection of the Little Sisters and their work. Cardinal Hayes made haste to assure her that this was not the situation at all. The work of the Little Sisters was invaluable and was both needed and appreciated.[22] In future each group would serve the Church according to their own special vocation.

Perhaps in retrospect the observation of Bishop Howard Hubbard of Albany is the insight and the healing needed here, "How could anything be so wrong since God has blessed both religious communities."[23]

It had never been Mother Angeline's intention to leave the Little Sisters of the Poor, much less to found a new religious congregation in the Church. It was her hope that she might be allowed to further her methods of caring for the elderly within her original vocation. During the anxious years of 1927 to 1929 Cardinal Hayes told Mother in an interview of December 1928: "Well, who knows, perhaps you may lead the way and many others will follow in your path later on."[24]

So many foundresses of new Communities sprung from the womb of already existing Institutes, felt a direct inspiration from God to make their decision. Not so with Mother Angeline. God's Will manifested itself in her life through an evolution of circumstances and ideas.

To transfer from one existing religious Congregation to another, much moreso to found a new one, is not an ordinary process in the spiritual development of an individual or a movement in the Church. On the other hand there are many examples of just such projects which have had the approval of the Church and the blessing of God.

Father Elio Gambari, S.M.M. a longtime officer of the Congregation for Religious and Secular Institutes wrote in his book, Religious Life:

> Transfer to another Institute is usually motivated by a desire for a form of life more responsive to a person's particular vocation, as for example, the contemplative life, or missionary life, sometimes it can be due to dissatisfaction or a lack of understanding in his own Community, or a too radical transformation of the Institute he is leaving. While the principle of fidelity to one's own Institute responds to the plan of God, the experience even of saints, proves that sometimes a transfer responds to God's plan.[25]

A few years before Mother M. Angeline Teresa had to suffer silently to receive the Will of God contrary to her own expectations another admirable American woman was led by God to make a similar discernment and decision. Mother Mary Teresa Tallon, the former Julia Teresa Tallon (1867–1954) who founded the Parish Visitors of Mary Immaculate in 1920.[26] Guided by her spiritual director she entered the Sisters of the Congregation of the Sisters of the Holy Cross at St. Mary's, Notre Dame, Indiana. For thirty-three years as a devout religious teacher she awaited God's Will in her behalf. She spoke of her hidden and "original vocation" as "the Cause" and testified that "it came straight from the Heart of her Beloved."[27] The following is taken from the Preface to the constitutions of the Parish Visitors of Mary Immaculate.

Foundation Graces

On July 2, 1900, while she was on retreat, Julia Teresa Tallon, then a Sister of the Holy Cross, received her first inspiration to follow God in a new vocation:

God had asked me to give myself to greater perfection and to train other souls to perfection of spirit, that He might rest in their recollected hearts and reign there as Supreme Lord and Master.

The fullness of the contemplative-missionary inspiration came on January 25, 1908:

God revealed to me clearly, at Holy Mass . . . what it was He wanted. I must establish an Institute where women would be trained to greater spiritual perfection and, being formed in the contemplative spirit, go out in search of the lost lambs to bring them back to the fold by means of Christian instruction. I saw God's will clearly and received strong assurances of His powerful protection. Jesus offered Himself as security for the work, and promised to supply by His infinite perfection the lack on my part.

The new institute, the Parish Visitors of Mary Immaculate was founded by Julia Teresa Tallon, now Mother Mary Teresa Tallon, on August 15, 1920, in New York City. Canonically erected as a New York diocesan religious congregation in April 1927, it was granted status as an Institute of pontifical rite on November 21, 1985.[28]

Another such call which has likewise benefited the Church and contemporary society is the admirable spiritual journey of Mother Teresa of Calcutta. She was born Ganxhe Agnes Bojaxhiu in 1910 at Skopie in Serbia. Compelled by an intense desire to be a missionary in India she joined the Sisters of Loreto, an Irish branch of the seventeenth century Institute of the Blessed Virgin Mary founded by the indomitable Mary Ward. As Sister Mary Teresa of the Child Jesus she made her first profession in India on May 24, 1931. On August 16, 1948 she left the Loreto Nuns to found the Missionaries of Charity. She went first to Patna but then returned in December to Calcutta where she stayed with the Little Sisters of the Poor until she established a house of her own. Her Sisters still observe as "Inspiration Day" the anniversary of her interior illumination on September 10, 1946 as she was en route to her annual retreat.

This is how it happened, I was travelling to Darjeeling by train when I heard the voice of God. I was sure it was God's voice. I was certain He was calling me. The message was clear: I must leave the convent to help the poor by living among them. This was a command, something to be done, something definite. I knew where I had to be. But I did not know how to get there.[29]

Here we have three intrepid women, each a Teresa, each called to leave the security of one religious Congregation to bring forth a new one. Two of them were graced with an express and certain indication of what was to be their role in God's providential plan. Mother M. Angeline Teresa, O.Carm. has left us in her ingenuous *Resume* absolutely no indication of any such heavenly light or consolation, simply in her own inimitable way stating: "No extraordinary occurrences, no visions."[30]

There is no indication of her own prolonged prayers before this action first contemplated during the annual retreat of 1927.[31] No mention of her repeated seeking of advice from the Cardinal, Bishops, retreat masters and spiritual directors in order to discern God's hidden Will. No hint of the heartache and self-examination a soul of her integrity must have wrestled with before making so painful a decision. "No extraordinary occurrences, no visions" is as revealing a self-disclosure possible of the wonderfully direct and untrammeled approach of Mother Angeline Teresa to all things whether divine or human. It is also a foreshadowing of her deep participation in the consummation of Carmelite spirituality which leads the soul into union with God by keeping nothing for one's self.

Fortified by the support of Cardinal Hayes and his concerned priestly representatives, they petitioned the Holy See in due process through the Mother General to be dispensed from their vows. This done, in prayerful serenity they awaited the next revelation of the Holy Spirit. In an unusual tribute, despite some restrictive measures, Mother Angeline was left in the office of superior until she withdrew from Our Lady's Home.[32]

NOTES

[1] *Recollections of the First Decade* (1929–1939) Ed. Jude Mead, C.P. pro manuscripto. unpublished. 29 individual recollections from Sisters who lived with Mother M. Angeline Teresa, O.Carm. Sisters: M. Bernadette de Lourdes, M. Elias, Regina Carmel, M. Gabriel, Mary of the Sacred Heart, M. Benigna Consolata, Elizabeth Marie of the Child Jesus, M. Angelica, Frances Michael, M. John of God, M. Adelaide Therese, Eugene Therese, M. Agatha Immaculate, Catherine Marie of the Sacred Heart, M. Rita Immaculate, Agnes Teresa of the Sacred Heart, M. Anthony of the Sacred Heart, M. Bernadette Immaculate, M. Grace of the Sacred Heart, M. Josita of the Sacred Heart, M. Kathleen of the Sacred Heart, Marie Therese of the Sacred Heart, Mary Aloysius, Michael Marie of the Sacred Heart, M. Andrew of the Blessed Sacrament, Mary Stephen, M. Jane Francis, Mary of the Angels, Mary Ann Rochford.

[2] Meltzer, Milton., *Brother Can You Spare a Dime? The Great Depression.* 1929–1933. Knopf. New York 1926.

[3] cf. *The Philosophy of Mother M. Angeline Teresa, O.Carm.* in *op. cit.* Mother M. Bernadette de Lourdes (Wisely) pp. 56,57.

[4] *Directions for the Mutual Relations Between Bishops and Religious in the Church.* AAS 70 (1978) pp. 473–506.

[5] "Foundation" Book p.1 line E.

[6] AANY Box P-4 Folder 7B, Msgr. Robert Keegan, April 15, 1929.

[7] "Foundation" Book p.1 line R to Z p.2 lines B to L.

[8] *Certificate of Citizenship, United States of America*, No. 3740098. Bridget McCrory, 66 Van Cortlandt Park So. Bronx, New York City, April 13, 1933. Charles Weiser, Clerk of Court.

[9] Pope John Paul II, *To the Bishops of Nigeria*. Lagos, February 16, 1982.

[10] *Ad gentes divinitus*, Vatican II, Decree on the Church's Missionary Activity, December 7, 1965. Also *Apostolicam Actuositatem*, Vatican II, Decree on the Apostolate of Lay People, November 18, 1965. Further implementation by Pope John Paul II. S.C.C. Postquam Apostoli, Norms for Cooperation among Local Churches and for a Better Distribution of the Clergy. March 25, 1980. Also *Catechesi Tradendae*, Catechesis in Our Time, October 16, 1979 n. 53.

[11] *Ad Gentes*, n. 11.

[12] *Ibid*. n. 22.

[13] Personal testimony, Sister M. Gabriel (Reis) O.Carm., Sister M. Bernadette de Lourdes (Wisely) O.Carm. Author's interview, Avila Motherhouse, January 9, 1989.

[14] *Sacramentary*, The Roman Missal p. 747 Catholic Book Publishing Co., New York, 1974 Thanksgiving Day Mass.

[15] Montgomery, Paul, L. *Nun to the Aged Marks Jubilee, New York Times*, March 20, 1964.

[16] *Author's Conversation*, Avila Motherhouse, August 9, 1984.

[17] "Foundation" Book, p.4, lines B-S.

[18] AANY Box P-4 Folder 7A.

[19] *Ibid*.

[20] *Ibid*.

[21] "Foundation" Book p.7 lines T-Y.

[22] AANY Box P-4 Folder 7A August 23, 1929 Cardinal Hayes to Mother Gertrude, L.S.P. Assistant General.

[23] Author's Personal Visit at Chancery Office, December 14, 1987.

[24] "Foundation" Book, p.5 lines J-L.

[25] Gambari, S.M.M. Elio. *Religious Life*. Trans. & updated, II Italian Edition, Daughters of St. Paul, Boston 1986. p. 581.

[26] Sister Rita Arlene, P.V.M.I., *Mother Mary Teresa Tallon*. Foundress and First General Superior of the Parish Visitors of Mary Immaculate. Marycrest. Monroe, N.Y. 1984 p.3.

[27] *Ibid*.

[28] Constitutions of the Congregation of the Parish Visitors of Mary Immaculate. Approved by the Congregation for Religious and Secular Institutes, 1985. Cf. *Preface*, p.5. Used with permission of Sister Francis Walter, P.V.M.I. General Superior. July 25, 1988.

[29] Mother Teresa of Calcutta. Cited in *Mother Teresa, The Early Years*. David Porter. Foreword by Malcolm Muggeridge. Eerdmans Publishing Company, Grand Rapids, Ia. 1986 p. 56.

[30] *Resume. op. cit.*, p. 1 #4.

[31] *Op. cit.*, #5.

[32] *Ibid*.

MOUNT CARMEL
In Spirit

The liturgy of the Church as it commemorates the dedication of a church edifice prays:

> God our Father,
> from living stones,
> your chosen people,
> you built an eternal temple
> to your glory.[1]

So too, when in the Providence of God, Mother M. Angeline Teresa, was moved to institute a new religious family in the bosom of the Church, besides all the required manifold formalities imperative in the process from Church and civil law, and of acquiring a place to live and carry on the apostolate, her most valued resource was those stalwart women who became her first six companions. They were the foundation stones, indeed the living stones, on which she was to build her ongoing mission of faith and charity. She was the youngest member of the pioneer group yet they unanimously accepted her as their leader, their model and their mother.

Before the actual separation from their former community as many as sixteen Sisters had petitioned to cast their lot with Mother Angeline.[2] Some of these formally withdrew their request made through His Eminence, Patrick Cardinal Hayes.[3] Others had second thoughts earlier on. However these six women became the nucleus of the new Congregation which circumstances had ultimately obliged Mother Angeline to originate. They were mature women who were well schooled in the religious life. They had long experience in the ministry of care for the aging. They were dedicated and competent. They knew the risks they were taking as they launched out into the unknown. On the other hand they were women of prayer, women of action, confident that their decision was right with God. They agreed in both mind and heart in the dream of Mother Angeline Teresa for a revolutionary forward looking program in wholistic care for elderly Americans. They remained always loyal to Mother Angeline as a person and in her compassionate design to improve and update her approach to the best possible geriatric therapy. In her turn Mother was staunchly loyal to each one of them. She shared with them her vision and gave them positions of trust, responsibility, and administration. They never let her down. They never turned away from their commitment to God and the Church. Each one persevered to the end of their lives in the service of the aged and infirm. United as they were in life and mission in death they lie together in Gate of Heaven cemetery in Hawthorn, New York. Mother Angeline Teresa, O.Carm. stood by the grave of each one of them and like the biblical Rachel, "mourned over her children because they were not" (Jer. 31, 15).

Mother M. Louise, O.Carm.

Mother M. Louise was the daughter of Ivo Doom and Octavie Deeru. She was born September 24, 1874 in Hooglede, Flanders, Belgium. In baptism she was called Marie Louise.[4] She entered as a postulant with the Little Sisters of the Poor at Bruges some time in 1893. She entered the novitiate September 7, 1894 at Anvers, Belgium where she made her first profession of vows December 8, 1896. After making triennial vows over a period of time she was admitted to Perpetual Profession April 29, 1912 at La Tour St. Joseph in France.[5]

In 1896 she came to America and served at Holy Family Home in Brooklyn. Subsequently she was assigned to St. Augustine's Home, Brooklyn in 1897; Somerville, Mass. in 1899; Our Lady's Home in the Bronx, N.Y. in 1912; returning to St. Augustine's in 1918, to Somerville in 1924 and Our Lady's Home, the Bronx in 1926. In company with Mother M. Angeline she left the Little Sisters August 9 ,1929.[6]

She opted to keep her same religious name in the new Community.[7] She was the first of the pioneer Sisters to be appointed a local superior at Mt. Carmel Villa on West 215th Street, New York in 1934. She became the superior/administrator of the first foundation outside of New York in Philadelphia, November 1, 1936. She became a close friend of Denis Cardinal Dougherty. In the three year period 1936 to 1938 the Carmelite Sisters opened three homes in the Archdiocese of Philadelphia. On August 5, 1936 she was named Second General Assistant of the nascent Congregation of the Carmelite Sisters.[8] She remained on the General Council until her resignation in 1946. Although confined to a wheel chair she remained on as local Superior of Sacred Heart Manor in Philadelphia where she died as the Sisters prayed the rosary at her bedside.[9]

Mother M. Leonie, O.Carm.

Among the Little Sisters of the Poor, Mother was known as Sister Leonie de La Conception.[10] She was the daughter of Martin Logan and Anne Tully born on June 14, 1877 in the Roxbury section of Boston, Mass. She was baptized in St. Patrick's Church, Roxbury June 17, 1877. John Cody and Catherine Cunningham were her godparents.[11] Her school records are not available but her further intellectual achievements indicate her academic ability.

She entered the Little Sisters of the Poor in Boston and then went down to New York June 19, 1903 to begin her novitiate at Queens. She made her first vows at the Queens Novitiate on December 8, 1904. Following her periods of temporary vows she made her Perpetual Profession at the Motherhouse, La Tour St. Joseph in France November 21, 1916. Afterwards she returned to the United States. Mother Leonie was missioned at St. Augustine's Home in Brooklyn in 1904. She came to the Newark Home in 1905. Finally, in 1911 she was sent to Our Lady's Home in the Bronx as local Councillor to Mother M. Angeline. With Mother Angeline she left the Little Sisters of the Poor on August 9, 1929.[12]

Mother M. Leonie, O.Carm. made her perpetual vows with the newly founded Carmelite Sisters on December 8, 1931. Shortly after this she became the local Assistant to Mother M. Angeline Teresa at St. Patrick's Home in the Bronx. At the first General Assembly of the new Institute she was named First Assistant to the Mother General, then Vicar General and local Superior at St. Patrick's. She held this office until she resigned in 1946.[13] She made the change from St. Patrick's to the new Motherhouse and Novitiate at Avila where she died September 22, 1947. Two of her remarks give an indication of both the beauty of her soul and of her character. "If you give a person even a glass of cold water put it on a plate and include a napkin."[14] And again, "Be kind and understanding with employees."[15]

Mother M. Colette of the Blessed Sacrament

Among the Little Sisters of the Poor Mother Colette was known as Sister Colette of St. Rose. Becoming a Carmelite she retained her religious name but changed her title to that of the Blessed Sacrament. She was born in Newry, (County Armagh and Down) Ireland February 10, 1878.[16] The daughter of Bernard Duffy and Ann Maguire and the first of their six children she was baptized Margaret. Her father died very young leaving her mother a widow struggling to bring up her family. She attended the parochial school taught by the Sisters of Mercy.[17] Upon leaving school, instead of continuing her education, she got a job to help her mother and family. Her leadership qualities were manifested early. The Protestant owners of the mills, the almost sole employers of the Catholics of Newry, made them come to work so early in the morning that on Holy Days most of them had to miss Mass. She and a girl friend approached the Bishop directly, a formidable task in those times. She explained that people who could not afford to take the day off because of their poverty were sorely tried. He looked at her intensely. He listened to her problem. He admired her courage. Then he acted ordering early Masses for the working folk at 5:00 in the morning.[18]

At the age of thirty-four when her family obligations were over she entered the Little Sisters of the Poor in Dublin and was sent to Paris as a postulant to the Notre Dame Home there.[19] She was received into the novitiate at La Tour on March 5, 1912. She was then thirty-four years old. On September 5, 1913, she made her first profession of vows. After her temporary vow period she made perpetual profession in the novitiate at Anvers, Belgium on December 23. She was first missioned in London, England and then in 1923 was assigned to Our Lady's Home in the Bronx.[20] Here she met again Mother M. Angeline with whom she had spent novitiate days in France. She was a Little Sister of the Poor for sixteen years until August 9, 1929 when she followed Mother M. Angeline.[21] Here she spent another twenty-seven years as a dedicated Carmelite in the service of the aged.

She enjoyed the confidence of Mother Angeline and went with her to Rome and was at her side in the private audience when Pope Pius XI blessed Mother, the new Community, and their aged residents.[22] In the General Assembly of the new Community in 1936 whe was appointed the third General Assistant. After helping with the Philadelphia foundation she opened St. Joseph's Home on Staten Island as Superior and Administrator November 13, 1938. In 1939 she led the first Carmelite Sisters to Fall River, Mass. She moved again on October 18, 1943 as Superior of the first Carmelite Home in the far west at Centralia in the State of Washington. At Mother Angeline's request she again returned to Fall River to open a second home in 1944 as the Diocesan authorities had asked for her officially.[23]

Elected as Third Assistant General for the Carmelite Sisters March 19, 1942, she continued her pilgrimage of opening new Homes of the Order. This time Mount Carmel Home in Manchester, N.H. September 26, 1949. She had a great respect for priests and always waited upon them with affection and respect. In return, she received the same from them. This most loyal daughter of Carmel died August 19, 1956 at Mount Carmel Home, Manchester.[24]

Mother Mary Teresa, O.Carm.

Mother Mary Teresa was the only one of the pioneer sisters who changed her religious name from the one she had received as a Little Sister of the Poor. Born October 9, 1887 in Richmond, Va., she was Rosina Schoof. Her parents were Joseph and Louise Koester.[25] In 1908 she entered the Little Sisters in Richmond, Va. She began her Novitiate at Queens, N.Y. on June 18, 1909 and was given the name Sister Alodie de St. Michel.[26] She made both her first profession December 8, 1910 and her perpetual profession January 16, 1921 at the same novitiate house in Queens Village, N.Y. She had served the aged first in St. Augustine's Home in Brooklyn and then October 1912 she came to Our Lady's Home in the Bronx. On August 9, 1929 she left with Mother M. Angeline.[27]

Mother M. Teresa, O.Carm. had a priest brother, Father Raphael Schoof, a Benedictine. He described his sister as "very outgoing and she always spoke her mind, yet she was always an example of charity and kindness."[28] He also cherished a memory of Mother M. Angeline Teresa, O.Carm. who when he was ordained May 31, 1940 presented him with a chalice and some beautiful vestments.[29]

Mother M. Teresa became the first novice-mistress of the fledgling Carmelite Community.[30] In 1934 she became Superior of Mt. Carmel Villa, New York. Later she made the foundation at St. Leo's Abbey, Florida, in 1940, taking over the domestic department and the boys' school. After this she founded Carmel Manor in Fort Thomas,Ky.and St. Joseph's Manor in St. Petersburg, Fla.In 1942 she was elected as the fourth Assistant General.[31] She died July 6, 1964 at Carmel Manor,Ky.[32] Of her, Mother M. Angeline Teresa, O.Carm. wrote, "She had always been a hard worker, truly dedicated and devoted to her vocation and the old people. There was no request I ever made that she did not try to fulfill, and the Congregation's interests were truly hers."[33]

Mother M. Alodie, O.Carm.

Among the Little Sisters of the Poor she was known as Sister Marie Alodie. At her birth on October 15, 1890 in Montreal, P.Q., Canada her parents, John Hutchison and Phoebe Irwin, had her baptized as Catherine.[34] About age twenty she entered the Little Sisters Home in Montreal. She entered the Novitiate at Queens, New York on December 12, 1911. She made her first profession of vows there on December 9, 1913.[35] After a period in which she renewed her vows she made her perpetual vows August 28, 1924 at

La Tour St. Joseph, France.[36] With the Little Sisters she was stationed at Troy, N.Y. in 1913, St. Augustine's in Brooklyn, N.Y. in 1915 and Paterson, N.J. in December 1919. Then in 1926 she came to Our Lady's Home, the Bronx, N.Y. where Mother Angeline was Superior. With Mother Angeline she separated from the Little Sisters August 9, 1929. [37]

As a member of the newly formed Community, she continued her "collections" for the aged poor. She was appointed Superior of Mount Carmel Villa in Philadelphia on September 15th, 1937.[38] After this she opened the new St. Joseph Home on Staten Island, N.Y. in 1941. Next she was Superior Administrator at Our Lady's Haven at Fairhaven, Mass. Toward the end of her life she resided at St. Patrick's Home in the Bronx where she died on August 14, 1959.[39]

Mother M. Alexis of Jesus, O.Carm.

Sister Alexis of St. Peter, as she was known as a Little Sister of the Poor was the second Canadian companion of Mother M. Angeline. Mary Josephine Dubè was born on May 21, 1883 at St. Flavie, P.Q.[40]. She was the daughter of Arthèmise Roy and Joseph Dubè. Of all the pioneer companions of Mother Angeline she seems to have the least amount of vital statistics. When she was only nineteen she entered the Little Sisters of the Poor Home in Montreal. From there she was sent to the American novitiate at Queens Village, N.Y. on October 10, 1912.[41] She received as her religious name Sister Alexis of St. Pierre. Having made her first profession on June 19, 1914 at Queens she passed through the various periods of temporary vows making her perpetual profession August 28, 1924 at the Motherhouse at La Tour St. Joseph, France.[42] Her assignments were Boston, Mass. 1914, New Haven, Ct. 1915, Sacred Heart Home, New York, December 1917, Holy Family Home, Brooklyn, 1922 and ultimately in February of 1928 to Our Lady's Home in the Bronx. With Mother M. Angeline and the other six she set out to begin religious life anew on August 9, 1929. She was the first of the original group to ask to be dispensed from her vows May 31, 1929.[43]

As a member of the incipient Carmelite Sisters she kept her original religious name but changed her title from St. Pierre to "of Jesus".[44] Her love for the aged poor was legendary. Although she exercised administrative positions as Assistant to Mother M. Angeline Teresa, O.Carm. at St. Patrick's, the Bronx, in 1936 and later for several years as Superior at Mount Carmel Villa in Philadelphia, she went to Mt. Carmel Home, N.Y.C. because of failing health.[45] She was an expert seamstress and returned to this humble work especially devoted to the "old men" wanting them to be well groomed. Since none of them had any income they were proud of the appearance she gave them. She was mending for them right up until the day before she died, February 24, 1945.[46]

Throughout the prolonged always delicate and sometimes painfull negotiations in preparing for the withdrawal from the original Community and the inauguration of the new Community there were two conditions which Mother M. Angeline insisted upon with both the Superiors of the Congregation and the Archdiocesan authorities representing the benevolent Cardinal Patrick Hayes. These were that the pioneer band would leave in a religious habit, different of course from that of the Little Sisters, because they were not returning to secular life but rather to continue their vocation. The second, that they would have a place to go to as a group approved by the Church.

In their final period in preparation for their departure, the Sisters made up for themselves a simple religious habit. At a later date Mother M. Angeline Teresa could write a description of it in her own hand to Cardinal Hayes:

"Description of Habit"

The habit is black, either serge or merino, with long sleeves about six inches wide. We wear a black scapular over Habit about two inches shorter, a black leather belt, to which is attached a fifteen decade rosary with a crucifix. A plain black cloak for going out, black leather shoes and woolen or cotton stockings, black. The headress consists of a little white head-cap, forehead band (symbol of Obedience) and a black veil, with white lining about six inches wide. Around the neck and over habit white (sic) gamp.

As to the place where they would go rumors ran rampant throughout the city. The Mother Provincial of the Little Sisters wrote to Cardinal Hayes:

If Your Eminence could but know all that has been said as to your propositions or to those of His Lordship Bishop Dunn, how assured our Sisters (the departing group. Editor's note) are seeing that you have given them Cardinal Farley's residence and Msgr. Breslin's house![48]

If these speculations from outsiders were true, along with others listed there would indeed have been cause for alarm. The fact of the matter was that when the separating Sisters left Our Lady's Home in the Bronx the modest place prepared for them was not ready. It had been arranged for them to spend the interim with the Dominican Sisters of the Congregation of Our Lady of the Rosary, Sparkill, N.Y. in one of their local missions in the city, St. Martin of Tours Convent. Again we have Mother M. Angeline Teresa's testimony in her own hand:

Although heartbroken at leaving a Community we loved and where we had spent many happy years and the dear old people whom it was our privilege to serve, we were much consoled by the kindness of these good Sisters who received us with open arms. The Superior General Mother M. Reginald, and the local Superior Sr. M. Alphonsus, made us feel that we were in our Father's House and in the company of His Saints. . . . We remained with these dear Sisters from August the 11th until September 3rd.[49]

It is interesting here to observe that Mother M. Angeline in her autographed account of the Foundation specifically states their departure/arrival date was August 11, 1929 whereas the *Extracts* from the General Archives of the Little Sisters give the date August 9, 1929 for leaving Our Lady's Home. The latter date was when the dispensations actually were signed.

NOTES

[1] *The Sacramentary*. Revised according to the second typical edition of the *Missale Romanum* 1975, March 1, 1985 for use in the dioceses of the U.S. of America. Cath. Book Pub. Co. N.Y. 1985. Common of the Dedication of a Church. B.p. 767.

[2] AANY P-4 Folder 7b.

[3] *Ibid.*

[4] *Extract*: GALSP Oct. 7, 1987 fasc. 2.

[5] *Ibid.*

[6] *Ibid.*

[7] *Monographs of the Pioneers of Carmel*, Sister M. Bernadette de Lourdes, O.Carm. (Kathleen Frances B. Wisely) pro manuscripto, unpaginated October 30, 1986 General Archives, Avila. *Mother M. Louise, O.Carm.*

[8] *Ibid.*

[9] *Ibid.*

[10] *Extract*: GALSP Oct. 7, 1987 fasc. 3.

[11] Baptismal Register, St. Patrick's Church, Roxbury, Mass. (Founded 1872) Conserved in the Archives of the Archdiocese of Boston. Official transcript sent July 26, 1988.

[12] *Extract*: GALSP. Oct. 7, 1987 fasc. 3.

[13] *Monographs ut supra cf. Mother M. Leonie, O.Carm.*

[14] *Ibid.*

[15] *Ibid.*

[16] *Extract*: GALSP. Oct. 7, 1987 fasc. 4.

[17] *Monographs ut supra* cf. Mother M. Colette, O.Carm.

[18] *Ibid.*

[19] *Extract*: GALSP. *op. cit.*

[20] *Ibid.*

[21] *Ibid.*

[22] *Monographs ut supra* cf. Mother M. Colette, O.Carm.

[23] *Ibid.*

[24] *Ibid.*

[25] *Extract*: GALSP. Oct. 7, 1987 fasc. 5.

[26] *Ibid.*

[27] *Ibid.*

[28] Author's personal visit: Rev. Raphael Schoof, O.S.B. St. Anthony's Church, San Antonio, Fl. Dec. 9, 1986.

[29] *Ibid.*

[30] *Monographs ut supra* cf. Mother M. Teresa, O.Carm.

[31] *Ibid.*

[32] *Ibid.*

[33] *Ibid.*

[34] *Extract*: GALSP. Oct. 7, 1987 fasc. 6.

[35] *Ibid.*

[36] *Ibid.*

[37] *Ibid.*

[38] *Monographs ut supra* cf. Mother M. Alodie, O.Carm.

[39] *Ibid.*

[40] *Extract*: GALSP. Oct. 7, 1987 fasc. 6.

[41] *Ibid.*

[42] *Ibid.*

[43] *Ibid.*

[44] *Monographs ut supra* cf. Mother M. Alexis of Jesus, O.Carm.

[45] *Ibid.*

[46] *Ibid.*

[47] AANY Box P-4 Folder 7A (April 15, 1931).

[48] AANY Box P-4 Folder 7B (May 27, 1929).

[49] EXHIBIT C: *"Foundations" Book,* Original Autograph Dated 1929–1930 St. Elizabeth Convent J.M.J. Page 11, line C.

MOUNT CARMEL
In Truth

The little new Community arrived at the very first place of their own, the old rectory of St. Elizabeth's parish, 4381 Broadway, New York City on September 3, 1929.[1] This is considered to be the actual foundation date for the Congregation of the Carmelite Sisters for the Aged and Infirm.

The very evening that Mother M. Angeline and the six pioneers arrived at St. Martin of Tours convent their devoted friend and sponsor Father Edwin Sinnott arrived to welcome them. He gathered "the little band"[2] into the parlor and wrote down for them a brief rule which they were to follow.[3] Of that courteous and prompt manifestation of loving concern Mother M. Angeline wrote, "was a balm to our sad hearts."[4]

Again Mother M. Angeline in her own handwriting best describes those eventful first days:

We arrived at St. Elizabeth's old Rectory September the 3rd and we were agreeably surprised to find seven beds in the house, which was providential in our case, as we were seven Sisters. There were also rugs on the floor, curtains on the windows, chairs, coal and wood in the cel(l)ar. We were so happy that first night to be in our own little Home together and felt that Our Dear Lord was watching over us in a very special manner. Father Sinnott gave each of the Sisters a crucifix for their rooms. Father Kelly gave us our first office books. The 4th of September, 1929, we had our first Mass in the old Church of St. Elizabeth celebrated by Reverend Father Sinnott who brought his own chalice, altar wine, linen, etc. Monsignor Breslin gave us a set of purple vestments, and a chalice. He was very kind and helpful to us on every occasion. The Paulist Fathers gave us our first ciborium from a lady, with whom we got acquainted only a short time before (Mrs. Anna Frick). Catholic Charities were our first benefactors, and have continued to provide for us very generously in spite of the many demands they daily receive. Father McEntegart gave the first check, $250, from Catholic Charities a few days before we took possession of this house to buy bedding, dishes, kitchen utensils, etc. Other benefactors who were more than kind to us were, Mr. and Mrs. Lane, Mr. Waters, Mrs. Flynn and her sister, Miss Dougherty, Mr. Farley, etc. Father Flanigan (sic) donated a beautiful Statue of the Little Flower, and also gave us a first class relic of St. Therese for our little chapel. Mother Teresa, Prioress of the Carmelite Monastery supplies us with altar breads gratis. Father Walsh, Superior General at Maryknoll, was also one of our best friends. On October 21st 1929 we had a Triduum which ended with the making of vows for one year. Father Sinnott obtained this favor for us, and gave us a very practical conference each day during the Triduum. The first few old people we received into our home were, Thomas Kelly, who heats up the house for us. Joseph Young, our doorkeeper, John Goldsberry a very pious old man, carpenter and odd jobs around, and Margaret Savage, a real good cook, who renders many services in the kitchen. The Seven First Sisters were Sister M. Leonie, Sister M. Louise, Sister M. Therese, Sister M. Colette of the Blessed Sacrament, Sister M. Alodie, Sister M. Alexis and Sister M. Angeline.[5]

What a treasure is this account in Mother M. Angeline's own hand. It was written hastily, so quickly indeed there are minor misspellings. Monsignor Patrick N. Breslin was Dean of the Bronx. Father McEntegart went on to be Most Reverend Bryan McEntegart, Bishop of Ogdensburg and later Brooklyn. From the beginning, Very Reverend Lawrence D. Flanagan, O.Carm., the Provincial of the New York Province of the Carmelites practically adopted this emerging Community of Sisters and actually prepared the way for them to affiliate later with the Ancient Order of Carmel. He had first met Mother Angeline at Our Lady's Home in the Bronx. Later on the Feast of St. Therese of the Child Jesus, October 3, 1928, he brought her a bouquet of roses blessed in honor of the saint. This had been a tremendous lift to Mother's sagging spirits in those troubled days. She never forgot this lovely Carmelite tradition and kept it with the Sisters all through the years.

How typical of Mother M. Angeline that she should indulgently list first the four aged original residents admitted to the new Home October 29, 1929. And then bring this touching account to a conclusion with the names of the intrepid first Sisters with her own in last place.

Looking back on these early days Mother Angeline recalled: "At the time I was called a revolutionary, but I went ahead with my plans."[6] An example of her "revolutionary" spirit came that summer of 1930 when in cooperation with the Catholic Charities of the Archdiocese of New York she took everyone, the Sisters and their elderly guests off on a vacation. The Burhkard estate in Palenville, New York in the Catskill Mountains became available and the pioneer group moved in from July 25th til October 10th. Such a change from the city was a godsend and everyone prospered in the mountain air and greenery. In those days such a move was unthinkable. Yet Mother's adaptability and inventive concern made the extraordinary seem commonplace and her good judgment prevailed.

The fulfillment of a growing need to be legally incorporated into the family of the Carmelite Order now begins to become a formal reality. Much of the process is contained in brief in the following letter in her own hand from Mother M. Angeline Teresa.[7]

St. Elizabeth
4381 Broadway
New York City
April 15, 1931

His Eminence Patrick Cardinal Hayes
Archbishop of New York.

Your Eminence:

Permit me to thank You for your great charity, and kindness, in receiving us last Monday in spite of the many other important demands on your time and Person. That little visit was for all of us an incomparable source of strength, light and guidance, I simply said to the Sisters "I can never again fear Our Lord after seeing His Representative on earth so inexhaustibly kind."

After gathering the Sisters together and discussing the different things we treated the other day, I am pleased to send you the following report.

That each and everyone is more than satisfied with the name, "Carmelite Sisters for the Aged and Infirm". They likewise are most anxious to be affiliated with the Carmelite Order, as Tertiaries, if Your Eminence approves. I spoke to Reverend Father Flanagan about this the day after our interview with Your Eminence, and he said it could be done, and that without difficulty, as their Father General is in New York at the present time. My, or rather I should say, our only aim in requesting this affiliation, is that of leaning up our work, so young and inexperienced, against one of the greatest religious families in the Church. I do not mean to withdraw from our Community its special mission, nor its peculiar character, much less to tamper with the future Constitutions that Your Eminence will give us, but that each one of us may participate in the spiritual treasures of the Order, without in any way prejudicing our duties of charity.

I am enclosing on separate paper the Sisters names, ages, and years of profession, also the description of the Habit. If there is any other information Your Eminence would like, I shall be only too pleased to send it.

Thanking Your Eminence once more, for all that has been done for us, especially during the past two years and assuring You of our religious respect and obedience.

> I am In Jesus and Mary
> Your Eminence's Obedient Child
> Sister M. Angeline Teresa.

As a result of this meeting with Cardinal Hayes each Sister wrote a personal letter to him petitioning his permission for "the privilege" of joining "the Carmelite Sisters for the Aged and Infirm." The originals dated April 13, 14 or 15 are preserved in the Archives of the Archdiocese of New York.[8]

On June 22, 1931 Cardinal Hayes wrote to Father Flanagan the Carmelite Provincial:

> I am enclosing herewith my approval of the petition of the Carmelite Sisters of the Aged and Infirm to the Holy See for authorization to make a foundation in this diocese[9]

The devoted attention and personal involvement of the Most Reverend Elias Magennis, O.Carm., Prior General of the Carmelite Order who returned to Rome only on June 3rd, 1931 brought rapid and favorable results.

Mother M. Angeline Teresa could send the following type-written letter:

> St. Elizabeth's Convent
> 4381 Broadway
> New York

His Eminence Patrick Cardinal Hayes
Archbishop of New York

Your Eminence:

We have just received a cablegram from Rome from Father Elias Magennis, (reading)
Can use name. Can receive subjects. Full recognition afterwards. Congregation writing Cardinal. (July 14, 1931)

We thank Your Eminence so very much for the most kind letter of approval, you gave Father Flanagan to be sent to Rome in our behalf, and we promise with the Grace of God to be docile instruments in Your hands, in our new field of endeavor in the Archdiocese of New York.

We are most anxious to get started, as we already have a long waiting list of old people. At present we feel that little equipment is necessary for the new house:

We will be more than willing to wait until financial circumstances permit further outlay.

In deepest appreciation for the many courtesies you have extended us, and reassuring Your Eminence of our religious respect and prayers,

> I am, In Jesus and Mary
> Your Eminence's Obedient Child
> (signed) Sister M. Angeline Teresa.[10]

The actual date of the reception of the Carmelite affiliation was July 16, 1931, the Feast of the Blessed Virgin Mary, Our Lady of Mount Carmel. In due time Father Elias Magennis, O.Carm. sent Mother Angeline Teresa a copy of the Carmelite Rule as well as a small figure dressed in the habit now approved for the Carmelite Sisters for the Aged and Infirm fashioned by the cloistered Carmelite Nuns of the monastery in Florence.

Cardinal Hayes did not delay to express his gratitude to Father Elias for his prompt and effective mediation in the affiliation of The Carmelite Sisters for the Aged and Infirm into the family of the Carmelite Order

> July 30, 1931

> Very Reverend Father Elias Magennis,O.C.C., Prior General
> Curia Generaslizia dei PP. Carmelitani
> Via Sforza Pallavicini, N. 10.,
> Rome (cf. footnote 13)
> Italy

My dear Father General:

I wish to thank you for your several communications and in particular, that of July 14th, with reference to the Carmelite Sisters for the Aged. I cannot tell you how pleased I am that your good offices have expedited the matter so satisfactorily.

I did not expect the Sacred Congregation to approve the new Community beyond authorizing me to organize it as a diocesan religious family. I did anticipate some difficulty in securing the permission because of the prestige of the Little Sisters of the Poor in the Sacred Congregation.

I certainly appreciate the gracious act of His Eminence Cardinal Lepicier.

I am now approving the purchase of the property in the Bronx for the Sisters, which I held up until I was sure of authorization from Rome.

> With a blessing, I am,
>
> Faithfully in Christ,
>
> (Patrick Cardinal Hayes)
>
> ARCHBISHOP OF NEW YORK[11]

The final and glorious event of this consolidation with the Carmelite Fathers of the Ancient Observance came with the Decree of Affiliation which is given here in full:

> We, Father Elias Magennis, a member of the Irish Province, humble Prior General, also Commissary and Apostolic Visitor, of the whole Order of the Brothers of the Blessed Virgin Mary of Mount Carmel, Mother of God.
>
> Since Religious Congregations of any Third Order, whether of men or women living in common and professing simple vows, should in virtue of Canon 494, be united to their Religious Order by the supreme Moderator of the First Order from which they derive their name and habit; therefore having considered the petition which Reverend Mother Angeline Teresa, Mother General of the Religious Congregation of Sisters of Our Lady of Mount Carmel for assistance to the Aged and Infirm, having recently presented to us with consent of the Ordinary of the place, that the aforesaid Congregation was established with the full approval of the aforementioned Ordinary in the Archdiocese of New York in the United States of America, and is now beginning to spread; by our authority we gladly grant the requested and ardently desired affiliation and from this time forth it shall share in all the indulgences, heretofore granted by the Apostolic See to our Order and which may be granted in the future.
>
> May the Father of all mercies sanction this affiliation and may the Mother of all Carmelites, foreseen by Elias in a cloud, preserve it. In the Name of the Father, and of the Son, and of the Holy Ghost. Amen.
>
> Dated at Rome at the College of St. Albert
> August 24, 1931.
>
> (signed) Father Elias Magennis,Prior General of the Carmelite Order
> Father Emmanuel Baranera Serra, Assistant General[12]

When Mother M. Angeline Teresa requested Cardinal Hayes to become affiliated with the Carmelite Fathers she described the Carmelite Order as "one of the greatest religious families in the Church."[13] She also stated her rationale for such a program, "That each one of us may participate in the spirit and spiritual treasures of the Order, without in any way prejudicing our duties of charity."[14]

The physical Mount Carmel so often recorded in the Scriptures is really a series of mountain peaks in northern Palestine now Israel. This chain runs some 15 miles. Its lofty summits and slopes which fall away to the Mediterranean sea are covered with greenery and flowers. It abounds in both sacred and profane history. But most especially it is the scene of the mission and miracles of the Prophet

Elijah. Seconding in his prayer and penance on this Holy Mountain of God came his first followers, the Sons of the Prophet. In turn arose the Christian hermits peopling its grottos with interior prayer and exterior penance. Within the framework of these mysteries blossomed devotion to the Blessed Virgin Mary of Mount Carmel and the traditional moral succession of the Order of Carmelites from the days of the prophet Elijah. Their ancient dwelling places clustered about the well of the prophet Elijah. St. Albert, Patriarch of Jerusalem, (1149–1214) who actually resided at Acre because Jerusalem was in Moslem hands, presented the Friars (Brothers) of Our Lady of Mount Carmel with their first rule of life sometime between 1206 and 1214. This Carmelite Rule was renewed by Pope Honorius III in 1226 and revised by Pope Innocent IV in 1247.[15] The same pontiff was to describe the dispersion of the Carmelites. "The inroads of the pagans have driven our beloved sons, the Hermits of Our Lady of Mount Carmel, to betake themselves, not without great affliction of spirit, to parts across the sea."[16] Henceforth the difficult scaling of the crags of the geographical Carmel becomes a mystical ascent to be participated in spiritually by Carmelites and their disciples worldwide according to the doctrine developed in St. John of the Cross.

The migration of the Carmelite Friars throughout Europe began first in Italy, then France and England where they were called the Whitefriars because of their white mantle and hood. It was inevitable that the seat of universal government of the Order would be set up in Rome.[17]

Towards the end of the sixteenth century St. Teresa of Avila (1515–1582) after instituting the reform of the Carmelite Nuns in 1562, with St. John of the Cross (1542–1591) undertook the reform of the Carmelite Friars. Both movements of the Teresian reform were called the Discalced since they went barefoot with sandals. St. John of the Cross made his solemn profession with the Discalced November 28, 1568. After intense negotiations and after the death of both founders, Pope Clement VIII on December 20, 1593 decreed the Discalced to be an independent and distinct religious Order.

The Carmelites of the Ancient Observance, sometimes referred to as the Calced, came to the United States during the Civil War. The members of the Irish Province came to New York in 1888. They undertook the parochial care of souls in Our Lady of the Scapular of Mount Carmel Parish. It would be difficult to evaluate adequately their compassionate care for these many years of the patients at Bellevue Hospital located in the parish. In 1931 Father Lawrence Flanagan, O.Carm., became Provincial of the newly established Province of St. Elias with headquarters in New York. It was he who befriended Mother M. Angeline and introduced her to the Most Reverend Elias Magennis, O.Carm.,[18] the Prior General who eventually received Mother M. Angeline and her first companions into the ranks of the Carmelite Order.

Even after the passing of so many years it is difficult to realize, much less express, what this gift and grace of affiliation for herself and her Sisters meant to Mother M. Angeline Teresa, O.Carm. as she and they began to ascend together the spiritual heights of Mount Carmel. Witness the unspeakable reward for those who are faithful in this ascent and reach its summit as taught by St. John of the Cross, Carmelite Doctor and Mystic in his paradigm of the Ascent of Mount Carmel:

"ONLY THE HONOR AND GLORY OF GOD DWELLS ON THIS MOUNT."[19]

NOTES

[1] EXHIBIT "C": "Foundation" Book. page 11, line T.

[2] *Ibid.* (line Mc)

[3] *Ibid.* (line M)

[4] *Ibid.* (line L)

[5] *Op. cit.* page 11, lines V through Z; page 12 lines C through Z; page 13, lines C to Z.

[6] Kay Leen in *The Catholic News* September 15, 1954.

[7] AANY Box P-4 Folder 7A NB—The Monday meeting was April 13, 1931 (ed. note)

[8] *Ibid.*

Sister Mary Leonie	April 13, 1931
Sister Mary Alexis of Jesus	April 14, 1931
Sister Mary Teresa	April 15, 1931
Sister M. Louise	undated
Sister Colette of the Most Blessed Sacrament	undated
Sister Alodie—petition missing (ed. note)	

[9] *Ibid.*

[10] *Ibid.*

[11] *Ibid.*

[12] AVGA

[13] AANY *op. cit.*

[14] *Ibid.*

[15] cf. Smet, Joachim, O.Carm., *The Carmelites. A History of the Brothers of Our Lady of Mount Carmel.* IV Vols. Carmelite Spiritual Center, Darien, Ill. (1975–1985) Vol. I, pp. 1–12.

[16] Pope Innocent IV., *Paganorum Incursus,* July 26, 1247; Bull. Carm., I, 8.

[17] McCaffrey, O.Carm. Rev. P.R. *The White Friars, An outline Carmelite History.*, Gill and Sons, Ltd. Dublin, 1926 p. 43.

[18] Most Reverend Elias Magennis, O. Carm. (1868-1937) was born in Ireland. At first he opted for the diocesan priesthood but entered the Irish Province of the Carmelites of the Ancient Observance in 1887 with an A.B. from the Royal University of Dublin and a licentiate in theology from Milltown Park, London. He was ordained a priest in 1894. He labored in Australia from 1898 until 1906. He returned to Ireland as novie-master from 1906-1909. He was elected Assistant General until 1919. He spent much of his term in the United States and was an outstanding leader in the cause of Irish Freedom.

Upon his election as Prior General, Pope Leo XIII said of him that he was destined to do great things for Carmel. He certainly did. His generalate from 1919-1931 has been called the Restoration. He made New York an independent Province and also Germany. He restored the Provinces of Holland, Australia, Spain and Poland. He returned the Carmelites to England and Portugal. He revived the Missionary Activity of the Order worldwide and opened new missions in Java and Brazil in concert with the Congregation for the Propagation of the Faith. He also brought the Carmelites back to the Holy Land. He directed the renewal of the Constitutions of the Order published in 1930. He revamped the educational system throughout the Order and revived the International College of St. Albert in Rome as "the scholastic center of the whole Order." He brought the cloistered Nuns, Carmelites of the Ancient Observance to the United States for the first time. He aggregated seven Institutes of Carmelite Sisters to the Order, the last being the Carmelite Sisters for the Aged and Infirm in 1931 to the role of the Third Order Secular. Himself an author of no mean ability he promoted the works of Carmelite scholars and writers including Blessed Titus Brandsma later a beatified martyr. Finally he undertook the renewal of the Carmelite calendar and began the revision of its liturgical books.

[19] St. John of the Cross, *Sketch of Mount Carmel, Collected writings of St. John of the Cross.* Trans. Kieran Kavanaugh, O.C.D. and Otilio Rodriguez, I.C.S. Publications. Institute of Carmelite Studies, Washington, D.C. 1973 p. 66

BRONX

On October 26, 1929 the stock market on Wall Street crashed. This single event began the Great Depression and changed the life style of countless Americans. Overnight, wealthy people became paupers. Banks failed, unemployment raged, once secure families were evicted from their homes, and bread lines became a commonplace across the country. There was a sense of paralysis from the lack of hope. Along with other institutions the Catholic Church suffered also. Huge debts had to be liquidated and new ones incurred in order to keep parochial schools open and respond to the demands made on the social services of the Church. The Church indeed suffered in and with her people.

It is a phenomenon both in the natural and supernatural order that at this precise point in history Mother M. Angeline Teresa and her six companions began their new venture. Like everyone else, their life and work was affected by the times. With no real financial security, they were rich in faith and hope. Frequently, when the aftermath of those days are evaluated, the perilous condition of the aged is omitted as a factor. Yet the aged were amongst those whose circumstances were most threatened. Life savings had been wiped out, securities had been massively devalued and many families could no longer support at home elderly members without any income.

Against this background the threefold rapid development of Mother Angeline's dream into reality is without precedent. First, the growth of her new religious family numerically. Next, the increase of elderly women and men who turned to her for their security, and to be honest, even for their survival. Finally, the acquisition of property, from the borrowed St. Elizabeth's old rectory, to purchasing land, buildings and construction of new ones, in the name of the fledgling Congregation of the Carmelite Sisters for the Aged and Infirm.

Under date of April 15, 1931 Mother Angeline sent Cardinal Hayes the following list of Sisters in the Community only a year and a half after its inception.

Sister M. Louise, Doome: 57 years of age and 35 years of Profession.

Sister M. Leonie, Logan: 54 years of age and 26 years of Profession.

Sister M. Therese, Schoof: 43 years of age and 20 years of Profession.

Sister M. Colette of the Blessed Sacrament,Duffy: 53 years of age and 18 years of Profession.

Sister M. Alodia, Hutchinson: 40 years of age and 18 years of Profession.

Sister M. Alexis of Jesus, Dube:48 years of age and 17 years of Profession.

Sister M. Frances Teresa, McKinnion: 39 years of age and 18 years of Profession.

Sister M. Edwin Martin, Kelly: 39 years of age and 18 years of Profession.

Sister M. Winifred, McGale: 37 years of age and 14 years of Profession.

Sister M. Angeline Teresa, McCrory: 37 years of age and 16 years of Profession. (cf. footnote [1])

By this time three other Little Sisters of the Poor had joined with Mother Angeline Teresa and her first six companions. There were some short term benefits from such action but to continue on this course would be aggravating two problems. Understandably a widening gap and a strained relationship between both Communities had been created. Moreover, the introduction and implementation of the innovative and charismatic ideals and philosophy of Mother Angeline Teresa and the Carmelite spirit would best be communicated to receptive new members. Cardinal Hayes was aware of these problems. By way of solution he instructed Mother Angeline in future not to receive any further members from the Little Sisters of the Poor into the new Carmelite community. He stated that he would no longer grant such a permission. He also notified the Provincial Superior of the Little Sisters of his decision.[2]

The zeal of Mother Angeline Teresa, O.Carm. for the aged was diffusive. Her personal dedication was inspiring. From the beginning young women were drawn through her to the new Carmelite Congregation. The first three recruits were received just a year and a half after the foundation. They were Mary Hearty from the Bronx, who upon her entrance was given the name Sister Mary Patrick of the Sacred Heart; Winifred Thompson from Philadelphia, who became Sister Mary Martin of Tours; and Mary Magdalene Koeble from New York who was called Sister Mary Thomas Aquin. All three entered January 6, 1931. The first two received the habit in the first ceremony of reception, September 8, 1931 presided over by Reverend Edwin Sinnott, the spiritual director of the Community. Sister Aquin, the youngest of the three, contracted polio and died tragically on August 30, 1931 at the age of twenty-three. The day the first two received the habit two more postulants arrived, Nora M. Shaughnessy who became Sister Mary Brendan and Catherine Stoll

who became Sister Mary Agnes.[3] Six other young ladies were waiting to join the Community but due to lack of accommodation they
had to delay until space was available at the Van Cortlandt complex. They were Mildred Joslin (Sister M. Regina), Anna Colgan
(Sister Margaret Mary), Mary Le Plante (Sister M. Veronica), Lillian
Cassidy (Sister M. Edward), and two blood sisters,Mary G. Amortegy
and Leonore Amortegy, who became in turn Sister M. Pauline and
Sister M. Celine.[4] These eight received the habit together on February 2, 1932, feast of the Purification of Our Lady, following a retreat
preached by Father Mel Daly, O.Carm.[5]

Meanwhile Mother Angeline Teresa had received three more elderly residents at St. Elizabeth's. Miss Mary McGrath, Miss Julia
Gorman and Mr. Patrick Maguire were the new members of the
family. The list of others seeking admission was daily growing
longer. St. Elizabeth's limitations were now becoming a hindrance
to the Community's expansion as well as to the apostolate for the
care of the aged.

It was understood from the beginning and in the nature of things
that St. Elizabeth's parish complex was to be a temporary arrangement for the Carmelite Sisters and their apostolate. No one dreamed
that the expansion would be so rapid and the need for a more
permanent arrangement would become imperative so soon.

Some five years later when the new Motherhouse, novitiate and
residence for the aged would be blessed, in retrospect Patrick Cardinal Hayes reflected on the extraordinary progress which brought
about the necessity for expansion.

> I express joy, great joy and happiness to come to St. Patrick's this
> morning. I have had my eyes open in surprise at the developments
> which have taken place. I have watched with solicitude the development
> and growth of this work, and now I rejoice today at seeing it. It is one of
> the most extraordinary developments of this large archdiocese. I did not
> think it possible, except the Lord would perform a miracle, to see the
> beginning and in a very few years to find this development, and it all
> taking place during 'the years of depression'. The only answer is prayer
> to the Wonderful Father in Heaven, Who has so wonderfully blessed
> this work. The development is not only material but it is also spiritual—
> a large Community of Sisters growing out of a small group of a few
> years ago, under the wonderful guidance of the Holy Spirit of God. I did
> not think it possible. There are other Communities crying out for the
> want of vocations, but here you find large numbers.
>
> Congratulations, Reverend Mother Angeline Teresa and Sisters. Really,
> in my years of administration of this large archdiocese, I have not known
> or met with any such other development that I could identify where

progress was made such as here. It is with a heart filled with gratitude that I say I have been privileged to see this. The work is God's, providing for those who have been compelled to leave their own home and spend their later years here in a house surrounded by good example.[6]

Cardinal Hayes, aware of the need for an expanded facility for the use of the Sisters and their apostolate, had encouraged Mother M. Angeline to look about for such a property. Monsignor Patrick N. Breslin and Father Edwin Sinnott, Mother's loyalest friends, arranged for her to visit various sites. She had her heart set on the Bronx which was geographically part of New York City and adjacent to excellent hospital services so often needed for the old people. After a long search she wrote to the Cardinal at the end of April:

> Having read the report of Catholic Charities we feel your burden is sufficiently heavy without additional expenses incurred by us. We have looked over the Bronx and have not found anything available for the present.
>
> If in your generosity and superior judgment you think Mamaroneck a suitable place we will gratefully accept the same.
>
> With deep appreciation of former kindness and assuring Your Eminence of our religious respect and prayers,
>
> I am in Jesus and Mary
> Your Eminence's Obedient Child,
>
> Sister M. Angeline Teresa.[7]

Once again Divine Providence favored Mother Angeline Teresa's confident prayers and in May a property with excellent potential was discovered in the Bronx. There was one acre of property located along Van Cortlandt Park South. The building itself was fairly modern, three stories high, and constructed of fire resistant brick. It had been built by the Radio Corporation of America to serve as an experimental laboratory. It was called the RCA Tower and was the receiving station for the first transatlantic radio broadcast from London March 14, 1924.[8]

On investigation it was found that several floors had been already divided into single rooms in accordance with the type of work done there. There was also a garage made of the same brick. It was evident that this plant no longer in use by the RCA corporation could be readily altered and adapted to the exigencies of a Motherhouse, novitiate and commodious quarters for fifty-four residents.

The Cardinal was notified and investigated the parcel of land and its buildings. He first sent Monsignor Robert Keegan from the Catholic Charities to inspect the site and report to him. Msgr. Keegan sent a glowing report on May 9, 1931.[9] In this survey he included the following items: the former use of the building; its construction material and form; its location on the property with provision for further expansion; the neighborhood near the reservoir, large public high schools, a new building of Hunter College and the Municipal Art Center all precluding any serious changes in the neighborhood. There was accessibility to the Jerome Avenue Subway at Mosholu Park Station; facilities, heavily wired for electricity along all walls adaptable for mechanical therapy treatment; heating system adequate for comfortable temperature and supply of hot water. Added to all this Keegan notes that there is a passenger elevator, a freight elevator and an elaborate air conditioning and ventilating system. His final estimation was that to reproduce the building at the present time would cost $140,000.[10] Enclosed in this fulsome report was also a map and a floor plan.

Mr. George Gillespie, the attorney for the Cardinal, also visited the complex at his request. These and other investigations were conducted by Rev. Bryan McEntegart, Rev. Joseph S. O'Connell and Rev. Thomas L. Brennock.

These preliminaries having been successfully accomplished the Cardinal himself visited the location. Having taken prudent counsel he wrote on July 30, 1931 that since the Sisters were now firmly established as a Religious Community, "I am now approving the purchase of the property in the Bronx for the Sisters."[11]

To the great joy of all concerned the building at 66 Van Cortlandt Park South, the Bronx, New York was purchased on August 15, 1931 for the sum of $200,000 and a down payment of $50,000.[12] The Carmelite Sisters for the Aged and Infirm now had a permanent haven for themselves and their beloved old folks. It might be of interest to note here one of the so many coincidental happenings in the life of Mother M. Angeline Teresa. Another religious community of women had tried unsuccessfully to obtain the RCA property. In the hope of securing it they had buried a religious medal in the ground. As the renovations began for the Carmelite Sisters it was uncovered. It was a medal of St. Therese of Lisieux, the Carmelite so loved by Mother![13]

While it is abundantly clear that Mother M. Angeline Teresa rejected the forms of institutionalism which were depersonalizing and regimentalized it was never her thought or charism to do away with the care of the aged in institutional settings but rather to reform the system so that these places would be true homes that would respect personal dignity with an emphasis on interested concern for each resident (her term) individually. At the very beginning of the new Religious Community, Msgr. Robert Keegan, representing the Archdiocesan Catholic Charities, who was such an admirer and supporter of Mother Angeline tried to insinuate another but alien dimension into her apostolate, viz., the service of the aged and sick in their private homes. In a covering note with his report to Cardinal Hayes under date of May 9, 1931 recommending without reserve the purchase of the facility at Van Cortlandt Park for St. Patrick's Home he intimated that the Carmelite Sisters should also be visiting Sisters for the aged poor infirm in their private homes.[14] In the actual text of his report to Cardinal Hayes for Catholic Charities under Title II, *Visiting Sisters for the Aged and Infirm* he goes on record that a separate convent be set up and at least four Sisters of the new Community be assigned to it for this work.[15] Typical of Mother Angeline's tact she never even adverted to this well meaning interference. It was no part of her dream and would have divided not only Sisters but also their area of concentration. It is equally important that Cardinal Hayes to whom the suggestion was made took no action on this point with Mother M. Angeline although he accepted the rest of the report as written.

Almost at once the work of renovation and preparation began. Mother M. Angeline Teresa as an act of both gratitude and recognition decided to call the new foundation, "St. Patrick's Home". In her usual deferential manner she first asked the Cardinal if she might and then wrote to thank him when he acquiesced. Everything was ready for occupancy by mid-September. Mother Angeline wrote to Cardinal Hayes:

> 4381 Broadway
> New York
> September 17th, 1931

His Eminence Patrick Cardinal Hayes
Archbishop of New York

Your Eminence,

On the eve of our departure for our new Home, which your Fatherly interest and care has provided for us, and those who are under our charge, we wish to express to You our deep gratitude for the many favors received through your bounty. Rest assured that you will have a daily remembrance in the prayers of our Community and we sincerely trust that we will be able to live up to the high ideals of Catholic Charities.

May we also be permitted to thank Your Eminence for allowing us to call our first Foundation, "St. Patrick's Home", it is a favor deeply appreciated by all our Sisters.

Assuring Your Eminence of our religious respect and Obedience, and asking your blessing.

> I am in Jesus and Mary
> Your Eminence's humble Servant,
> Sister M. Angeline Teresa.[16]

The actual date of the transfer of the Sisters, novices, postulants and their aged residents from what surely had been the cradle of the Congregation St. Elizabeth's Rectory occurred on September 29, 1931.[17] Even after their settling in workmen continued to finish the remodelling.

The building had been redesigned in order to render both possible and practical Mother Angeline Teresa's ideal of a residence for the aged poor. It was to be an American home, not an institution. There were no evidences of physical restraint or incarceration. The residents were to be free to come and go provided their health permitted. This meant that by simply notifying the Sisters, as good order would require, they were free to visit friends, go out for a meal, go shopping or even go to a movie. They were also encouraged to share their talents for the welfare of all, as noted above, and a real family spirit became the happy result.

It was Mother herself who laid out the modifications of the new building. The best areas were given over to the residents. Living quarters were arranged for use in single occupancy, double occupancy and to make room for others on the long waiting list a few rooms were designed for three or four compatible persons. Each room was dedicated to a special saint. There were comfortable chairs in every room. Married couples lived together in their own room as they had done at home for so many years. No item of comfort for the residents had been omitted, a sanitary kitchen, cheery dining rooms, a laundry and sewing room. There were spacious recreation rooms for groups and small parlors for private visiting as well as the offices needed for administration. Mother Angeline's office was near to the residents and her door was always open for them to come to her. The chapel albeit small was the heart of St. Patrick's Home. Although residents of any denomination were received all were welcome to be present at Holy Mass, Benediction of the Blessed Sacrament and any of the spiritual exercises of the Sisters.

The far ends of the third floor became the novitiate and convent. The first, under the patronage of the Little Flower was the novitiate. The other end was the convent for the Sisters under the title of Our

Lady of Mount Carmel. Even the attic was utilized for the novices' recreation and typing room, and storage.

The functions which today have been departmentalized and professionalized for skilled personnel were lovingly performed by the Sisters. The admissions office interviewed and evaluated new applicants. Another Sister took care of social and recreational needs of the residents. A properly qualified Sister watched over nursing service. The food services were managed by another Sister with special supervision by Mother herself for the menus of feast days and holidays. A physician was at hand and frequently visited anyone who was ill or needed attention. Of course there was a resident Chaplain to look after the old people and to assist the Sisters in their spiritual needs.

Amidst this complex activity the project was finally ready to be blessed with a public ceremony. This was held December 16, 1931. Cardinal Hayes dedicated the new Home to St. Patrick and blessed the new complex. Although he was involved with the project from the beginning he was really astounded at what Mother Angeline had accomplished in such a short time. This was obvious from his remarks: "I have often heard of the good Sisters working miracles, but I never believed that anyone could make the changes that have been made here in such a short time."[18] His Eminence also took advantage of the occasion to remark that the Carmelite Sisters for the Aged and Infirm were the first Religious Congregation to be founded in America solely for the care of the aging.

Some twenty-five years later Mother Angeline Teresa looked back with pixie humor as she recalled the momentous occasion of the opening of her first home.

> Our first applicant was a frail old gentleman of eighty. From his pocket he drew out two hundred single dollar bills. They were soiled and worn. By the looks of them they must have been in circulation as long as himself. Placing them carefully on the table before me, he said: 'Mother, I want you to take this money and keep me for the rest of my life and bury me.' The old gentleman seemed to have about six months of life left in him, and it seemed like a good offer at the time. I accepted it and gave him a home. Twenty years later he was still with us! And true to my promise, I buried him at the ripe old age of 100. He got his money's worth.[19]

Off to such a glowing start, Mother Angeline's dream expanded rapidly before her eyes. The number of vocations continued to increase, attracting not a few professionally trained women. The census of the aged residents in the house, both men and women, stretched the projected capacity of the house, and the need for physical expansion could not be put off.

It was decided that the only way to go was up. Three more stories would be added to the original building. A revised civil corporation was founded establishing formally "St. Patrick's Home for the Aged and Infirm" located in Bronx County. Cardinal Hayes was the President, Monsignor Patrick Breslin, Vice President, Reverend Edward Sinnott, Second Vice President, Mother M. Angeline Teresa, O.Carm., Treasurer and Sister M. Leonie, O.Carm. Assistant Treasurer, under date of February 23, 1935. On July 23, 1935 they met at the Chancery Office, 477 Madison Avenue, New York, to approve the new construction and to borrow $60,000. When the contract was signed by Mother M. Angeline Teresa on August 20th, 1935, the costs had risen to $71,981. The construction undertaken by Mr. Frank O'Hare of the O'Hare Construction Company began almost at once. As a result the three floor addition was finished, furnished and functional. The blessing of the new facility took place just five years after the Carmelite Sisters had moved from temporary headquarters at St. Elizabeth's to their first permanent home at St. Patrick's. Again it was Cardinal Hayes who presided over the ceremony accompanied by many diocesan and religious priests. Perhaps this article in the New York *Catholic News* best describes the event: "Institution opened by the Carmelite Sisters five years ago makes notable progress—His Eminence lauds work of the Community—New quarters provide model home for older persons."[20]

The number of Novices moved Mother Angeline to continue her expansion program. The original garage had been used for storage. Now it was emptied, extended twenty feet and two stories were added to accommodate forty-six novices in two dormitory floors. The ground floor contained the office of the Novice Mistress, recreation and work rooms. It was ready for occupancy and blessing October 31, 1937. Most Reverend John Collins, a missionary Bishop from Liberia who was a house guest of Cardinal Hayes officiated. At this time also two porches which had been added to the Main Building for the use of the elderly residents were also blessed as well as a lovely Grotto of Our Lady of Lourdes.

Cardinal Patrick Hayes died September 4, 1938.[21] Perhaps nowhere was his life and labor better described than in an address he made for the Catholic Charities of New York Campaign:

> The Golden Rule of doing to others as we would have others do unto us is not as high or as noble as doing MORE for others than they can ever possibly do for us, because God Himself ALREADY has done more for us than we can ever possibly do for Him.[22]

However his loving concern and fatherly care was continued apace by his successor, Archbishop, later Francis Cardinal Spellman. Following the treasured example of his predecessor, Cardinal Hayes, Cardinal Spellman[23] was a trusted friend and firm supporter of Mother Angeline Teresa and her Carmelite Sisters. If indeed, true love is letting go, he encouraged Mother Angeline to move the Motherhouse outside the Archdiocese when she had the opportunity to obtain a non-pareilled house and property. In his almost-thirty-year career as Archbishop of New York he allowed Mother to make an unprecedented five new foundations. In the appeal made in 1957 to have the Community raised to pontifical status he not only wrote a favorable letter but even moreso he sent an authentic document giving the valid history and development of the Carmelite Sisters against any detractors.[24] Countless news items testify to his presence at almost every dedication of a new foundation, every personal jubilee of Mother and each Congregational milestone of the Carmelite Sisters. It was he who won for Mother Angeline the papal honor *Pro Ecclesia et Pontifice* which he bestowed on her in the name of the Holy Father in his residence on Saturday July 1, 1961.[25] Despite his many *encomia* for Mother Angeline, Cardinal Francis Spellman proved his words by thoughtful, gentle actions until his death December 2, 1967.

When he took over in 1939, the exigencies of the times called for an increase in the care for chronically ill aged in need of skilled medical and nursing attention. Cardinal Spellman at Mother Angeline's request approved a radically expanded extension for such facilities at St. Patrick's. The proposed renovations were estimated at $1,600,000, a staggering sum. Undaunted Mother Angeline assisted by Mother M. Aloysius, O.Carm. the Superior and Administrator of St. Patrick's Home undertook this program. As a sign of the acceptance of the work of the Carmelite Sisters under the Hill-Burton Bill a federal grant of $300,000 was received. Shortly after this Cardinal Spellman invited Mother Angeline Teresa, O.Carm. to his office on Madison Avenue. She was accompanied by Mother M. Aloysius. He presented Mother Angeline with his check for $100,000 toward the new building. This was but the continuation of his many kindnesses to Mother Angeline and her Carmelite Sisters. Typical of the gratitude and respect of Mother Angeline Teresa, the new building, six stories high at its completion, was named the Cardinal Spellman Building. It was dedicated on June 7, 1959 by the Cardinal himself.

Monsignor Francis F. Reh, later Bishop, addressed the assembly:

> That twenty-eight years ago a young religious Superioress and her tiny band of adventurers for Christ saw a dream realized, to provide a home

for those without a home. It was not an institution, a shelter, merely supplying the physical needs of those who might not be able to provide these for themselves. It was a dream to create a true home. It must be a home more permanent than any hotel or residence, wherein security would replace the growing concern, that anxiety, that dread of the aging for the days when mounting years may leave them not only alone but incapable of helping themselves ... And it was here that the Congregation of the Carmelite Sisters for the Aged and Infirm under the leadership of Mother M. Angeline Teresa found their dream realized.[26]

The crowning joy in Mother Angeline's lifetime for her beloved first home St. Patrick's was the new free standing convent in keeping with the contemporary ideal that one should not live where one works. The new convent, another six story building, contained a Chapel, Community Room, Refectory, office space, sleeping quarters and an elevator, prepared not only for staff Sisters but also for sisters who were retired. It was dedicated March 4, 1971 by His Eminence Terence Cardinal Cooke. First to her dismay and then to her humble joy the new convent was dedicated to Mother M. Angeline Teresa, O.Carm. herself.

Throughout the years of steady expansion, St. Patrick's has grown and fulfilled the fondest hopes and dreams of the Foundress and present Mother General of the Carmelite Sisters, Reverend Mother M. Angeline Teresa. We, her Carmelite daughters, wish to express our love and appreciation for her dynamic leadership by dedicating this newest building to her. Bricks and mortar can raise the house from its foundation, but only the vibrant lives of dedicated souls can make that house a true home dedicated to the love and service of our fellow man.

To our exemplar, then, whose noble heart has set the pace of courage and action in the face of obstacles, we dedicate this Convent, this Chapel, these rooms, which will serve to carry on her most cherished ideals of service to others.[27]

For a synopsized account of the growth and development of Mother M. Angeline Teresa's first foundation St. Patrick's Home the following extract is presented here.

Extract

"Our beloved Foundress and First Superior General was Administrator of Saint Patrick's Home from 1931 to 1946. In 1946 she moved to our present Motherhouse, Avila-on-Hudson, Germantown, New York. During these years at St. Patrick's she had the opportunity to observe first hand how her unique concepts of individualized care for older persons improved the quality of their lives.

Saint Patrick's Home has served as a model for all the foundations made from this first home. The basic philosophy of care has passed the test of time and has proved to be satisfying and comforting to persons as they advance in age and have specific needs. The following chronology of Saint Patrick's Home tells its own story.

Saint Patrick's Home was purchased August 15, 1931. Dedicated: December 16, 1931 by His Eminence, Patrick Cardinal Hayes.

1st. Expansion 1934—Chapel and office on First Floor.
Convent—Second Floor.
Refectory on ground floor.
Blessed by Monsignor Patrick Breslin.

2nd. Expansion 1936—Three additional stories added to original building. Dedicated September 30th, 1936, by His Eminence Patrick Cardinal Hayes.

3rd. Expansion 1937—Two porches added to original building October 31, 1937.

4th. Expansion 1937—An old garage enlarged and converted into a separate Novitiate Building October 31, 1937.

5th. Expansion 1938—An all purpose room was added to the Noviate building, dedicated to the Infant of Prague in 1938.

6th. Expansion 1957—A new building was erected and dedicated to His Eminence "Francis Cardinal Spellman". It was blessed by Cardinal Spellman on June 7th, 1959.

7th. Expansion 1970—A free standing Convent was built and dedicated to Mother M. Angeline Teresa—Foundress. This was blessed by Cardinal Cooke, March 4, 1971.[28]

8th. Expansion 1987–1989—A dynamic building program for a new eight story facility was undertaken. The first phase was the demolition of the existing chapel, laundry and administration building to maximize the area for construction without interrupting the total care of the present aged residents.

The new building was designed not only to continue the specialized apostolate of St. Patrick's Home, viz. the finest geriatric services for the Aged and Infirm, but also to introduce two ancillary services both innovative and futuristic.

1) An approved non-residential health care center fully equipped for an updated Adult Day Care Program.

2) Moreover a facility for an Intergenerational Program with a fully equipped Child Day Care Center. Here the values and benefits of an older generation can be shared with those of a new and coming generation in a balanced supervised milieu.

The second phase was the transferal of the residents to the new quarters and the reception of new residents. The former structure was removed and an enlarged parking facility added.

In this eighth expansion of the original St. Patrick's Home the dream of Mother M. Angeline Teresa ever to reach out to the Aging and the poor of every category has been both retrenched and contemporized.[29]

NOTES

[1] AANY Box P4 Folder 7A (April 15, 1931).

[2] AANY Box P4 Folder 7B (January 11, 1933).

[3] AVGA—*Category Book* page 1 and 2.

[4] *Ibid.*

[5] Details supplied by Sister M. Bernadette, O.Carm. and Sister M. Elias, O.Carm., two oldest members of the Community who made their own novitiate with these sisters. Conversation with the author November 14, 1988 at Avila.

[6] Patrick Cardinal Hayes quoted in *Catholic News*, (New York) October 3, 1936.

[7] AANY Box P1 Folder 5 (April 30, 1931).

[8] AANY Report to Cardinal May 9, 1931.

[9] AANY Box P1 Folder 5 (May 9, 1931).

[10] *Ibid.*

[11] AANY *op. cit.* Letter to Fr. Elias Magennis in Rome. July 30, 1931.

[12] AVGA—*Memorandum*—St. Patrick's Home File.

[13] *Ibid.*

[14] AANY Box P1 Folder 5.

[15] *Ibid.*

[16] Wisely, *op. cit.* p. 82.

[17] *Catholic News* (NY) December 26, 1931.

[18] *Catholic News* (NY) October 3, 1936.

[19] Kay Leen in *The Catholic News* September 15, 1954.

[20] *Ibid.*

[21] This simple biographical note can in no way begin to describe the life and work of His Eminence Patrick Cardinal Hayes, the Cardinal of Charities. The son of Daniel and Mary (Gleason) he was born November 20, 1867 at City Hall Place in New York City. He attended La Salle High School. Then, Manhattan College where he excelled in the classics and mathematics. He graduated in 1888, the president of the class and also the Athletic Association. He attended the seminary of St. Sulpice and old St. Joseph's Seminary at Troy. He was ordained a priest on September 8, 1892. He attended the Catholic University of America for two years of advanced studies in Theology. In 1902 he became secretary for Archbishop John Farley, later Cardinal. He became Chancellor of the Archdiocese of New York in 1903. October 28, 1914 he became Auxiliary Bishop of New York and Titular Bishop of Tagaste. On November 29, 1917 he was appointed Bishop Ordinary of the U.S. Armed Forces. He became the Archbishop of New York, March 10, 1919. On March 6, 1924 he was elevated to the Cardinalate under the title of Sancta Maria in Via. He was involved personally and officially with Mother M. Angeline Teresa, O.Carm. and her work from 1929 to his death, September 4, 1938.

[22] Radio Address—New York Catholic Charities Campaign, May 11, 1924.

[23] Francis Cardinal Spellman was born May 4, 1889 at Whitman Massachusetts the son of William and Ellen Conway. He attended Dyer Grammar School and graduated from Whitman High School in 1907. He graduated from Fordham University June 14, 1911. His academic record was excellent and he received the coveted award, the Hughes Medal for Religion. Encouraged by Monsignor Gill of Brockton, Mass. he began his studies for the priesthood at the North American College, Rome, in the fall of 1911. He was ordained a priest May 14, 1916 by Most Reverend Giuseppe Ceppetelli, Patriarch of Constantinople, at the Church of the Apollinaire. After some local assignments in the Archdiocese of Boston, he volunteered and was accepted as a chaplain for the United States Army only to be directed at the last moment by William Cardinal O'Connell to the staff of the *Boston Pilot* instead. Then the Chancery Office in 1922. November 2, 1925 he returned to Rome as an attache in the Vatican Secretariat of State, the first American ever to be so honored. During this period he became a close personal friend of Eugenio Cardinal Pacelli, later Pope Pius XII. On July 30, 1932 he was appointed Auxiliary Bishop of Boston and was consecrated in Rome September 8, 1932. He was named Archbishop of New York April 15, 1939. On December 11, 1939 he was appointed Military Vicar for the Armed Forces of the United States a position in which he distinguished himself until his death. He also served the Church during World War II by his close association with President F.D. Roosevelt. In the Consistory of February 18, 1946 he was created a Cardinal under the title of SS. John and Paul

the 4th century Basilica of the Passionist Fathers on the Celian Hill. He died December 2, 1967.

[24] SCRIS Archives Box N 62 1.

[25] cf. *The Catholic News*, July 8, 1961.

[26] *Catholic News*, (NY) March 7, 1959.

[27] AVGA—*Dedication Program*, March 4, 1971.

[28] AVGA—cf. *Memorandum* note 12.

[29] Author's update addition: January 21, 1989.

AVILA

A concise barometer indicating the need and the acceptance of Mother Angeline Teresa's philosophy for the care of the aged and the dedication of the Carmelite Sisters to this specific apostolate is the expansion of her foundations. This began early on and was made possible by the extraordinary number of vocations which came to the infant Congregation. Before enumerating these foundations in chronological sequence the pride of place must go to St. Teresa's Motherhouse. Before becoming the property of the Carmelite Sisters the estate was called "Ridgely" or "Tivoli on (the) Hudson", located on Woods Road in the Village of Tivoli, Town of Clermont, County of Columbia, State of New York.[1] The Property Deed was listed from Sarah Jewett Marsh, of 1220 Park Avenue and Julia Giles of 214 East 62nd Street, in the City, County and State of New York and the Carmelite Sisters for the Aged and Infirm, a New York membership corporation with office at No. 66 Van Cortlandt Park South in the County of Bronx and State of New York.[2] The Bill of Sale listed the same two parties and besides two parcels of land containing 86 acres also were included some 31 pieces of farm equipment individually catalogued,among which were a 1928 McCormick Tractor (18 years old), a 1928 Dodge Suburban Wagon (same age) and a 1930 Ford 2 ton truck with lattice body (16 years old). The transaction was dated December 3, 1946.[3] The Wall Street Firm of Appleton, Rice and Perrin were the Attorneys for the sellers. The actual cost was $40,000. In no time Tivoli on Hudson became Avila on Hudson. A 1946 real estate broker's brochure from *Previews Incorporated* profusely illustrated describes the estate as, "A rare combination of traditional charm, historical background, and all prerequisites of the present day life in this fine estate, which in addition to its rich heritage offers 86 acres of diversified land that commands extensive views from its 1/4 mile frontage on the Hudson River."[4] The Sisters of the Holy Cross had already made a down payment of $4,000 to the owners of this property. In return for relinquishing their rights to the property this $4,000 was returned to them and the sum of 400 plus dollars was also repaid which represented the price of a new tractor which they had purchased for the property.[5]

The genesis of the personal efforts of Mother M. Angeline Teresa to seek, find, and establish by ecclesiastical authority this Mother-house, Generalate and Novitiate of the Carmelite Sisters for the Aged and Infirm are best presented by herself in her Circular Letter under date of December 13, 1946 from St. Patrick's Home in the Bronx announcing to the whole Community the purchase and establishment of their new Mother House:

The Purpose of This Letter . . . .

All good things are worth waiting for, aren't they? Well—we have waited—we have persevered in prayer and pleading, petitions without end, and lo! and behold! God has answered our prayers in His own good time and His own inimitable way. Rejoice with me and be glad that your prayers have brought such good things to pass to our little Carmel. I promised to tell you all about the big intention that has kept all of you so busy saying extra prayers and making Novenas'ad infinitum', and, true to my word, I am sending you a full account of the purchase of our new Mother House and Novitiate. I want you to join with me in thanking the Little King at Midnight Mass for doing so much for us.

The Hardships We Suffered . . . .

It was not easy. We began to hunt up property that would be suitable. By suitable, I mean, not too far away from the City, yet secluded; not too small for our purposes, yet not too big for our purse. That was indeed a large order especially in these times of inflated values but as you will presently find out, no order is too large that prayer cannot purchase.

We went to see the Hudson River Naval Academy in Irvington, just a few miles from Tarrytown. It seemed to be made for us. The grounds were truly beautiful, it was only a half-hour from St. Patrick's it had seclusion, it would house a sufficient number and—best of all—the price was reasonable. Full of hope, storming Heaven through the intercession of the Little Flower whose Feast was coming very soon, we submitted all the facts to the Chancery Office. Archbishop McIntyre thought that everything was fine, but—we could not have it! Why?? It was located in Westchester County which was overflowing with tax-exempt property owned by Religious. What could we do? Was this not a sure sign that God did not intend this delightful place for us? We were disappointed, but felt that the Little Flower would not forsake us entirely. She did not want to take all the credit and had referred the entire matter to her Holy Mother, St. Teresa, who had plenty of experience in getting new foundations. So, we too turned to the great Teresa and in a solemn Novena in which the Cloistered Carmelites joined us, we sang the Hymn with bursting lungs and hopeful hearts. We promised that if we received something suitable through her intercession, that our Mother House would forevermore bear her illustrious name.

At this time we stumbled, purely through chance, upon a wonderful piece of property located at Hyde Park. This time we made sure that we were looking in the right territory, and Archbishop McIntyre assured us that Dutchess, Putnam and Rockland Counties would be just fine. Hyde Park, you know, is in Dutchess County. I do not want to waste time describing to you the superlative qualities that this property possessed, but, suffice it to say, that after we had lined everything up in good order and practically had all our plans made for moving in, Archbhishop McIntyre again stamped the seal of his disapproval upon our high hopes. We could not have it. Why?? It was practically next door to the Cardinal Farley Military Academy, the Jesuits were in Hyde Park, the Marists were in Hyde Park and to have the Carmelites in Hyde Park would be just a little too much!

This does not give you the true picture of the many jaunts we made to see properties that were not suitable at all or that were far too expensive for our lean purse. We leave all that to your good imaginations. Now, let me tell you how we found . . . .

The Answer to Our Prayers . . . .

We were tempted over and over to give up. Nothing seemed to be going our way at all. When we seemed to have a prize within our grasp—one word sent it spinning away from us forever. But Teresa of Avila was never one to give up, and remember, she was backing us up all the way. So, was it any wonder that at the darkest moment—when we felt that perhaps God was not going to answer our prayers the way we hoped He would—a dear friend of St. Teresa's, Bishop Gibbons by name, stepped into the picture. We received a call to the effect that there was a beautiful property in his diocese a few miles from Tivoli. It was for sale at a very reasonable price and he intended to tell Archbishop McIntyre about it. This coincided with a meeting with the Archbishop who told us about the property and gave directions in his own handwriting as to how we could get there. 'Go up there,' he said, 'and look it over. From Bishop Gibbon's description it is a real buy. Let me know how you like it.' We gasped. This property was not even in the New York Archdiocese and here was Archbishop McIntyre telling us to look at it, in fact, sending us up there with his blessing! To be certain, I asked, 'Your Excellency, this is not in the Archdiocese. Is it alright to look at it with the intention of purchasing?' 'Perfectly alright, Mother,' the Archbishop rejoined in his precise way. 'Hurry now and get there before it's too dark to see anything'. It was then a few minutes of twelve and we turned the car towards the Taconic Parkway and speeded in the direction of Tivoli. We saw only a little of the property that day because we had no one to guide us, but we did get into the Main House and went through all the rooms. We liked the view, we liked the grounds, we liked the whole thing! Best of all, the price was within our limited range—$40,000 for several fine buildings and 86 Acres of land. By the time we paid for a few extras, it jumped to $42,000 odd and we still have some repairs to take into consideration. But we were able to pay CASH and that means everything to us. Let me have the pleasure of taking you through Avila-on-the-Hudson, the new Mother House of the Carmelite Sisters and the Home of the Little Flower Novitiate. The full name, of course, is 'St. Teresa's Mother House'.

The Main House . . . .

Nineteen rooms in all. The basement has the kitchen, store room, Oil Burner. The main floor contains a beautiful Library which will serve as our Chapel, a Living Room, Breakfast Room for our Chaplain, Reception Room, Refectory, Pantry and spacious Halls. The second floor. . . . four large rooms, two smaller ones, all wall-papered in tasteful designs. Four lavatories. The third floor. . . . four large rooms, four smaller ones, two lavatories.

The structure is in the style of an Italian Villa, true to type. Balconies adorn several windows. The building itself is entirely of brick with a white stucco facing. The location is on a hill overlooking the lordly Hudson at one of its most fascinating points—where one can view the majestic Catskills in all their splendor.

. . .

THE GREAT QUESTION . . . .

When are we moving? We hope——early in 1947.

THE INVITATION

Are you interested enough in all that I have told you to come and see for yourselves? If so, you are cordially invited at some future date which will be made definite later on, to witness for yourselves how God answers prayer and how He can not be outdone in generosity! Will you come?

AND NOW, MY PERSONAL GREETING . . . .

May God Bless you, my dearly beloved daughters in Carmel. You are truly the greatest consolation that I have when things go wrong as they so often do. You are the ones I depend on to draw down with your fervent prayers, penances and sacrifices, all those rich blessings which we need so much. You have never failed me in the past and I know that I can count on each and every one of you for the future.

. . .

With a final 'Thank-you' from a grateful and overflowing heart, I am,

Your devoted Mother in Carmel,

(signed Mother M. Angeline Teresa,O.Carm.)[6]

Even before the formalities of purchasing the Tivoli estate, there were rigorous canonical requirements which had to be complied with. Bishop Edmund F. Gibbons readily signified his willingness for Mother Angeline Teresa to acquire the property since the Carmelite Sisters for the Aged and Infirm were already working in the Albany diocese, indeed even in his residence since 1944. However, to transfer the Motherhouse and the General Administration presupposed a further situation since the jurisdiction of the Cardinal Archbishop of New York over a presently diocesan Congregation could no longer be maintained. At the same time proper jursidiction would have to be transferred and accepted by the Bishop of Albany who would become the new ecclesiastical superior. Cardinal Spellman who had become Mother Angeline's close personal friend and father to the Community must also relinquish his authority. After being notified by Bishop James McIntyre, who had directed the Sisters to Tivoli, and being further reassured by Father Francis F. Reh who had been appointed ecclesiastical superior of the Carmelite Sisters, regarding the advantages of the house, the property and the potential, the Cardinal granted his permission. Bishop Gibbons, in turn, graciously accepted his responsibility in a letter under date of November 26, 1946.[7] Thereafter Bishop Gibbons[8] exercised an active and paternal interest in the affairs of the Carmelite Sisters, a tradition graciously carried on by his successors . . . up to and including the present Ordinary, Most Reverend Howard J. Hubbard, D.D., who knew Mother Angeline Teresa personally and in her last days showed her every courtesy. He is now actively engaged in sponsoring the process for the introduction of the cause to raise Mother M. Angeline to the honors of the altar.

An almost immediate earnest of this concern was evidenced when he came down to Avila to bless the chapel on February 11, 1947. Originally it was the library but had been liturgically decorated by Mr. Anthony Savarese a noted artist friend of Mother from New York City. Her thirty-three novices were coming up to Avila by bus in order to be present for the blessing and to move in also. On the way up from St. Patrick's in the Bronx they encountered a real snowstorm. When the bus driver left the main road and was trying to ascend an ice-covered hill on a narrow dirt road close to the new Motherhouse the bus skidded into a snow bank and abruptly died. The rest of the journey was completed on foot with each one carrying their luggage and their few earthly possessions.[9]

Mother Angeline Teresa's first concern was for a proper chapel. Having obtained Bishop Gibbons' ready permission, she collected funds and on October 15, 1952, less than five years after coming to Avila, the new chapel was blessed. Designed by the architectural firm of Gander Brothers, it was modified Georgian style in red brick. Again Anthony Savarese designed the carved wood altars, communion rail, and Way of the Cross. He also supplied the stained glass windows and the pews which were decoratively divided simulating monastic choir stalls. First Bishop Gibbons blessed the lower area laid out as refectory, kitchen and store rooms. After this he blessed the outside of the chapel. Finally the interior of the chapel was blessed and the clergy, the Mother General, the Carmelite Sisters, visiting religious and the benefactors entered for a Solemn Mass at which Bishop Gibbons presided. Father Thomas Tooher was the celebrant. Rev. Joseph Ryan was Deacon and Father John Hughes, S.J. Subdeacon. Father William Mel Daly, O.Carm. gave a moving sermon. Bishop Gibbons spoke of the transformation of Avila. He cautioned the Sisters not to stop now but to get busy with a novitiate building as the Novices were still sleeping over the garage.

The next expansion at Avila was the Novitiate building connected by an enclosed corridor with the chapel. No longer need the novices go outside in inclement weather. For Mother Angeline Teresa, to will was to do. The challenge offered by the Bishop was taken seriously and on November 1, 1954 a five-story novitiate building with private rooms for 75 novices, classrooms and reception rooms was finished. Father William Russell, O.Carm., Prior Provincial of the Carmelites dedicated the facility to St. Therese, the Little Flower. Father James Wilders, chaplain at the Mary Manning Walsh Home, preached for the occasion.

Since all the Carmelite Sisters come home to Avila for their annual retreat, Mother Angeline Teresa desired to make them welcome, feel at home and be free for the period of spiritual exercises. This inspired her next project, the Mount Carmel Retreat House connected with the Chapel and novitiate. It was ready to be blessed on April 3, 1961. Constructed of red brick, melding in perfectly with the previous buildings of the complex, it stands five stories high with sixty individual rooms for the Sister Retreatants, a spiritual library, restful lounge area and even a snack bar to supply every need of soul, mind and body in this House of Prayer. It was dedicated on April 3, 1961 by Bishop Frederick Hall, a Mill Hill Missionary.[10]

Having taken good care of God and His service, the novices and the retreatant Sisters, it was almost inevitable that Mother's next concern would be a private wing for her beloved priests, the respected chaplains, the Retreat Masters and visiting priests. Besides five private rooms there is a suite for the chaplain, a common lounge and a dining room.

On the same day, November 1, 1967, when the priests' wing was blessed so was Mother Angeline Teresa's final gift to Avila and the Sisters who were always in her mind and heart. This was Carmel Hall, a commodious building containing an assembly hall, stage, gymnasium and cafeteria installations. Its uses for the Community have been endless: General Chapters, workshops, lectures and entertainments—even special liturgies when the chapel was inadequate for the great number of pilgrims. Bishop Edward J. McGinn of Albany performed the double blessing.

On October 15, 1980 the Teresian Library dedicated to St. Teresa of Avila and Mother Angeline Teresa was opened and dedicated by Father Eugene Robitaille, SS.CC.[11] It holds over three thousand reference and technical books of theology, spirituality, gerontology and geriatrics along with a selected periodical section.

Avila is a monument. A monument of love, of concern, of response to felt needs and of Mother M. Angeline Teresa herself. St. Teresa's Motherhouse is most inherently also the house of Mother M. Angeline Teresa, Foundress of the Congregation of the Carmelite Sisters for the Aged and Infirm.

NOTES

[1] cf. Columbia County Clerk's Office, ss *Satisfaction of Mortgage* recorded August 17, 1987, 3:30 p.m. Book no. 91 p. 332 by Donald G. Tracy, Clerk. AVGA.

[2] State of New York, Columbia County Clerk's Office. Recorded on the 10th day of December, 1946 at 9:05 a.m. Book no. 279 of Deeds at page 178. Inscribed Grant A. Miller. AVGA.

[3] Original Bill of Sale. Notarized by Joseph A. Cole, Notary Public. State of New York. AVGA.

[4] *Previews Listing*, Brochure No. 41570 Broker, Lloyd Boice, Germantown, N.Y.

⁵ Letter to Mother M. Angeline Teresa from Edward V. Mallon, Attorney at Law, 489 Fifth Avenue, New York under date of December 3, 1946. Original AVGA.

⁶ *Circular Letters*, Num. 41, Vol. I.

⁷ ADAL File: Carmelite Sisters for the Aged Infirm. Folder #2.

⁸ *Biographical Note*: Most Reverend Edmund F. Gibbons installed as sixth Bishop of Albany April 1, 1919. He served as Bishop longer than any other prelate. Born Sept. 16, 1868 in Hartsdale, N.Y. The family moved to Albany and then later to Buffalo. He studied at Niagara University and Our Lady of the Angels Seminary. In October 1887 he moved to the North American College at Rome where he obtained his Doctor of Sacred Theology Degree. On May 27, 1893 he was ordained a priest in the Basilica of St. John Lateran. Returning to Buffalo he fulfilled several pastorates, was Secretary to Bishop Ryan and was Diocesan Superintendent of Schools for 16 years. February 1, 1919 he was named Bishop of Albany by Pope Benedict XV. He was consecrated in the Buffalo Cathedral March 25, 1919. He instituted 52 new parishes, 82 grammar schools, 22 High Schools and two Colleges, St. Rose and St. Bernadine of Sienna. He established the Diocesan newspaper *The Evangelist*. He built St. Clare's Hospital in Schenectady and expanded the other three Catholic Hospitals. He inaugurated Mater Christi Minor Seminary and was a leader in social and educational endeavors for both the capitol city and state. The number of religious Orders of both men and women multiplied in the Diocese. He brought the Carmelite Sisters into the Diocese for his Bishop's House, welcomed their Motherhouse and Generalate and gave them charge of the domestic department of his seminary. He obtained Pontifical Jurisdiction for them also. After 35 years as Bishop he retired. His long and productive life ended at his death in 1964. cf. ADAL, *Profiles of the Former Bishops of Albany*.

⁹ Sister M. Bernadette de Lourdes (Wisely) O.Carm. *Blessing of Avila*. Monograph. February 11, 1972. AVGA Archival Box 1.

¹⁰ *Avila Newsletter*, January 1962.

¹¹ Dedicatory Placque at Library Entrance, Avila.

UNITED STATES

The first foundation of Mother M. Angeline Teresa, O.Carm. for her Carmelite Sisters for the Aged and Infirm which was made on September 3, 1929 at the old St. Elizabeth Rectory, 4381 Broadway, New York has been chronicled in Chapter the Fifth. In due time, following the imperative of necessity caused by internal growth and external expansion of the apostolate, the second foundation of the Congregation was made by Mother Angeline Teresa at St. Patrick's Home, 66 Van Cortlandt Park South, the Bronx, New York, to which the Community transferred on September 29, 1931. The significance of this first permanent home has been thoroughly demonstrated in Chapter the Eighth along with a schema of its multiple improvements and development. In the preceding chapter the acquisition of the first permanent Motherhouse, Generalate and Novitiate at St. Teresa's Motherhouse, Avila on Hudson, Woods Road, Germantown, New York, has been narrated along with its subsequent building programs, all initiated by Mother Angeline Teresa herself after securing the property and moving up to equip it for habitation by the Sisters on January 13, 1947.[1]

Among Mother's personal and historical papers in the General Archives of the Congregation is a *Memorandum* drawn up by herself explaining why her zeal impelled her to reach out to new foundations so early on in the development of her Congregation.[2]

REASONS FOR DESIRING TO SPREAD INTO OTHER VINEYARDS:

No. 1 God has blessed us with many vocations, and we have therefore sufficient Sisters ready for the work of "Caring for the Aged and Infirm."

No. 2 There is a long list of applications, some of whom are from your city . . . we know there is no home in your City doing just the kind of work we endeavor to do.

AGAIN:

(a) *It is the honest answer of the Community to give the Aged, who are without means, a home; and at the same time give a home to those Aged Pesons who are fortunate enough as to possess a few dollars of this world's goods.*

(b)   *To provide a Home for all Creeds, where the feeling of home will be stressed . . . a home with only such regulations as might be found in any well-regulated, right-living AND LOVING FAMILY . . . A HOME WHERE THE Aged have their own guests at will as well as the privilege to come and go at their ease: a home where the Aged are at HOME.*

"Our Congregation is directly under the control of the Diocese or Archdiocese in which it labors". Incidently, too, there is no allegiance to a foreign Motherhouse: we are purely American in our ideals and methods of administration, being founded in New York under the guidance of His Eminence, Patrick Cardinal Hayes, Archbishop of New York, for the particular purpose of creating "homes" in the full sense of the term for the American Middle Class people.[3]

The end product of this zealous projection is seen in the following chronological record.

Mount Carmel Villa third Foundation. The first to spring from St. Patrick's Home. Located at West 215th Street and Park Terrace East, New York City. First Mass August 22, 1934. Mother Teresa, one of the first companions, was first superior/administrator. Approved by Patrick Cardinal Hayes. It was in operation just over a year. Among the early Sisters it was called the "forgotten foundation".[4]

Mount Carmel Home fourth Foundation. Former St. Ambrose School, 539 West 54th Street, New York City in an area called "Hell's Kitchen". Opened November 21, 1935 when Mother M. Teresa moved down with the residents from the closed Villa as superior/administrator. Sponsored by Cardinal Hayes. Closed in 1981.

Mount Carmel Villa fifth Foundation. First foundation outside of New York. The former Egan Mansion at 5420 Chester Avenue, Philadelphia, Pennsylvania. At request of Denis Cardinal Dougherty. Opened November 1, 1936 with Mother Mary Louise, O.Carm. of the original pioneers as superior/administrator. On Cardinal Dougherty's first visit, to the mortification of the Sisters, their best chair gave way under the prelate's weight. The home was closed in 1953.

Sacred Heart Manor sixth Foundation. Second in Archdiocese of Philadelphia. Located at 6445 Germantown Avenue, Philadelphia, Pennsylvania. Opened October 17, 1937. Mother M. Alodie, one of the original seven sisters was superior/administrator. Sponsored by Denis Cardinal Dougherty.

St. Agnes Residence seventh Foundation. The third in three years in Philadelphia. Located at 8329 Stenton Avenue, Chestnut Hill, Philadelphia, Pennsylvania. Blessed on January 21, 1938 on Mother

Angeline Teresa's birthday in her presence. Mother M. Louise became the first superior/administrator. It was closed in 1957.[5]

St. Joseph's Home eighth Foundation. The fifth in New York City. Located at 123 Lilypond Avenue, Staten Island, New York. Opening date November 13, 1938. Mother M. Colette was named first superior/administrator, one of Mother Angeline Teresa's first companions. The home had been arranged with Mother Angeline Teresa by Patrick Cardinal Hayes who had died September 4, 1938. Dedicated by Monsignor Michael J. LaVelle. Closed in 1955.

Catholic Memorial Home ninth Foundation. Established July 1, 1939 at 2446 Highland Avenue in Fall River, Massachusetts by Bishop James E. Cassidy after a special visit to Mother Angeline Teresa at St. Patrick's in the Bronx at the recommendation of Cardinal Hayes. This foundation was unique since besides the Home for aged men and women a completely separate building was for a hostel for retired priests. It was blessed the next day, July 2, 1939 and was the first free standing residence for clergy in the United States. Mother M. Colette was named the first superior/administrator of this double foundation.[6]

Our Lady of Providence Seminary tenth Foundation. At request of Bishop Francis P. Keough the Carmelite Sisters for the first time undertook a seminary domestic department prompted by Mother Angeline Teresa's love for priests. Permission granted by Archbishop Francis Spellman, August 12, 1941. Opened August 15, 1941. Mother M. Brendan first superior. Seminary located at 485 Mt.Pleasant Avenue, Providence, Rhode Island. Closed in 1950.

Queen of Carmel Convent eleventh Foundation. Attached to St. Leo Benedictine Abbey, St. Leo, Florida. Invited to take up the domestic department for the Fathers and Boys School. Abbot Francis Sadlier OSB received the Sisters September 12, 1941 with approval of Bishop Joseph P. Hurley of St. Augustine. Because of the benign influence of the Carmelites the enrollment increased from 50 to 239 boys. Sisters remained about 11 years. Now St. Leo's College with a marble memorial plaque erected on campus in their memory. Mother M. Teresa, one of the first group, became superior. Closed in 1952.

Cure of Ars Hospice twelfth Foundation. A second hospice for the clergy this time in the Diocese of Scranton was opened at Brackney, Pennsylvania at the request of Bishop William J. Hafey. Mother Marie de Lourdes was the first superior/administrator. The Carmelite Sisters took up this work September 15, 1941. They remained until the facility was closed by the Diocese in 1949.

St. Joseph Seminary thirteenth Foundation. Located at Dunwoodie, Yonkers, New York. Carmelite Sisters requested to assume the Domestic

Department at the request of Archbishop, later Cardinal, Francis J. Spellman. Opened on April 28, 1943. The first superior was Mother Mary Joseph. This program was concluded as of June, 1969.

St. Luke's Infirmary fourteenth Foundation. Located at 701 H Street, Centralia, State of Washington in the then Diocese of Seattle at the invitation of Bishop Gerald Shaughnessy, October 18, 1943. Mother M. Colette was the first superior/administrator in this furthest foundation. Due to misunderstanding of the type of person to be admitted Mother withdrew the Sisters in 1945.[7]

Cathedral Faculty House fifteenth Foundation. Undertaken at request of Archbishop Francis J. Spellman serving the Diocesan priests on the staff of Cathedral High School at 352 Riverside Drive. Opened December 28, 1943 in New York City with Mother M. Regina Carmel as superior. Closed in 1969.

Bishop's Residence sixteenth Foundation. At the request of Bishop Edmund F. Gibbons the Carmelite Sisters assumed the domestic department at 465 State Street, Albany, New York on April 11, 1944. Mother M. Regina Carmel was superior. This operation continued until 1977.

St. Mary's Day Nursery seventeenth Foundation. Opened January 21, 1945. Mother M. Regina Carmel as first superior. Special concession to Samuel Cardinal Stritch of Chicago. Located at 655 West 44th Street. Sometimes called "Settlement House". Closed 1955.

Our Lady's Haven eighteenth Foundation. Located at Fairhaven, Massachusetts. Second foundation in Fall River Diocese with Bishop James E. Cassidy. Opened February 2, 1945 at 71 Center Street with Mother M. Colette as superior/administrator. Carmelite Sisters left this facility in 1985.

Diocesan Mission House nineteenth Foundation. At request of Samuel Cardinal Stritch this second foundation in Chicago was opened December 28, 1945 at 4821 South Ellis Avenue with Mother Cecilia Therese as superior/administrator. This was a domestic department which continued until 1948.

St. Teresa's Motherhouse twentieth Foundation. Avila on Hudson. February 11, 1947. Notice already given *ut supra*.

Bishop's Residence twenty-first Foundation. Located at 901 West State Street in Trenton, New Jersey. Requested for domestic services by Bishop William Griffin, the Carmelite Sisters with Sister Colette Marie, superior, took up their work on May 1, 1947. The Sisters were recalled in 1959.

St. Raphael's Home twenty-second Foundation. Located at 1550 Roxbury

Road, Columbus, Ohio. It was the first institution undertaken by Bishop Michael J. Ready and given to Mother M. Angeline Teresa as an outright gift so anxious was he to have the Carmelite Sisters in his diocese. They came January 25, 1948 with Mother M. Regina Carmel as superior/administrator.

St. Rita's Home twenty-third Foundation. On March 6, 1949 a second Carmelite Home, St. Rita's was opened at 1415 East Broad Street, Columbus, Ohio by the same zealous Bishop Ready. Sister Mary Agnes, superior/administrator and the sisters opened the facility on March 6, 1949.

St. Margaret Mary House twenty-fourth Foundation. Located at 3033 P Street, Washington D.C., a former Home for Aged Ladies had been merged with an adjoining property called St. Margaret Mary House. Monsignor Edward Buckley, the founder, died and the property was turned over to the Archdiocese. In 1949 Archbishop (later Cardinal) Patrick O'Boyle invited Mother Angeline Teresa to take over these two Georgetown buildings. She accepted them at once and September 9, 1949 the Carmelites began their apostolate with Mother Mary Gabriel as superior/administrator. Renovations and expansion were imperative. A new facility replaced both these buildings in 1957.

St. Francis Home twenty-fifth Foundation. Dedicated September 24, 1949, this was the first Carmelite Home in New Hampshire. It was one of two offered to Mother Angeline Teresa. Located in Laconia, New Hampshire in the Manchester Diocese run by Bishop Matthew J. Brady. Mother M. Aloysius was the first superior/administrator. The Carmelite Sisters withdrew in 1985.

Mount Carmel Home twenty-sixth Foundation. Located at 519 Bridge Street, Manchester, New Hampshire. This second home offered by Bishop Matthew J. Brady to Mother Angeline Teresa was dedicated September 26, 1949 just two days after its predecessor. Mother M. Colette was the first superior/administrator. Before the Carmelite Sisters withdrew in 1985 the name was changed to St. Teresa's Manor.

Carmel Manor twenty-seventh Foundation. This home opened on December 13, 1949 in Fort Thomas, Kentucky in the Diocese of Covington just across the Ohio River from Cincinnati. Shortly after a new building was erected followed by a residence for retired priests. Bishop William T. Mulloy contracted with Mother Angeline Teresa for the foundation with Mother M. Teresa as first superior/administrator. Bishop Richard J. Ackerman, C.S.Sp. developed the retired priests' residence.

Sacred Heart Home twenty-eighth Foundation. This was the third foundation in Chicago and the first Home for the Aged which was dedicated June 8, 1950 at 1550 S. Albany Street. Again, it was Samuel Cardinal Stritch who urged Mother M. Angeline to begin this work with Mother M. Ignatius Loyola as superior/administrator. This home was closed in 1972.[8]

Bishop's Residence twenty-ninth Foundation. Bishop Michael J. Ready who had been so generous to Mother Angeline Teresa requested Sisters to manage his household located at 188 East Broad Street, Columbus, Ohio. Mother Mary Alice, superior, came with the Carmelite Sisters September 8, 1950. The Sisters withdrew in 1957.

Villa Maria thirtieth Foundation. This was the second Florida foundation of Mother Angeline Teresa. Established April 12, 1951 at 1050 N.E. 125th Street, North Miami, Dade County, Florida. Archbishop Joseph P. Hurley of St. Augustine contracted with Mother Angeline Teresa. Mother Mary Martin, among the early candidates for the Carmelite Sisters was the superior/administrator. Carmelites withdrew in 1958.[9]

St. Joseph's Manor thirty-first Foundation. Third Florida house. At 2335 Lakeview Avenue South, St. Petersburg. Opened April 14, 1951. Mother Mary Teresa, first superior/administrator. Sponsored by Archbishop Joseph P. Hurley. Correspondence with Bishop (later Archbishop of Louisville) Thomas J. McDonough, Auxiliary of St. Augustine in 1951 when Archbishop Hurley was in Yugoslavia. Home closed in 1958.[10]

St. Mary's Home thirty-second Foundation. Located at 278 Broadway, Youngstown, Ohio. Opened July 13, 1952 and was blessed by Bishop Emmet M. Walsh. Mother M. Josephine Immaculate was the first superior/administrator. After the last infirm resident was placed elsewhere, St. Mary's Home was closed in 1972.[11]

Mary Manning Walsh Home thirty-third Foundation. This was the seventh foundation in New York City. It was the renovated former New York Orthopedic Hospital at 420 East 59th Street in Manhattan. It was formally dedicated on September 28, 1952 by Francis Cardinal Spellman. It was the largest Home of Mother Angeline Teresa to date. Mother M. Bernadette de Lourdes was the first superior/administrator. It was replaced by an entirely new building on another lot. It is a 16-story building at 1339 York Avenue between 71st and 72nd Streets for 362 residents. The Carmelite Sisters and their residents took possession in 1969.

St. Patrick's Manor thirty-fourth Foundation. Opened at Boston, Massachusetts on June 10, 1953. Mother M. Angeline Teresa was invited by Archbishop (later Cardinal) Richard J. Cushing to extend her work to the Archdiocese. The first building was the former Hotel Lafayette at the prestigious address of 333 Commonwealth Avenue in the heart of the city. Mother Angeline Teresa stayed on supervising personally the transformation. Mother M. Eileen was the first superior/administrator. Seventeen years later on May 17, 1970 a new facility for 292 residents was blessed by Cardinal Cushing at Framingham, Massachusetts.

Marian Manor thirty-fifth Foundation. In the first Marian Year of 1954 Archbishop Cushing asked Mother Angeline Teresa to take over the former Carney Hospital complex at 130 Dorchester Street, South Boston, Massachusetts. Ready for 150 residents it was opened on May 7, 1954 with Mother Maria Paul as the superior/administrator.

Welty Memorial Home thirty-sixth Foundation. The first in West Virginia. Invitation for this home extended to Mother Angeline Teresa by one of her New York friends, Bishop Thomas J. McDonnell, Coadjutor Bishop of Wheeling. She took over an existing home originally given by Clara Welty. When the Fort Henry bridge was built the original mansion was taken over by the State. A new building was purchased at 1252 National Road and extended. It was to this home that the Carmelite Sisters came to conduct the home, January 8, 1954. Mother Elizabeth Eugene was the first superior/administrator. The Sisters withdrew in 1961.

Mater Christi Seminary thirty-seventh Foundation. At the request of Bishop Edmund Gibbons of Albany, Mother Angeline Teresa responded by accepting the domestic Department of Mater Christi Minor Seminary at 1134 New Scotland Avenue, Albany on September 8, 1954. Mother Mary Alice was the first superior/administrator. The seminary was closed in 1972 at which time the Sisters withdrew.

Kahl Memorial Home thirty-eighth Foundation. Bishop Ralph Leo Hayes asked Mother Angeline Teresa to staff a home for the aged in the Diocese of Davenport, Iowa to be opened in the Kahl mansion 1101 West 9th Street which had been donated to the diocese by the Kahl family. It stood on a majestic hill overlooking the Mississippi River. The home was dedicated with the Carmelite Sisters present February 17, 1955. Mother M. Stephen was the first superior/administrator.

Josephine Baird Home thirty-ninth Foundation. This was the eighth foundation in New York City. Opened on March 20, 1955, with the permission of Francis Cardinal Spellman, located at 341 West 55th Street, New York City. Mother M. Josita was first superior/administrator. This facility was closed in 1972.

Carmel Hall fortieth Foundation. Edward Cardinal Mooney directed Monsignor Bernard Kearns to urge Mother Angeline Teresa to come as soon as possible to inspect the Detroit Hotel for a Carmelite Home in December, 1954. After her visit Mother wrote on January 21, (her birthday!) 1955 that she was willing to undertake this project.[12] Located at 2560 Woodward Avenue it accomodated 509 aged residents. By far the largest home to date. The Sisters took up occupancy May 29, 1955. Mother Regina Carmel was the first superior/administrator. The Sisters were withdrawn in 1979.

Carroll Manor forty-first Foundation. Successor to St. Margaret Mary House.[13] A newly constructed facility for 244 residents located at 4922 La Salle Road, Hyattsville, Maryland directly on the northeast boundary of the District of Columbia. Dedicated November 23, 1957 by Archbishop (later Cardinal) Patrick O'Boyle, first Archbishop of the Washington Archdiocese in the presence of Mother Angeline Teresa. First superior/administrator, Mother Frances Michael.

St. Ann Home forty-second Foundation. Third Carmelite home in New Hampshire. Sponsored by Bishop Matthew F. Brady of Manchester who requested another foundation from Mother Angeline Teresa. Dedicated as a newly constructed facility on November 2, 1956. Located at 194 Dover Point Road, Dover, New Hampshire, it accomodated 50 residents. Mother Mary Immaculate was first superior/administrator.

Madonna Residence forty-third Foundation. First Carmelite Foundation in Brooklyn, New York although Mother Angeline had labored previously in the Diocese as a Little Sister of the Poor. The former Knights of Columbus Building at One Prospect Park West was suitably adapted to take care of 290 aged residents. It was blessed on February 11, 1962 by Bishop Bryan McEntegart. Mother Ignatius Loyola became its first superior/administrator.

St. Joseph's Manor forty-fourth Foundation. Although the project of Bishop (later Cardinal) Lawrence Shehan with Mother M. Angeline Teresa, the new facility for 300 aged residents was blessed on October 2, 1960 by Archbishop Henry J. O'Brien of Hartford. Located at 6448 Main Street, Trumbull, Connecticut in the Diocese of Bridgeport. Mother M. Bernadette de Lourdes was the first superior/administrator. The scope of care for the aged here has expanded to Independent Living in homes, apartments; Intermediate skilled and chronic nursing care; and a Day Care center for the elderly.

Lourdes Residence forty-fifth Foundation. Formerly the Lake Court Hotel 315 South Flagler Drive, West Palm Beach, Florida. Bishop Coleman F. Carroll of Miami (later an Archdiocese in 1968) invited Mother Angeline Teresa to examine the building and possibly make a Carmelite Home of it. Mother agreed and under the title of Lourdes Residence it was dedicated on February 5, 1961. Mother Mary Immaculate was the first superior/administrator. By 1975 it became obsolete and inadequate. The

Sisters closed it down. It was demolished and on the same spot through the magnificent generosity of Mrs. John (Noreen F. Condon) McKeen, rebuilt and called the Lourdes Noreen McKeen Residence for Geriatric Care.

St. Margaret Hall forty-sixth Foundation. This was Mother Angeline Teresa's fourth home in the state of Ohio. Located at 1960 Madison Avenue in Cincinnati, it was the project of Archbishop Karl J. Alter. It was greatly supported by Sir Walter Schott, K.S.G. and after his death by his wife and two sons. It opened October 3, 1962 for some 150 elderly. Mother Regina Carmel was its first superior/administrator.

Our Lady's Manor forty-seventh Foundation. This first European venture of Mother M. Angeline Teresa into Ireland, the land of her birth was a dream fulfilled. The good reputation of the kind of care given the aging by Mother Angeline Teresa's Sisters was the occasion for His Grace, Doctor John C. McQuaid, Archbishop of Dublin, to offer a foundation.[14] On April 11, 1960 Doctor McQuaid was informed by realtors that they intended to put up for sale Bulloch Castle with 2.5 acres of property at Dalkey, County Dublin right on Dublin Bay. On May 31, Mother Angeline was informed the property was available, and she should send a delegation to ascertain whether it was suitable for one of her homes. On July 14, 1960 the Archbishop wrote that the Diocesan Council had approved his proposal for such a home for about 50 adults.[15] The property was bought and on May 6, 1963 the Carmelite Sisters went to Dublin, remodeling was begun, and on May 27, 1965, Archbishop McQuaid blessed a newly built Our Lady's Manor. Mother M. Eileen was first superior/administrator.

Bethania forty-eighth Foundation. This was the second house of the Carmelite Sisters outside the United States. On January 8, 1964 Mother Angeline Teresa wrote to Bishop William A. Scully for his advice and consent to take over an existing home for the aged in Dunoon, Scotland.[16] She had been asked to do this by Bishop Stephen McGill of the Diocese of Argyll and the Isles, with its See City at Oban. On January 10, 1964 Bishop Scully responded affirmatively.[17] The Carmelite Sisters began their work on June 17, 1964. Mother Mary Ann was the superior / administrator. Four Sisters of a secular institute called Mater Dei who had formerly conducted Bethania, entered the Carmelite Sisters at Avila. The Carmelite Sisters withdrew in 1974.

Ferncliff Residence forty-ninth Foundation. The genesis of this Carmelite Home is a gift made to Francis Cardinal Spellman by Mrs. Vincent Astor of Rhinebeck, New York. The Astor mansion on River Road, in Rhinebeck, New York, situated in a large plot became a residence for 20 elderly people. Mother Angeline Teresa assisted at the dedication by Francis

Cardinal Spellman, January 6, 1965. The first superior/administrator was Mother Armand Marian. By 1973 a new building accommodated 320 elderly residents.

The Pennsylvania fiftieth Foundation. Adjacent to the Lourdes-Noreen McKeen Residence stands the Pennsylvania Hotel with its 210 rooms. It was acquired by the Carmelite Sisters and dedicated by Bishop Coleman F. Carroll, January 17,1965. The unique situation of both houses now under one administrator makes transfers between both facilities possible. Mother M. Josita became the first superior/ administrator.

Garvey Manor fifty-first Foundation. Named after Bishop Eugene Garvey, the first Bishop of Altoona, Pennsylvania, Bishop J. Carroll McCormick requested a home in his Diocese. As a result, Garvey Manor with accommodations for 150 residents on Logan Boulevard, Hollidaysburg, Pennsylvania was blessed June 24, 1955. It adjoins the Diocesan Office complex. Mother M. Stephen was the first superior/administrator.

St. Patrick's Residence fifty-second Foundation. At the invitation of the saintly Bishop Romeo Blanchette, then Auxiliary of Joliet, Illinois, Mother Angeline Teresa accepted the projected home for the Diocese. The Louis Joliet Hotel at 22 East Clinton Street in downtown Joliet was converted into St. Patrick's Residence and was opened June 27, 1965. There was room for 197 residents. Mother Daniel Marie became the first superior/ administrator. Keeping the same name the Sisters and residents moved into a new suburban facility, 1400 Brookdale Road, Naperville, Illinois in 1989.

Mount Carmel Nursing Home fifty-third Foundation. At the request of Bishop Ernest Primeau, sixth Bishop of Manchester, Mother Angeline Teresa accepted a fourth Home in New Hampshire. Located at 235 Myrtle Street, Manchester, New Hampshire with room for 120 residents, it was dedicated September 14, 1969. Mother M. Harriet Therese became the first superior/administrator.

Ozanam Hall fifty-fourth Foundation. Named after Frederick Ozanam, the remarkable layman who founded the St. Vincent de Paul Society, the second Carmelite Home in the Brooklyn-Queens Diocese, stands at 42–41 201st Street in the Bayside section. It is built on a property where another Ozanam Home stood until 1950 when it closed. The money from its sale was to be used to replace it at the same site. The money was skillfully invested and used for the new Ozanam Hall with its accomodations for 432 residents at various care levels. It was blessed November 22, 1971 by Bishop Francis Mugavero who had cooperated with Mother Angeline Teresa in this project. Mother Ignatius Loyola was the first superior/ administrator.

St. Joseph Nursing Home fifty-fifth Foundation. This home is unique in the development of Mother Angeline Teresa's apostolate. The concept and invitation came first through a dedicated laywoman, Mrs. Walter J. Heenan. When Mother agreed to staff such a home, a Board of Directors was set up with Bishop David Cunningham, who blessed the new facility for 120 aged residents, located at 2535 Genesee Street, Utica, New York on December 13, 1971. Mother Armand Marian became its first superior/administrator.

Villa Teresa fifty-sixth Foundation. Mother Angeline Teresa prepared this foundation with Bishop George L. Leech, Bishop of Harrisburg who presided at the groundbreaking, but had retired by the time Bishop Joseph T. Daley dedicated the newly erected building September 13, 1973. High on a hill at 1051 Avila Road the five-story cruciform building houses 180 aged residents. Mother M. Stephen was first superior/administrator.

Carmel Richmond fifty-seventh Foundation. Located at 88 Old Town Road, Borough of Richmond, Staten Island, this facility for 300 aged residents was dedicated October 29, 1974 by Terence Cardinal Cooke in the presence of Mother Angeline Teresa. Mother Fidelis Patricia was the first superior/administrator.

Teresian House fifty-eighth Foundation. Although the first Carmelite Home for the Aged in Albany, it was the fourth foundation in the Diocese. A joint effort of Mother Angeline Teresa and Bishop Edwin B. Broderick,[8] the newly constructed facility for 300 elderly residents on Washington Avenue Extension was blessed on October 30th, 1974. The first superior/administrator of Teresian House was Mother Mel Therese.

Little Flower Manor fifty-ninth Foundation. This was Mother Angeline Teresa's last foundation in her lifetime. The name for this home was selected by Bishop J. Carroll McCormick because of his personal devotion to St. Therese of Lisieux. When he was Bishop of Altoona Mother Angeline had opened a home there. As Bishop of Scranton, he welcomed her to Wilkes-Barre. This new home was part of his Project Expansion to celebrate the 100th Anniversary of his Diocese. Located prominently on a hill above the city at 200 South Meade Street, it accomodates 127 residents and was blessed November 29, 1974. Mother Angeline appointed Mother Therese Regina as the home's first superior/administrator.

Interspersed with this phenomenal development of the Carmelite Sisters for the Aged and Infirm were three landmark celebrations.

25th ANNIVERSARY OF FOUNDATION
The official celebration took place in St. Patrick's Cathedral, New

York on September 21, 1954. The actual date of the founding was September 3, 1929. At the time it was not the practice to have non-diocesan celebrations at St. Patrick's such as jubilees of a particular religious Congregation, but Cardinal Spellman, being a great friend of Mother Angeline Teresa because of the New York origins of the Carmelite Sisters for the Aged and Infirm, wanted the anniversary to be celebrated at the Cathedral and he himself offered the Pontifical Mass of Thanksgiving. Monsignor James Lynch, P.A., was the preacher.[19]

40th ANNIVERSARY FOUNDATION

The "Ruby Jubilee", the fortieth anniversary of the foundation of the Congregation of the Carmelite Sisters for the Aged and Infirm was observed September 6, 1969 at St. Teresa's Motherhouse, Avila on Hudson. Terence Cardinal Cooke made the long trip from the city to be the principal celebrant at the Mass. Four Bishops including Bishop Edwin B. Broderick, the Bishop of Albany, concelebrated the Thanksgiving Mass. Very Reverend Lawrence Mooney, O.Carm., Prior Provincial of the Carmelite Fathers was present and Father William Mel Daly, O.Carm. was the homilist. The sanctuary was filled with clergy both diocesan and religious while the Chapel overflowed with Carmelite Sisters, visiting religious and laity. A luncheon followed in Carmel Hall, the latest building added to the Motherhouse complex by Mother M. Angline Teresa.[20]

50th ANNIVERSARY FOUNDATION

The 50th anniversary of the founding of the Congregation of the Carmelite Sisters for the Aged and Infirm occured on September 3, 1979. At Mother Angeline Teresa's request, the event took place September 8, 1979 on the nearest feast of Our Lady. There was a Pontifical Mass in St. Patrick's Cathedral, New York, with Terence Cardinal Cooke as the principal celebrant. Father William Mel Daly, O.Carm. was the preacher. In attendance were three Cardinals, 27 Bishops, 70 priests, a host of Carmelite Sisters, members of Mother Angeline Teresa's own family, the McCrory's, two aged residents from each of the New York homes as representing all the others, along with visiting religious Brothers and Sisters with a vast crowd of the laity filling the Cathedral to capacity. A luncheon followed at the nearby Waldorf Astoria Hotel during which Monsignor James J. Murray, Director of the Archdiocesan Charities, was the toastmaster. Mother Angeline Teresa was not present at this twofold celebration due to distance and her advanced age. She shared the joy of the moment by viewing pictures and hearing tapes of what took place both at the liturgy and luncheon. Messages were received from Pope John Paul II, Jimmy Carter, the president of the United States, and many other ecclesiastical and civic leaders.[21]

In the death of Francis Cardinal Spellman, December 2, 1967 the Church and the Archdiocese of New York lost an outstanding churchman and vigorous leader in the service of God and country. This was proven by the countless testimonials received from admirers from all levels of society including such personages as President Lyndon B. Johnson and His Holiness, Pope Paul VI.

On March 8, 1968 Most Reverend Terence Cooke was appointed Archbishop of New York.[22] He was installed April 4 of the same year. Just a year later he was created Cardinal. Like all of his predecessors from the time of Cardinal Hayes, he was devoted to Mother M. Angeline Teresa and a great supporter of the Carmelite Sisters for the Aged and Infirm. Unlike his predecessors, he was personally acquainted with Mother from the early days of his priesthood. As a young priest Director of the Catholic Youth Organization, he met Mother Angeline Teresa, O.Carm. and when the Mary Manning Walsh Home opened in 1952, he served with Mother M. Bernadette de Lourdes, O.Carm. in forming a committee for training the staff and volunteers in the special needs and care of the elderly. He worked with this program giving some of the orientation and in-service training. Hence when he gave the homily for Mother Angeline's Golden Jubilee of Profession March 19, 1964 at St. Patrick's Home in the Bronx in the presence of Cardinal Spellman he could orate,

> Mother Angeline was decades before her time in the dreams she had of ways and means to preserve the spirit of independence of the elderly who need care. Thanks be to God, she served as a faithful instrument of His grace in establishing a special Community to serve the aging of all classes and circumstances. God alone knew the tremendous needs that there would be in a few short years for this important work.

> Mother Angeline Teresa and her companions experienced painful trials and hardships. Some doubted the need for the work they had in mind. Many doubted the validity of their method of caring for the aged. The courageous faith of the Carmelite Sisters was sustained by a deep interior life as they accepted God's plan without question. In the midst of early difficulties, the Sisters were consoled by the faithful friendship of a number of priests. From the earliest days to the present the Carmelite Sisters have been known for their reverence and respect for the priesthood. Of course Mother Angeline leads all the Sisters in the warmth of the hospitality for priests.

In conclusion Monsignor Terence Cooke exhorted:

> May Mother Angeline, as an angel of consolation, have many more fruitful years among us as a pioneer, a leader, an apostle, an instrument of God's charity toward the elderly and as a Mother to us all.[23]

As a manifestation of his esteem for Mother Angeline he obtained for her a second Papal Award, the Benemerenti Medal under date of September 10, 1978.

On the glorious occasion of the Fiftieth anniversary of the foundation of the Carmelite Sisters for the Aged and Infirm, Terence Cardinal Cooke was the principal celebrant at the Jubilee Mass in St. Patrick's Cathedral. In advance he wrote to Mother Angeline on September 3, 1979,

> It is a pleasure for me to join with the priests, religious and laity of the Archdiocese of New York, in expressing congratulations to you and all the Carmelite Sisters for the Aged and Infirm, on the occasion of the Golden Jubilee celebration of the foundation of your Religious Community. From humble beginnings in 1929, first at St. Elizabeth's in Washington Heights, and then at St. Patrick's Home in the northwest Bronx, your Community has been an inspiration in caring for our beloved aged, not only in New York, but throughout the United States and even overseas. The devoted persevering efforts of the Carmelite Sisters have established in the Providence of God, a tradition of loving service which will have a lasting effect on future generations. With so many people whom you have served over the years, I give thanks to God for you and your Community as you reach this milestone in your history. Under the patronage of Our Lady of Mount Carmel and St. Teresa of Avila, may the Lord continue to bless your apostolate.[24]

Besides the many personal services rendered to Cardinal Cooke by Mother Angeline was the additional courtesy that she cared for his aunt, Mary Gannon, at Mary Manning Walsh Home until she died.

The prayer of the Faithful at the Golden Jubilee Mass at St. Patrick's Cathedral read by Mother Angeline Teresa's nephew John J. McCrory, really rounds out the long and loving relationship between Mother Angeline Teresa and the great Archdiocese of New York, and its benificent Ordinaries:

> (For) "The many Cardinals, Bishops and priests of the Church who have helped the Carmelite Sisters over the past fifty years. We recall in a special way this morning the late Patrick Cardinal Hayes (1924–1938), Francis Cardinal Spellman (1946–1967), and our friend and principal Celebrant at this Mass of Thanksgiving, Terence Cardinal Cooke."[25]

Through these milestones of progress Mother Angeline Teresa, O.Carm. saw her work blessed, her Community developed and her dream come true, as silver turned to ruby, and ruby into gold before her very eyes.

NOTES

[1] Mother Angeline Teresa herself cooked for this first group. They went out to Mass at St. Sylvia's Church, Tivoli. Sister M. Gabriel (Reis) O.Carm., member of the group. Personal Interview with author, Avila Motherhouse. January 16, 1989.

[2] cf. Sister M. Bernadette de Lourdes (Wisely) O.Carm. *Book of Foundation*. 1929–1974. Incomplete, unpaginated manuscript. Begun 1988. Account of St. Patrick's Home. AVGA (Ed. note. Apparently this *Memorandum* was addressed to an inquiring Bishop) This manuscript not to be confused with Exhibit C. Foundation Book in Mother Angeline Teresa's own hand 1929–1930.

[3] *Ibid*. cf. St. Patrick's Account.

[4] *Ibid*. cf. Mount Carmel Villa Account.

[5] John Cardinal O'Hara, C.S.C., Letter, February 11, 1957. Permission for Mother Angeline Teresa to sell St. Agnes Property. AAPH File: Carmelite Sisters.

[6] Contract for Foundation, July 9, 1939. Signed: Bishop James E. Cassidy and Mother M. Angeline Teresa. ADFR. File: Carmelite Sisters.

[7] *Collection Special Correspondence*: Mother M. Angeline Teresa, O.Carm. and Sister Assumpta Marie, O.Carm. 1938–1971. Item 6 AVGA.

[8] AACH N.B. Papers and records of the Cardinal Stritch Era (1939–1958) uncatalogued.

[9] AASA The entire State of Florida was one Diocese in 1951. cf. Archives of St. Augustine at Jacksonville. Consulted Archdiocese of Miami chancery and Catholic Center. AAMI.

[10] ADSP Letters discovered in Archives of St. Petersburg subsequent to author's research are from Mother M. Teresa (Schoof) O.Carm., not Mother M. Angeline Teresa.

[11] *The Vindicator*, Diocesan Newspaper, Youngstown, OH affirms opening date of Foundation July 13, 1952. cf. (6–27–52 also 7–3–52). Same source sets September 4, 1970 (9–4–70) for the departure of Carmelite Sisters. ADYO.

[12] AADT File: Carmelite Sisters. Folder #1. Letter of January 21, 1955.

[13] AVGA Golden Jubilee Program, September 8, 1979.

[14] ADUB Diocesan Archives Dublin. Personal response from Archvist Daniel Sheehy, dated 18 June 1987.

[15] *Ibid.*

[16] ADAL File: Carmelite Sisters for Aged and Infirm. Folder #2.

[17] ADAL *ibid.*

[18] Most Reverend Edwin J. Broderick the eighth Bishop of Albany was born in the Bronx January 16, 1917. His parents were Patrick and Margaret M. Broderick. As a student at Regis High School he discerned his vocation. He attended the minor seminary at Cathedral College in the city. He then attended St. Joseph Seminary at Dunwoodie. He was ordained on May 30, 1942 by Cardinal Spellman in St. Patrick's Cathedral. He taught history at Cardinal Hayes High School and received a Master of Arts degree from Fordham in 1951 and a Doctorate in English in 1951. He became the first full time Director of radio and television in the Archdiocese of New York. In 1954 Pope Pius XII appointed him U.S. representative on the Pontifical Commission for television. He was named Monsignor the same year. In 1964 he became the Rector of Dunwoodie Seminary. He was ordained Titular Bishop of Tizica and Auxiliary Bishop of New York April 21, 1967. On March 20, 1969 he was named Bishop of Albany. He resigned the See in May 1967 to become the Director of Catholic Relief services. He wrote of his long association with Mother M. Angeline Teresa, O.Carm.: "My first meeting with Mother Angeline was in 1966 when in a choral group with several other Dunwoodie first philosophers I visited St. Patrick's Home to entertain the guests . . . When our program ended she thanked our chorus and invited the dear Seminarians to a morsel of food. It turned out to be a banquet. Thirty years later I became the Bishop of Albany. On the occasions I visited Avila, Mother would greet me at the front door . . . It was then I realized her attractive virtues, her sense of joy in service, her good-will, optimism and generosity were still so vibrant."

[19] AVGA 25th Anniversary account in Chronicle of celebration, September 21, 1954. Also text of sermon preached by Msgr. James J. Lynch, P.A. at St. Patrick's Cathedral.

[20] AVGA 40th Anniversary account in *Highlights of 1969*. Pub. Germantown, N.Y. Also collection of photos and memorabilia.

[21] AVGA 50th Anniversary account in *Golden Jubilee Program* pub. Avila, Germantown, N.Y. September 3, 1979.

[22] Biographical note. Terence Cardinal Cooke was born in New York March 1, 1921. The son of Michael Cooke and Margaret Gannon. He attended Cathedral College in New York and St. Joseph's Seminary in Dunwoodie. He was ordained a priest December 1, 1945. His first as-

signment was St. Athanasius in the Bronx, and St. Agatha's Home in Nanuet. He attended Catholic University in Washington in 1947, and was the Director of the Catholic Youth Organization for Catholic Charities from 1949–1954. He was at Fordham University from 1949–1956. In 1954 he became Procurator at Dunwoodie Seminary. In 1957 he became the Secretary to Cardinal Spellman. In 1956 he became a member of the Board for the Carmelite Sisters for the Aged and Infirm. In 1957 he was named Monsignor. In 1958 he was made Vice-Chancellor of the New York Archdiocese. In 1960 he became Chancellor. In 1965 he became Vicar General of the Archdiocese. On December 13, 1965, he was ordained the titular Bishop of Summa and Auxiliary Bishop of New York. He became Archbishop of the See of New York on March 8, 1968—the first alumnus of Dunwoodie Seminary to become Archbishop of New York. He was installed as Archbishop and appointed Military Vicar for the United States Armed Forces April 24, 1968. One year later he was created Cardinal on April 28, 1969 under the Title of the Basilica of SS. John and Paul attached to the Generalate of the Passionists in Rome. He enriched his titular Basilica with an elevator. His ability was further recognized as he was appointed to the Roman Congregations for Bishops, for the Oriental Churches, and for the Evangelization of Peoples. He also served on two Pontifical Commissions for Migration and Tourism. He endured his terminal illness with edifying patience and fortitude. He died October 6, 1983. So much was he loved and his virtue recognized that the initial process to present his cause for beatification is being sponsored by the Archdiocese of New York.

[23] AVGA *Homily* March 19, 1954, Upright File number 1.

[24] AVGA Upright File number 1.

[25] AVGA Golden Jubilee Program, September 8, 1979.

ROME

Perhaps no other city in the world presents so many faces and facets to so many people as Rome, the eternal city on the Tiber. Some relish its antiquities. Others revere its relics of Christian martyrs and numerous saints. Still more revel in its whirl of art, music, culture, cuisine and high fashion. Mother Angeline Teresa's recording pen reveals that for her Rome was the very core of her Catholic Faith. She saw it as a promising field for her zealous apostolate for the aged among the amiable Italian people. Finally, it was the magnet under which the paternal protection of the Supreme Pontiff her nascent little Congregation might blossom into full stature by attaining pontifical jurisdiction.

Mother Angeline Teresa's first trip to Rome followed her participation in the 1932 International Eucharistic Congress in Dublin. This journey, which included a trip to Scotland to visit her mother, was an unexpected windfall, for Mother Angeline so early in the life of her struggling Community. It was sponsored by Patrick Cardinal Hayes who wanted Mother to be presented to Pope Pius XI and who personally arranged a July audience for her in Rome. Catholic Charities supplied the passage for Mother herself and her traveling companion, Mother Colette.[1]

In her own hand and in her own inimitable way Mother Angeline Teresa kept a daily journal of persons and events throughout the pilgrimage.[2] As seen through her eyes one can see her almost childlike sense of wonder and subtle humor. She actually turned this voyage into an occasion of public relations for her new Community. The 4 prelates and 129 priests traveling on the S.S. Dresden were deeply impressed with her solid piety. As she begged prayers for herself, her recently established Congregation and their apostolate for the aged she left an indelible memory which led to many of her later foundations.[3]

In her journal[4] she narrates shipboard incidents spiritual and mundane. She is overwhelmed with the abundance of Masses at sea and rose early to be present at as many as possible. In one of her letters written from the ship she states that she attended fifteen

Masses.[5] Social amenities are recorded. Afternoon teas and evening "sing alongs" with one Irish air after another lasting far into the night after the nuns had retired. Only once at one such musicale was her usual dignified calm shaken. One priestly practical joker let go a wind-up mechanical mouse in her direction. When she saw it she jumped up and practically fell onto the lap of a venerable old Bishop returning to China who was seated next to her. Everyone convulsed with laughter at her momentary distress. As soon as she realized the joke she joined in the merriment herself with no rancor at all.[6]

With great reverence she told of the solemnities of the Eucharistic Congress held at Phoenix Park in Dublin manifesting subconsciously her own deep devotion to the Blessed Sacrament. Her Dublin visit ended with time spent with her beloved Carmelite Fathers. The next event was the visit with her Mother whom she had not seen since she left the family hearth twenty years before. She wrote: "To say I was received with open arms & spoiled during my three weeks there would be a faint expression of the reality."[7]

At this time also she visited with Canon Taylor, her old friend and confessor, who underwrote a visit for her to Lisieux en route to Rome.[8]

Arriving in Rome she was greeted by the former Prior General of the Carmelite Fathers of the Ancient Observance who had so graciously affiliated the whole Congregation of the Carmelite Sisters, Most Reverend Elias Magennis. They stayed with the "Blue Sisters," actually the Little Company of Mary, at their Calvary Hospital on Via San Stefano Rotondo.[9] They visited the Major Basilicas and other places dear to Christian faith and devotion.

The climax came on July 21 when the two American Carmelites were given a private audience with Pope Pius XI. They appeared in white mantles supplied by the Carmelite Fathers as they had left their own in Scotland.[10] Mother was able to converse freely with the Pope in French. At the end of the audience the Holy Father placed his hands on Mother's head blessing her, the Sisters, their relatives and friends. Of the historical and moving visit with the Pope Mother M. Angeline Teresa could write with confidence: "I have no more fear for the future, now that we have the Blessing of Christ's Vicar."[11]

Mother Angeline Teresa left Rome by train on July 23, 1932. Returning through France and Scotland, she came back to the States on August 10th, 1932.

Mother Angeline's second Roman project, namely a foundation in Rome itself, officially surfaced for the first time barely eight years after the foundation of her Congregation. The minutes of the meeting of the General Council, July 17, 1937 record the following:

MEMORANDUM of Very Rev. Hilary Mary
D'oswald, Superior-General, Carmelite
Fathers, Ancient Observance—July 17, 1937
Talk of Roman FOUNDATION

The Very Reverend Hilary Mary D'oswald, O.CARM.,
Superior-General, Carmelite Fathers, was in New York—he had been visiting the different houses of his community, and through the kindness of the Very Rev. Father Flanagan, Provincial-Local, he came to visit Saint Patrick's Home.

The Father General said the Community Mass, and after breakfast, we all assembled in the Reception Room to be presented to him individually by Reverend Mother. He was glad to learn of our growth and of our Foundations and Prospective Foundations.

Reverend Mother mentioned to him that *we would like to make a *FOUNDATION in ROME**, the Father General said if she really meant it he would take it up with Cardinal Marchetti, Vicar of Rome, and the Protector of the Carmelite Order. Rev. Mother assured him that she was in earnest.

After telling us many interesting things, he reminded us that we should build Spiritual-interior foundations within ourselves; admonished us to become steeped in Religious Principles and to labor zealously for the Glory of God—the TRUE vocation of every Carmelite. He promised to keep us especially in his prayers: he couldn't forget us.

The Father General then went over to see the Novitiate Building now in the last stages of construction.

Carmelite Sisters for the Aged and Infirm,
66 Van Cortlandt Park, South, Bronx, NYC.

July 17, 1937[12]

A follow-up on this project surfaces in another memorandum at a subsequent General Council meeting dated December 18, 1937:

MEMORANDUM of CABLEGRAM FROM ROME*
December Eighteenth, 1 9 3 7 !

On the Feast of the Expectation of the Blessed Virgin Mary, December eighteenth, 1937, Reverend Mother M. Angeline Teresa, received a Cablegram from the

Very Reverend Father General, O.CARM.,(Very Rev. Hilary M. D'oswald, O.CARM) *Rome*, ITALY . . . . saying that he had been in communication with His Eminence, Cardinal Marchetti, Vicar of Rome, and that he (Cardinal Marchetti) was *open to our establishing a Foundation in ROME*.

A letter from the Father-General during the Christmas Holidays explained the Cablegram in detail. The Carmelites in Rome thought it would be better if Reverend Mother could come to Rome and learn something of the proposition from a closer view of things, and have a personal interview with Cardinal Marchetti himself.

Correspondence continued with the Very Rev. Father-General on this subject.[13]

Pursuing this project even more urgently, Mother Angeline informed the full Council on February 28, 1938:

PROSPECTIVE FOUNDATION in ROME: Rev. Mother acquainted the Counsellors with the fact that we had been in constant communication with the Father-General relative to our *Eventually coming to Rome*; and as a result she felt that she should see Our Cardinal Hayes on the subject. Even if His Eminence could not see our leaving for Rome in the near future, Rev. Mother felt he would permit her to go and see Cardinal Marchetti and the condition of things in Rome; as only by really seeing the persons and the places could anything definite be determined. All were in favor of the move. The Meeting came to a close after saying the usual concluding prayers.[14]

Another entry in the General Council Minutes book on March 21, 1938 observes:

b) That since Rev. Mother M. Angeline Teresa had received the Cardinal's permission to go to Rome to see about the ROMAN Foundation, she would sail April second, 1938, taking Sister M. Collette [sic] as companion.[15]

Thus came about Mother Angeline's second visit to Rome. The high point of this journey was a private audience with Pope Pius XI arranged by the aforesaid Cardinal Marchetti. The Holy Father gave a special blessing including the entire Congregation: Motherhouse, Novitiate, and branch houses. As a token of his paternal affection the Pontiff gave Mother Angeline Teresa his white skull cap, to which was attaced his personal name card. This papal gift is still treasured by the Carmelite Sisters.[16] After visiting further with the Prior General of the Carmelites of the Ancient Observance in Rome, Mother and Sister Colette returned by train to Paris, then Scotland and home by ship the end of May.

The last entry regarding the Roman Foundation in the Minutes Book of the General Council is entered on June 3, 1938:

Reverend Mother returned from Europe the last week in May, and this was the first date convenient for the assembling of the COUNCIL. All the Counsellors were present, and Rev. Mother M. Angeline Teresa, O.CARM., after Opening the Meeting with Prayer gave a verbal account of the

a) *TRIP TO ROME:* which briefly—we could not undertake a Foundation there this year. Secondly, it was thought advisable to send two Sisters at first to learn the language and the ways of the people before attempting anything further. The Carmelite Fathers were renting a villa for a few months to see what steps could be taken on this side of the globe (they were very anxious to rush the procedure), in order that the Sisters would have a place near them if they could come to Rome that year. All this was left an open issue, as nothing could be determined just now.[17]

All this exciting preparation came to a halt with the outbreak of World War II in Europe in 1939. The crises that followed in the United States and the demands put on the Sisters by post war expansion of the Church in America caused this Roman Foundation to be sidetracked.

Mother Angeline Teresa returned to Rome many times thereafter but always in the interests of her Carmelite Sisters for the Aged and Infirm. At Cardinal Hayes' impetus she visited Rome in 1932 and 1938. Urged by Bishop Gibbons of Albany she visited Rome in 1950. This was the Holy Year for the Universal Church and the 700th Anniversary of the traditional date for the reception of the brown scapular of Our Lady of Mount Carmel by St. Simon Stock. At every Roman visit she paid her loving respects to the Pope and never omitted a courtesy visit of gratitude to the Prior General of the Carmelite Fathers.

Again in 1953 she was the guest of Archbishop (later Cardinal) Richard J. Cushing of Boston whose pilgrimage left on the S.S. New Amsterdam from Boston. At the audience with the Holy Father on September 8, 1953 Pope Pius XII delayed to talk to Mother for over ten minutes. In 1957 Mother went to Milan to attend the International Gerontological Congress, after which she went down to Rome. Her private audience, again with Pope Pius XII, was July 24th at the Vatican since the Pope had not yet left for his summer residence at Castel Gandolfo.

In 1964 in the course of her canonical visitation of the houses of the Congregation in Ireland and Scotland Mother again went down to Rome. This time she spoke with Pope Paul VI. Afterwards she visited the Congregation for Religious several times, and called on Most Reverend Kilian Healy, O.Carm. the Prior General of her beloved Carmelite Order.

Besides her dearest wish to have a geographical foundation in Rome, Mother M. Angeline Teresa pursued earnestly Roman (Pontifical) approbation for her Carmelite Congregation. The first step toward such approbation is the approval of the Bishop of the place where the Community is founded.

In the approach to Roman approval for a Religious institute there are two jurisdictions which function concommitently,as it were. First, there is the absolute jurisdiction of ecclesiastical authority. This is the Bishop, and the Holy See, operating usually through the Congregation for Institutes of Consecrated Life and Societies of Apostolic Life.[18] Then there is the internal development within the religious community itself. This religious maturity is fostered by General Chapters or periodic meetings through which the Community monitors its life style and discipline; the enactment of particular legislation; and the elections of its legitimate Superiors.[19]

Cardinal Hayes had approved Mother Angeline's original Community on September 3, 1929 and their affiliation with the Carmelite Order took place on the Feast of Our Lady of Mt. Carmel, July 16, 1931. These were the events which established them as a religious Institute in the Church. Patrick Cardinal Hayes,who had watched their rapid development,saw the need for them to take over now their internal government. He accomplished this by having the Carmelite Sisters first General Assembly held at St. Patrick's Home in the Bronx on August 5, 1936. Providentially this was actually the seventh anniversary of their canonical separation from the Little Sisters of the Poor. Using his competent authority he appointed the superiors for the Congregation who would then be competent to be members of their next official Chapter. Mother M. Angeline described this historic event herself:

REPORT OF FIRST APPOINTMENTS MADE BY HIS EMINENCE,
PATRICK CARDINAL HAYES, AT ST. PATRICK'S HOME
August 5, 1936

The following is an account of the appointments made by His Eminence, Patrick Cardinal Hayes at St. Patrick's Home, on August 5th, Feast of Our Lady of the Snow and also the SEVENTH anniversary of the founding of the Community.

Representing His Eminence, the Cardinal, was the Right Rev. Monsignor Patrick N. Breslin, Rector of Our Lady of Mercy Church and Dean of the Bronx. Monsignor Breslin opened the day by celebrating Mass in honor of Our Lady of the Snow in St. Patrick's Chapel, at which time he delivered a touching sermon on 'personal love' for Our Blessed

Mother. Present in the Chapel were the Sisters, Novices, Postulants and the Old People, the guests of the Home.

Immediately after Mass, the Community of Professed Sisters repaired to the Community Room where Monsignor Breslin addressed the Sisters and told them of the Cardinal's wishes. Monsignor's address was opened with a short prayer, after which he told the assembled Sisters that he came in the Name, and with the Authority of His Eminence to announce the names of those appointed to Office in the Congregation.

The Rev. Mother M. Angeline Teresa, O.Carm., Foundress of the Community, is SUPERIOR-GENERAL for life;

The Rev. Mother M. Angeline Teresa, O.Carm., Motherhouse Superior (St. Patrick's Home is Motherhouse of the Congregation)

Sister M. Leonie, O.Carm., is FIRST ASSISTANT

Sister M. Louise, O.Carm.,is SECOND ASSISTANT

Sister M. Colette, O.Carm., is THIRD ASSISTANT

Sister M. Teresa, O.Carm., is FOURTH ASSISTANT and Superior of Mt. Carmel Home for three years.

After the appointments made by His Eminence, all raised their hearts to God in prayer, thanking Him for the Wise choice on the part of His Eminence; and then each Sister publicly pledged her fealty to the newly-made Mother General of the Community.

AUGUST 5th, 1936

MOTHER M. ANGELINE TERESA, O.CARM.[20]

It was an unusual and remarkable decision on the part of the Cardinal Archbishop of New York to appoint Mother Angeline Teresa as Superior General for life, surely a testimony of the great esteem in which he held her. The other officials had been appointed for a period of three years. Mother Angeline's own reaction is once again an evidence of her own humility and obedience to Canon Law since she never afterwards insisted on this prerogative, but rather submitted herself for free election by the Sisters at every following Chapter. Due notice of this newsworthy General Assembly was given in the *New York Times*, highlighting Mother M.Angeline's lifetime appointment. The identifying caption erroneously read, "First General Chapter Held of Carmelite Sisters."[21]

Shortly after the First General Assembly on August 11, 1936, the three religious resident at St. Patrick's Home in the Bronx, Mothers Leonie, Louise and Colette, who had been named Assistants, wrote to Cardinal Hayes expressing their gratitude and joy at the results of the Assembly, especially Mother M. Angeline Teresa's lifelong office as Superior General. The Cardinal responded to them under date of August 19, 1936:

> I pray that God may grant Reverend Mother Angeline many years to guide the Community and continue the splendid work that she is doing.[22]

The first canonical General Chapter of the Carmelite Sisters was held at St. Patrick's Home and Motherhouse from March 17-March 20, 1942. Before this Chapter the local communities of each house selected two Sisters during the third week of February as delegates to accompany the local Superior. Father (later Monsignor) James B. Roberts assisted the Sisters before the Chapter and during the sessions. Reverend Francis X. Shea was the delegate for the Archbishop. The formularies for vows, temporary, perpetual and renewal were revised. Adjustments were made regarding the procedures for convoking and conducting future Chapters regarding delegates, elections, and amending the Constitutions. A contract was approved to be signed by incoming postulants insuring free services. At the same session it was voted to amend the Constitutions by adding "Caring for Seminarians and Aged Priests" to the original apostolate of the Community. At the Second Session on March 19, 1942 Mother M. Angeline Teresa was elected by twenty-four of the twenty-five possible votes as Superior General. At the time there were thirty-seven Novices and nineteen postulants.[23]

Second General Chapter—1948

The Second General Chapter held from November 24—November 26, 1948 was the first Chapter to be held at the new Motherhouse at Avila on Hudson. Most Reverend Edmund F. Gibbons, Bishop of Albany, accompanied by Reverend Joseph Kelly, Vicar for Religious, presided over the elections and remained through the Chapter. The first matter of business was the election of the Superior General and the General Councillors. Mother M. Angeline Teresa was re-elected Mother General with twenty-eight of a possible thirty votes. The Chapter of Affairs made some revisions in the Constitutions and the compilation of a Customs Book to preserve Carmelite traditions and practices not found in the Constitutions. The Chapter then closed and at the time there were twelve Novices and twelve Postulants.[24]

The Extraordinary Chapter of 1949

An extraordinary General Chapter was convoked for October 19, 1949. Mother and the Sisters assembled at Avila-on-Hudson, Germantown, N.Y. The reason for this special chapter was a directive from the Sacred Congregation for Religious at the Vatican asking for a review of the legislation of all religious communities. As it happened, the Most Reverend Edmund F. Gibbons announced that having consulted with a canonical expert, Rev. Ferdinand Mayer, O.F.M. Conv. of St. Anthony's Monastery, Rensselaer, N.Y., he felt that proposed changes made by the recent Chapter of 1948 were adequate for the present directives. Each Sister was presented with a double column of the original Constitutions approved by Cardinal Hayes on January 12, 1934 matched with the changes proposed by the Chapter of 1948. The Capitulars unanimously accepted the proposed changes. It was also decided that copies of the revised Constitutions be sent to the Bishops in whose Dioceses Carmelite Homes were located. Bishop Gibbons closed the Extraordinary Chapter with Benediction of the Blessed Sacrament.[25]

Third General Chapter 1954

The Carmelite Sisters conducted their Third General Chapter at St. Teresa's Motherhouse, Avila, September 19–November 13, 1954. The Vicar For Religious of the Albany Diocese, Reverend Joseph P. Kelly, was the official delegate of Bishop Gibbons. Before the election Father Kelly instructed the members of the Chapter that according to the Constitutions, Mother M. Angeline Teresa was ineligible for re-election. If anyone wanted her again they must use the term *postulate* on their ballot and two-thirds majority was required. On the first ballot Mother Angeline was postulated by forty-three votes out of a possible forty-four. Because of the need for approval from Rome for the postulation to be accepted, the Chapter was suspended on September 20, 1954 and the Chapter members went home. On his return to the Diocese on September 22, Bishop Edmund F. Gibbons approved Mother's postulation and sent due notice to Rome. An affirmative telegram came from Rome on November 9, 1954 and the delegates were recalled to Avila for November 13, 1954. First the General Councillors were elected. The importance of the Marian Year was noted. A Vocation Director was appointed and a modification of the veil to a soft one without the long celluloid insert was approved. On November 14, 1954 the first two-part Chapter was closed. There were twenty Novices and eighteen postulants.[26]

Fourth General Chapter 1960

The Fourth General Chapter of the Carmelite Sisters was convened at St. Teresa's Motherhouse at Avila from September 19–21. Bishop William A. Scully came for the elections accompanied by his secretary, Monsignor James G. Hart. On September 20, elections were held and to the surprise of no one, Mother Angeline Teresa was postulated on the first ballot. This Chapter made history as it was the first one as a Congregation of Pontifical Right. Mother's long-time dream and the goal of all her efforts had come to glorious fruition when, on July 16, 1957, the Feast of Our Lady of Mount Carmel, the "Decree of Praise" erecting the Congregation of the Carmelite Sisters for the Aged and Infirm of Germantown, New York was promulgated by Valerius Cardinal Valeriani of the Sacred Congregation for Religious. This was the greatest event that had taken place between this and the Chapter of 1954. At this Chapter a two-year novitiate was formally introduced. As the Chapter came to a close it was noted that there were fifty novices and thirty postulants.[27]

The Fifth General Chapter 1966

While the blessed objective of Pontifical Approbation had come to pass before the last Chapter, it will complete the juridical development of the Carmelite Sisters as they continue to grow and develop in the subsequent Chapters. The Fifth General Chapter was convoked at Avila-on-Hudson September 12, through September 23, 1966. The theme given in advance was Spiritual Renewal according to the Documents of Vatican II Council and the Carmelite heritage. A unique aspect of this Chapter was that the Most Reverend Edward J. Maginn, the Apostolic Administrator of the Albany Diocese, presided at the elections. Mother M. Angeline Teresa, O.Carm. was once again postulated on the first ballot. When Bishop Maginn announced the result of the vote to the Community he added that Ildebrando Cardinal Antoniutti, Prefect of the Congregation for Religious at Rome, in view of Mother Angeline's remarkable qualities of leadership and wisdom, was authorizing her postulation in advance if it would be the choice of the Chapter. The business of the Chapter continued with discussions on the modification of the habit; definitive standards for continuing dedicated care of the aged; evaluating Community recreation; reorganizing Community prayers; and restoring both the Carmelette (High School Volunteers) Program and uniforms. Thus, one of the longer Chapters came to a close. There were in the Congregation eighty-five novices and forty-one postulants.[28]

Sixth General Chapter 1972

The Sixth General Chapter was convened by Mother Angeline Teresa at St. Teresa's Motherhouse from September 6 through September 16th, 1972. It was unique in the fact that two prolonged pre-Chapter meetings preceded it, the first in February, the second in

July. Mother Angeline Teresa invited Father Jude Mead to act as facilitator and then after the elections to prepare the Interim Directives for the Community. Bishop Edwin Broderick presided at the election in which Mother Angeline was again postulated on September 8, 1972. Other observations concerning this will be made further on. The great task of the Chapter is best described in Mother Angeline's presentation of the Interim Directives to the Community:

> . . . The months, days and hours of work by the Chapter members are crystallized in this book entitled Consuming Zeal. It is a Community book, for each Sister's opinion was consulted beforehand, and the delegates sent to the Chapter as the representatives of the Sisters, worked long and hard.

> . . . I thank God for having lived to see this day when our Sisters could produce such a document. Let us read, study and contemplate this rule of life.

> . . . This is a handbook of our Carmelite Spirit and tradition. May God give each of us the grace to persevere, to conform to the pattern of Christ set for us on the Mount, and to be loyal and generous daughters of the Church.[29]

Although the Chapter closed on September 16, 1972[30] the Chapter document was speedily printed and each Sister had her own copy by January 4, 1973. To appreciate Mother Angeline's acute participation in these Interim Directives, when the moderator approached her about the title she said the theme for the whole Chapter had been Zeal and she wanted that concept kept. When "Consuming" was suggested as a modifier she was delighted. Also at the front of the text it was again suggested to her by the moderator that there be a Declaration of Ecclesial Status that is the intent of the Congregation. She accepted the following readily except she asked, "Could we not add Carmelite to the habit?"

> The Congregation of the Carmelite Sisters for the Aged and Infirm, St. Teresa Motherhouse, Avila-on-Hudson, New York, is and shall remain a Religious Institute as currently defined by the Church, with the norms of:

> Public profession of the vows of Obedience, Poverty and Chastity.
> Common life for all members.
> Wearing a distinctively religious CARMELITE habit, a visible sign of their consecration to God and to the service of the People of God.

> Enactment of the VI General Chapter, September 1972.

Seventh General Chapter 1978

Mother M. Angeline Teresa convoked the Seventh General Chapter of the Carmelite Sisters to be held at Avila, September 7th through September 21, 1978. On February 6, 1978 she sent a letter to each of the delegates informing them that she, with the unanimous consent of the General Council, had asked Father Jude Mead, C.P. to be advisor and consultant to the Seventh General Chapter, and had sent this information to the Sacred Congregation for Religious in Rome.[31] He met in preparatory session with the members of the General Council.

There can be no doubt that the Seventh General Chapter was the most emotionally fraught in the almost fifty-year history of the Congregation. Mother Angeline was now eighty-five years old. Her health was becoming more fragile. It could hardly be expected that she could withstand another six-year term as Superior General. While speculation abounded Mother Angeline, typically, kept her own counsel. Among the Sisters there were troubled emotions and mixed feelings. Some wanted to keep her at any cost. Others felt it cruel to think of burdening her again at this late hour. Above all no one wanted to hurt her or have her feel rejected. The facilitator reminded the Sisters how in past history so many founders and foundresses were neglected, unknown and even put out of the Orders they had founded. To make it clear to everyone inside and outside the Community, he suggested that the first act of the upcoming Chapter be a Decree of Recognition of Mother Angeline as the Superior General Emerita for life with all its privileges and that she be declared the true and only Foundress of the Congregation after Our Lady of Mount Carmel.[32] The concept was acceptable at once. The Decree of Recognition was drawn up and presented to the Chapter delegates at a pre-chapter meeting. On June 7, 1978 Mother M. Michael Rosarie, O.Carm., Vicar General, explained the nature of the Decree to the delegates and asked them to keep its message a secret as they wanted it to be a surprise for Mother.[33]

When the delegates assembled on September 7 for the Chapter, Mother Michael Rosarie read a beautiful greeting to all from Mother Angeline Teresa. Mother M. Bernadette de Lourdes then presented the text of the Decree of Recognition to be voted as the first Chapter item next day. Then Mother Angeline Teresa had a surprise for the delegates. She presented a touching letter withdrawing her name from election. The entire text is presented here as it was read to the assembly in the Chapel the evening of September 7th by Mother Michael Rosarie:

9 August 1978

Dear Members of the Council,

As the General Chapter draws closer, I am hereby writing to let you know that I do not wish to be considered for the Office of Mother General.

At the same time I am requesting that you go ahead with all that is necessary to run the Chapter efficiently, relying on the Grace of God and the inspiration of the Holy Spirit. I am confident that God will be with us now just as He has been with us for the past forty-nine years.

The Ordinary of the Diocese of Albany, His Excellency Bishop H. Hubbard has already been notified about the Chapter, and he will be here on September 8th. I know that you will arrange for the Mass of the Holy Spirit, and all that is necessary for the elections.

I know that at this time work must be done on our Rule and Constitutions, and it is important that we do so in accordance with the wishes of Rome. "Stay with Rome" is my advice to you during these days of confusion and change, particularly now as a tribute to our late lamented Pope Paul the Sixth and as a gesture of loyalty to the incoming Holy Father.

I also know that you will do all in your power to make the Delegates and all who come to the Chapter comfortable and be sure they are warm and that there is plenty of food in the house.

I ask God to give His Wisdom and Understanding to whomever He ordains will be my successor, and I will do all in my power to help especially by my prayers.

I thank each one of you for your dedication and loyalty over the past six years, and I pray God and Our Lady of Mount Carmel to reward and shower you with blessings.

With my deep gratitude and prayers, I am,

Your devoted Mother in Carmel,

(Mother M. Angeline Teresa Ord.Carm.,)[34]

Thus consoled, the Chapter proceeded on the next day to elect Mother M. Michael Rosarie (Devaney), O.Carm., as Superior General. Even this event was rendered less painful by a typical Mother Angeline intrusion. After all the ballots were collected and still unopened the two tellers were dispatched from the Chapter Hall by Bishop Hubbard to Mother M. Angeline's room for her vote. Sister M. Lois Joseph and Sister Noreen Thomas went off to receive Mother's secret vote. The capitulars awaited their return. Time passed tortuously slowly. Tension grew greater and greater. No one knew what happened or what was going on. After almost half an hour the two tellers returned with one hand as long as the other. They simply announced that Mother chose to abstain from voting so as not in any way to influence the Chapter. "But," they added, "Mother made us sit down and have a cup of tea!" The assembly, including Bishop Hubbard, broke into a release of laughter. Nothing was wrong. Indeed everything was right and Mother M. Angeline was still in every sense "her own woman".

Then there was the solemn announcement of the election to the Community by Bishop Hubbard who took the occasion to praise Mother Michael, Mother Angeline and the great work done by the Carmelite Sisters. Then Benediction of the Blessed Sacrament followed. Immediately afterwards, everyone, Bishop, priests, Mother Michael, delegates and the local Community went up to Mother Angeline's room to present her with the special Decree of Recognition reproduced in its entirety in the appendix. This outstanding event of the Chapter ended up significantly with Mother M. Angeline's beautiful remark, "No where are there better Sisters than my own!"[35]

EIGHTH GENERAL CHAPTER 1984

This Chapter, the first without Mother M. Angeline Teresa, O.Carm's presence, was held September 1 through September 21, 1984. Most Reverend Howard J. Hubbard, Bishop of Albany, presided and Mother Michael Rosarie was re-elected on the first ballot.[36]

NOTES

[1] Sister M. Bernadette de Lourdes (Wisely) O.Carm. and Sister M. Gabriel (Reis) O.Carm. Personal Interview. January 21, 1989. Avila Motherhouse.

[2] *Exhibit E.* Mother M. Angeline Teresa, *My Trip Abroad*, 1st trip to Europe, June 12–August 5, 1932. 17 pages.

[3] Prelates: Archbishop Beckman, Bishops Toolen, Rummell, and Kohlman.

[4] *Exhibit E.* cf. note 2.

[5] *Circular Letters.* Letter 7, Vol. I p. 2 June 19, 1932.

[6] Letter 5, Vol. I, p. 5 June 17, 1932.

[7] *Exhibit E.* p.4.

[8] Letter 11 Vol. I p. 2.

[9] *Exhibit E.* p. 5.

[10] *Ibid.* p. 10.

[11] Letter 12, Vol. I, p. 1 June 21, 1932.

[12] AVGA Vertical File #2, "Foundations." cf. *Rome Foundation*.

[13] *Ibid.*

[14] *Ibid.*

[15] *Ibid.*

[16] *Ibid.*

[17] *Rome Foundation* cf. note 12.

[18] This designation became official February 1, 1989. From 1967 this office was known as the Congregation for Religious and Secular Institutes. It was previously called the Sacred Congregation for Religious.

[19] Cf. Pope Paul VI, *Ecclesiae Sanctae*, Intro. August 6, 1966.

[20] AVGA Chapter Records, August 5, 1936.

[21] Cf. *New York Times*, August 6, 1936.

[22] AVGA Chapter Records, August 11, 1936.

[23] AVGA *op. cit.*, March 20, 1942.

[24] AVGA *op. cit.*, Nov. 26, 1948.

[25] AVGA *op. cit.*, October 19, 1949.

[26] AVGA *op. cit.*, November 14, 1954.

[27] AVGA *op. cit.*, September 21, 1960.

[28] AVGA *op. cit.*, September 23, 1966.

[29] *Consuming Zeal*, VI General Chapter Directives, Carmelite Sisters, Germantown NY, October 15, 1972.

[30] AVGA Chapter Records, September 16, 1972.

[31] AVGA *op. cit.*, February 6, 1972.

[32] AVGA *op. cit.*, April 29, 1972.

[33] AVGA *op. cit.*, June 7, 1972.

[34] AVGA *Promotor's File*, Drawer #1. August 9, 1972. Composed by Rev. John Lamont, O.Carm. under direct instruction as to whom it would be directed, points to be included, and manner of presentation, from

Mother M. Angeline herself after a spiritual conference apart from confession.

[35] AVGA Chapter Records, September 8, 1972.

[36] AVGA *op. cit.*, September 3, 1984.

CENACLE

Keeping apace with the extraordinary progress of her charismatic ideal Mother M. Angeline Teresa, O.Carm. witnessed phenomenal expansion in vocations, houses and juridical status. Hence she earnestly strove for herself and the Community to parallel equal development in spiritual realities. Certainly she meditated on the cautionary verse of the psalmist:

Unless the Lord build the house, they labor in vain that build it. Ps. 127:1

For Mother M. Angeline there could be no real religious life without a sound basis of prayer and no real spirituality unless rooted in the Scripture and the sacramental life of the Church. In a sense she thus anticipated and subsequently incorporated the norms for the prayer life of religious succinctly outlined in the Vatican II Decree on the Renewal of Religious Life:

The members of each institute, therefore, should seek and love above all else God who has first loved us (cf. 1 Jn.4:10). In all circumstances they should take care to foster a life hidden with Christ in God (cf. Col.3:3), which is the source and stimulus of love of the neighbor, for the salvation of the world and the up-building of the Church. Even the very practice of the evangelical counsels is animated and governed by this charity.

For this reason, members of institutes should assiduously cultivate the spirit of prayer, and prayer itself, drawing on the authentic sources of Christian Spirituality. In the first place, let them have the sacred scripture at hand daily, so that they might learn 'the surpassing worth of knowing Christ Jesus.' (Phil.3:8) by reading and meditating on the divine scriptures. They should perform the sacred liturgy, especially the holy mystery of the Eucharist, with their hearts and their lips, according to the mind of the Church, and they should nourish their spiritual lives from this richest of sources.

Thus, refreshed at the table of the divine law and of the sacred altar, let them love the members of Christ as brothers; let them reverence and love their pastors in a filial spirit; let them more and more live and think with the Church, and let them dedicate themselves wholeheartedly to its mission.[1]

Among countless apt quotations from the pen of Mother M. Angeline Teresa let the following suffice:

> How are you living your life of prayer? Carmelites have always been renowned for their spirit of prayer. Unless our activity stems from prayer, it is useless. It is in prayer that we obtain the graces we need to do our work well for Christ and to be faithful Religious.[2]

> Prayer means finding Christ by uniting ourselves to Him each morning at the Holy Sacrifice of the Mass; by saying our Office and other prayers with the Community; by making our meditation. Surely there are many opportunities to 'raise our minds and hearts to God in prayer,' not only in the Chapel but as we go about serving the old people in His Name. We have so much to say to each other. Wouldn't it be good to spend some time talking with God? A prayerful Religious finds God everywhere and speaks to him all day long.[3]

> Because it is the mind of the Church that the Divine Office of the Church be the official prayer of Religious we will now say these inspiring prayers beginning on December 8th. The schedule of Community Prayers has been changed and the new one has been sent to each house. Outside the Divine Office there will be very few vocal prayers. You may continue any of our Community Prayers privately if you decide to do so, and there is also time allotted for private devotions and extra spiritual reading. Lauds will be part of our morning prayers; Vespers the evening prayer, and Compline part of our night prayers. These parts of the Office are not time consuming and there should be no difficulty in getting them in. I sincerely pray that through these inspiring prayers of the Church all of us will be so united in prayer that our Carmelite Congregation may once again become a united spiritual family dedicated to Christ in serving the Aged and in supporting one another.[4]

> Holy Scripture is the reading I most love. It does my soul more good than any other spiritual book. It is the best of all food for my soul. Not by bread alone does man live but by every word that comes from the Mouth of God.[5]

Before treating of the spirituality of Mother Angeline, a brief evaluation of the fonts of her practice of prayer will be useful. As noted, the first font of her prayer life was the sacred scripture and the liturgy. The second font was the Spiritual Exercises of St. Ignatius. According to the practice of the Little Sisters, she returned to the Motherhouse to prepare for Final Vows. During this second novitiate at La Tour in France a certain Jesuit whom she simply identifies as Father "T" gave the retreat in preparation for her final profession in 1925.[6] Although the retreat lasted only eight days, the director carefully kept the integrity of the originally intended four-week plan. There was the use of the acts of the intellect in reasoning and the acts of the will in manifesting one's love. The exercises were divided into four parts. In the first phase there is the consideration and contemplation of sin. In the second phase the life of Christ up to Palm Sunday inclusive is considered. The third phase treats of the Passion and death of Christ the Lord. The fourth and final phase concerns the Resurrection and Ascension of Our Lord and concludes with Three Methods of Prayer.[7] These latter directives treat in the first Method of the Ten Commandments, the Seven Capital Sins, the three Powers of the Soul, and the five Senses of the Body. In the second Method Contemplation of the full meaning of each word of a given prayer, e.g., the Our Father. The third Method is the measured rhythmical recitation of the Our Father, Hail Mary, Soul of Christ, the Creed or the Hail Holy Queen, taking each word as before but accommodated to each breath or respiration during which the word is prayed mentally.[8] The Spiritual Exercises of St. Ignatius outlined above are a series of meditations composed by the saint between 1521 and 1548. They rank among the great classics of Christian spirituality. Because of their being an inexhaustible fountain of solid piety, Pope Pius XI declared St. Ignatius to be the heavenly patron of spiritual exercises and retreats July 22, 1922. The same Pontiff in his encyclical letter *Mens Nostra* of December 20, 1929 recommended the Ignatian Exercises to all the faithful.[9]

The following are the retreat resolutions made by Mother Angeline at the close of her profession retreat April 20, 1925:

> Our Lord speaks—"My beloved, my bride—live by your Rule. If you live by your Rule you will be like a consecrated host; your Rule makes you God's servant, consecrated in love."

Novitiate Resolutions

1) I wish to be here on earth, as a lily among thorns, even among the pain of the thorns that I may always remain gentle and loving.

2) I wish to increase and not diminish the practice of virtue in my daily life.

3) Perform 30 small acts of love or sacrifice to more worthily receive Christ in Holy Communion the following day.

4) I wish to discard and keep my mind away from all useless and idle thoughts.

5) As I go up and down the stairs throughout the day I will say the invocation, 'Jesus, Mary and Joseph,' for the poor souls in Purgatory.

6) I will make frequent acts of love in the presence of my God.

7) Each time I pass by a doorway I will reiterate, 'My God, it is your little, insignificant one passing by.'

8) Each morning when Our Lord comes to rest on my tongue in Holy Communion I will ask Him to grant that I may never offend Him by sins of the tongue. I'm sure He will grant my request.

9) I desire, with the grace of God, to obey at all times and in all things on the supernatural level, in order to please God alone in the small things as well as in greater things.

10) Each day I will recite 7 Hail Mary's in honor of the 7 sorrows of Our Blessed Mother in order to obtain the grace of perseverance. I will frequently renew my perpetual vows, especially during the consecration of the Mass.

11) I wish to remain silent especially during times of pain, hurt and contradictions in my daily life.

12) With the grace of God I will endeavor to make the lives of my Little Sisters happy by helping them in any way I can and by good example.

Easter Sunday—1st day of retreat.
Thought: 'Peace be with you'—the words which Our Lord addressed to his apostles.

It is in this peace that we must begin this retreat, which is so important because it is preparing us for Perpetual Vows; this threefold blessed day on which we pronounce our Perpetual Vows, whereby we rediscover our baptismal innocence. In other words, if we should die after pronouncing those vows we would go straight to Heaven. As a matter of fact, each time we renew these vows, that same condition exists. What a grace and a joy for Religious.

Our last period of formation is ending; we now only need to put into practice all that we have learned.

Thought: It takes less time and more courage to become a saint.

2nd day: 'God alone' was the maxim of the Saints.

3rd day: 'What does it profit a man to gain the world and lose his soul in the process.'

4th day: Venial sin causes death in our soul.

5th day: Our Lord, our Friend. He wants our love. Our Lord, our Model. How often do we ask ourselves what Jesus would do if He were in our place.

In the mystery of the Annunciation our Blessed Mother is our model of prayer.

In the mystery of the Visitation our Blessed Mother is the model of active ministry.

6th day: The birth of Our Lord—vow and virtue of poverty.

Thought: Always ask for all permissions.

The Holy Family of Nazareth—Jesus is our model of obedience. Thought: The value and worth of our life is depicted in our obedience.

7th day: The Holy Family of Nazareth—our model of charity. God gives His choicest blessings only to those who are charitable. Thought: Life owes me nothing; I am the last.

Our apostolic zeal must be to save souls. The Church depends on us to save the souls of our elderly, but we cannot give what we do not possess, that is, if we don't possess God in our own lives we cannot give Him to others.

The storm on the Sea of Galilee—*Thought*: We must never be discouraged in temptations but rather we must maintain great faith in God and do our best, and then Jesus will take us by the hand as He did with St. Peter.

8th day: The Passion of Our Lord—In His Passion He made the sacrifice of His life, His dearest friends, and even His Holy Mother. He sacrificed His reputation and His honor.

Thought: We should seek only to please God, for God and eternity are all that matter.

Be faithful to your particular examen and reflect on a well-chosen topic.

Resolutions of retreat:
Not to make too many resolutions but to select those we feel most in need of having, selected either through advice or from our own experience.

Thought: As you leave the Novitiate remember not to get too involved in worldly affairs but maintain your interior life and remain closely united to the good God, for as long as possible.

Be especially careful during the first year for the evil one will try to distract you from the good influences of your novitiate days.

We must always follow our Rule and Constitutions as they were taught us in the novitiate. We must remain united with our Motherhouse in order to preserve the fervor of our novitiate days.

9th day: There is much joy in the Religious Life. Since we have the joyous privilege of professing our perpetual vows during the alleluia season of the liturgical calendar, let us make an effort to preserve the joy within.

10th day: Heaven is everlasting joy, seeing God and His Blessed Mother for eternity.

Dear Father, through the Immaculate Heart of Mary, I offer you Jesus, your most beloved Son, and I offer myself in Him, with Him, and through Him for all your intentions and in the name of all your creation (Ind. 300 days).

Sweet Heart of Jesus grant that I may love thee more and more (300 days).

Agonizing heart of Jesus have pity on the dying.

All for you Sacred Heart of Jesus (300 days).

Sacred Heart of Jesus I believe in your love for me (300 days).

Sacred heart of Jesus, source of all purity, have mercy on us (300 days).

Eucharistic Heart of Jesus, have mercy on us.

Sacred Heart of Jesus, your kingdom come (300 days).

Sacred Heart of Jesus, be my love.

Perseverance is not seen as never being tempted and never falling but rather by beginning again even though we may fall 10 or 50 times a day.

Perseverance is therefore to always begin again and never to be discouraged (in the sense of giving up).

Advice from the Retreat Master: 1st—Resolution of retreat—always have faith in the goodness and mercy of Christ. He loves you very much and He's all yours.

2nd—The first year following the novitiate, continue to live as a novice in silence, reflection and in the interior life.

3rd—Always remain open with your Superiors and confessors and things will go well. No matter what may happen never become discouraged; a well-disposed heart who loves sincerely is more than her spouse expects of her.

4th—You are on an express train for Heaven. Never doubt this. If you continue on this journey that you have begun with sincerity and good intentions, and if you remain as you are at the end of this retreat and of your novitiate you will not only be a good little sister, but also a great saint. I hope you live to see the day when you have reached the degree of sanctity which Our Lord expects of you.

5th—You have made a very good retreat, from what I have seen; now go out in the joy of alleluia.

6th—Keep your heart for God alone as it is too small for other affections and too large to want anyone else to fill it but God alone.

7th—Each month recollect yourself in a day of retreat, examine the resolutions you have made in this retreat and at the end of your novitiate and reflect on the fervor with which you are living them.

Father T.S.J.   April 20, 1925

Tour St. Joseph.[10]

The next basic reference for the spirituality of Mother M. Angeline Teresa is the doctrine of St. Francis De Sales, especially in his *Introduction to the Devout Life*.[11] This was published first in 1609. Bridget McCrory would have been introduced to this spiritual masterpiece early on since so many of the priests of both Ireland and Scotland had come to the knowledge of Salesian spirituality from their French seminary professors. During her formation period for the religious life in France the priests who were spiritual directors and confessors would likewise have been steeped in the doctrine of the gentle Bishop of Geneva. In her conferences to her own novices and circular letters to her Community St. Francis De Sales is quoted frequently and with a conversant familiarity.[12] From his preface the saint himself describes this work:

> I have divided this Introduction into five parts. In the first I endeavor by remonstrance and exercises to convert Philothea's (Philothea signifies a soul loving or in love with God) simple desire into a solid resolution. She at last makes this by a firm protestation after her general confession followed by most Holy Communion, in which she gives herself up to her savior and happily enters into His holy love. This done, to lead her further on, I show her the two great means by which she may unite herself more and more to His Divine Majesty: the use of the sacraments, by which our Good God comes to us, and holy prayer by which He attracts us to Himself. It is to this that I devote the second part. In the third part I show her how she ought to exercise herself in several virtues most needed for her advancement, not stopping except for some particular advice which she could hardly have received elsewhere or discovered for herself. In the fourth part I expose to her view some of the snares of her enemies, showing her how she may escape them and proceed forward. In the fifth and last part I cause her to retire a little, in order to refresh herself, recover her breath, and repair her strength, so that she may afterwards more happily gain ground and advance in a devout life.[13]

St. Francis De Sales, the man and his writings, are characterized by simplicity of style, directness of approach and gentle sensitivity. Since Mother Angeline was possessed of these same virtuous qualities herself[14] she found an enduring rapport with this spiritual Doctor of the Church.

When God in his Providence called Mother M. Angeline Teresa to found her own religious family, almost immediately aggregated into the family of Carmel, she had already imbibed the Carmelite spirit through her devotion and study of the writings of the great St. Teresa of Jesus of Avila, begun as a teenager and nurtured over the years.[15] Citations from this great Carmelite Foundress and Mystic were threaded through the daily instructions which Mother Angeline gave to the postulants and novices and appear frequently throughout her circular letters and conferences to the Sisters. It is also significant that when she transferred to her own new Community, while keeping her religious name Angeline, she added to it the name Teresa.

Perhaps Mother Angeline Teresa's most tender devotion was to St. Therese of the Child Jesus and her spiritual approach of "the Little Way."[16] Her autobiography, *The Story of a Soul* was a favorite spiritual reading book also.[17] Mother Angeline became a close friend of Canon Thomas Nimmo Taylor, later Monsignor. He put the village of Carfin, Scotland both on the map and in the public eye by his monumental Grotto erected in honor of Our Lady of Lourdes begun on September 20, 1920.[18] Canon Taylor also undertook to spread devotion to St. Therese of Lisieux throughout the English-speaking world. When the preliminary investigation of the process of her beatification was held at Lisieux in 1911, Canon Taylor was one of the principal witnesses to the fame of her sanctity among the English-speaking people.[19] In 1912 he published his translation of her autobiography. A statue of the Little Flower was erected at the Carfin Grotto in 1923. Canon Taylor deepened Mother Angeline's devotion to St. Therese and made it possible for her to join him in a pilgrimage to Lisieux July 14 to 18, 1932 when she visited Scotland after the Eucharistic Congress in Dublin that year. At Lisieux, Mother delighted in seeing St. Therese's First Commuion dress, her reception dress, her long golden hair, artifacts of penance, her habit, scapular so much like her own, and the white choir mantle.[20] United in love and devotion to the Little Flower these two corresponded until the Canon died in his ninetieth year December 1963. The following undated petitions in Mother M. Angeline Teresa's own hand show how much she had taken to heart the "Little Way" of St. Therese of Lisieux:

Petitions to the Little Flower

1st. Please help me to become a saint.

2nd. Grace of a happy death for myself and all who are dear to me.

3rd. To see you at least once before I die please, if I am not too unworthy of your love dear Little Flower.

4th. Grace to make all my Sisters very happy in their holy vocation.

5th. Grace to love God as you did.

6th. Grace to follow my Spouse in your little way.

7th. To see the will of God in everything.

8th. To always please God and my Superiors in God.

9th. Never to commit a deliberate venial sin and final perseverance.[21]

The Upper Room or the Cenacle is the symbol in salvation history of the interior life of the Church. Here Jesus celebrated the first Eucharist and established his priesthood. Here Jesus appeared to his apostles after his resurrection. Here the eleven apostles waited in unity of mind persevering in continuous prayer with the holy women and Mary the Mother of Jesus. In presenting Mother M. Angeline Teresa's reflections on prayer as the basis of her community's unity and evaluating the sources of her spirituality and sharing in the outpouring of the Holy Spirit in her new Pentecost, the symbol of the Cenacle puts it all together as the Acts of the Apostles witnesses:

All these joined in continuous prayer, together with several women, including Mary the Mother of Jesus, and with his brothers (Acts 1:14).

NOTES

[1] *Perfectae Caritatis*. Decree on the Up To Date Renewal of the Religious Life. Num. 6. October 28, 1965 Vatican II.

[2] Mother M. Angeline Teresa, O.Carm. Circular Letter, November 1969. Num. 141, Vol. IV.

[3] *Ibid*.

[4] *Ibid*. N.B. Up until this time the Sisters had recited the Little Office of the Blessed Virgin Mary.

[5] Mother M. Angeline Teresa, O.Carm. EXIHIBIT D. *Diary* in her own hand. page February 14 final paragraph.

[6] Mother M. Angeline Teresa, O.Carm. Autograph *Retreat Notes*, April 20, 1925. AVGA.

[7] *The Spiritual Exercises of St. Ignatius*, Transl Louis J. Puhl, S.J. Newman Press, Westminster, MD. 1963 cf. nos. 3 and 4.

[8] *Ibid*. nos. 238 ff; 252 ff; 258 ff.

[9] *The Papal Encyclicals*, Ed. Claudia Carlen, I.H.M. Consortium Books, McGrath Publishing Co., Vol. III 1903–1939, Raleigh, 1981.

[10] Mother M. Angeline Teresa, O.Carm. *Retraite 1925 a La Tour St. Joseph,* Trans. Sister M. Gerard Daniel, O.Carm. AVGA.

[11] St. Francis De Sales, *Introduction to the Devout Life,* Trans. and Ed. John K. Ryan, Harper and Brothers, Publishers, New York, 1949.

[12] Personal Interview. Sister M. Bernadette De Lourdes (Wisely) O.Carm. Avila Motherhouse, January 10, 1989. Also cf. EXHIBIT D. *Diary* page February 6.

[13] St. Francis De Sales, *op. cit.* cf. "The Author's Preface," Annecy, Feast of St. Mary Magdalene 1609.

[14] *Recollections of the First Decade,* cf. Chapter V note 1.

[15] Cf. Chapter III note 5.

[16] *Autobiography of St. Therese of Lisieux,* "L'histoire d'une Ame." Trans. Ronald Knox, P.J. Kenedy and Sons, New York 1958 p. 230.

[17] *Ibid.* p. 28

[18] McGhee, Susan, *The Carfin Grotto, The First Sixty Years,* Carfin, Motherwell, 1981 p. 5.

[19] *St. Francis Xavier's Parish Carfin 1862–1962, Centenary Book.* page 20.

[20] Mother M. Angeline Teresa, O.Carm. Circular Letter, Rome, 1932, Vol. I, num. 11.

[21] Mother M. Angeline Teresa, O.Carm., (Autograph) *Petitions to the Little Flower.* Single sheet. Undated. AVGA.

[22] Exhibit D. Mother M. Angeline Teresa, O.Carm. *Diary,* February 2 through February 14, ca. 1905.

MOUNT OF BEATITUDES

In the preceding chapter under the salvation history symbol of the Cenacle, the fonts of Mother Angeline Teresa's prayer and spiritual life were recalled. Now under another rich symbol of the history of salvation, namely the Mount of Beatitudes, her own teaching on prayer is presented. The actual Mount of Beatitudes is situated at the upper end of the Sea of Galilee in the area of Tabgha. In the spiritual sense of the Scriptures it is the pulpit from which Jesus teaches His new age and His instruction on prayer. As Moses gave the Decaloque from the Mount so Jesus gives His new law. After teaching His disciples how to become blessed or, according to some scholars, how to become happy,[1] Jesus eventually taught the disciples His own prayer, the Our Father.[2] It is quite germane to our comparison also that Mother sees prayer as *True Happiness*.

The following excerpts from Mother Angeline Teresa's Diary reflections on the nature of Prayer in her own hand reveal the essence of her thoughts:

Four Principal Degrees of Prayer

1st Quietude, is an advanced but incomplete state of Union, in which the soul still loses, more or less frequently the thought of God, and in which the effect of grace, though already very strong, is not yet so strong as to render impossible all distractions.

II. Full Union, when the Divine action is so powerful that the soul is wholly occupied with it and no outside thought can turn one from it; the senses, however, remain free, and retain their relation to the exterior world.

III. Ecstasy, which has its peculiar character, the breaking of relations with the outside world, the inhibiting of voluntary movements. So luminous now becomes the sense of the presence of God and so vivid the consciousness of being united to Him, that there results the suspension of the interior faculties, and even the binding of the exterior senses. St. Teresa thus describes one form of Ecstasy. God, anticipating all thought and all interior preparation descends on you with an impetuosity so sudden and so strong that you feel yourself swept away as if by a cloud or an eagle, and transported you know not whither. But as you know not whither you are going, your feeble nature experiences in this moment, otherwise so delicious, I know not what fright at the beginning. The soul therefore must show much more courage and resolution than in the preceding states. The enjoyment of God in His Three-Fold Existence becomes now conscious, and almost uninterrupted. When a soul possesses the love of God and the certitude of being in a state of grace, its condition cannot remain secret, but is translated to the exterior with an invincible force, and with a brilliancy with which even the blindest cannot fail to be struck.

Ordinary Prayer

There is only one way of learning to pray, and that is to pray often, fill up our days with aspirations, and little ejaculatory prayers. It is a sure sign of our nearness to God for our holiness will be in proportion to our love and thought of Him all day long. We never pray alone, of this we are sure, whenever we pray rightly. There is One dwelling in us (the Holy Ghost). He is our access to the Father; He forms the Word in our hearts. He is the Spirit in whom we pray at all times. Prayer is the union of one who is not with the One who is. It is nothing else but being on terms of friendship with God, frequently conversing in secret with Him Who we know loves us. I think the best of all prayer is just to kneel or sit quietly and let Jesus pour Himself into our souls. It is such a delight to listen to Him, to be silent, and give His grace and love full liberty to act within us. It is very simple, think of God Who dwells within us, Whose temple we are, since He dwells in our soul; His prayer is ours, and we should desire to partake of it unceasingly.

(Mother comments:)

Little by little our soul becomes accustomed to live in His blessed company, realizing that it bears within itself a little Heaven, in which the God of love has made His Home. Not only in solitude but in the company of others and in the performing of our ordinary duties, we can preserve this solitude of the heart and familiarly converse with God. Those who from necessity are obliged to converse with the world, can even in the streets and public places possess solitude of the heart, and remain united with God. St. Catherine of Sienna was able to find God in the midst of her household duties in which her parents kept her employed in order to withdraw her from devotional exercises. In the midst of all these occupations she remained retired within her heart, which she called her little "Cell," and there she conversed continually with her Spouse. St. Frances de Sales also said, "I have made a temple of my soul and I live there with my good Master." And when St. Chantal asked him, "Are you long without thinking of God," he replied, "Sometimes nearly a quarter of an hour." How could souls thus united to God fail to always do God's work? When embarrassed concerning difficult or doubtful questions let us recollect ourselves in God, and if we can go before the Blessed Sacrament and ask Counsel and light, and arrange everything with God before treating with men. If we pray well, God ·with His grace and light will always be with us, and cause all that we do to turn to His glory. It is an old custom with the Servants of God, always to have some little prayers ready, and to be darting them up to Heaven frequently during the day, lifting their minds to God, from out of the filth of this world. He who adopts this plan will get great fruit with little pains. Nothing helps us more than this constant spirit of prayer, for the great thing is to become Saints. We should go to God with the same love and confidence with which a little child approaches its mother. God loves this simplicity. He has no need of learned men for the success of His works. On the contrary, He more frequently chooses those who go to Him with simplicity like the Apostles for His greatest designs.

True Happiness

The secret of happiness for me is self-forgetfulness, and continual self-denial. My love of God should be strong enough to destroy all love for self, and to bear weariness and sickness with no outward sign. I will watch against over-eagerness at my work, knowing that it will advance in proportion with the intensity of my union with God. In the midst of all kinds of distractions, I will try to remain at least interiorly calm and recollected, in the little heaven of my soul, because when I get excited and hurry over anything, try as I may I cannot raise my soul in prayer. I love the simple gaze and the consuming of love that I feel in my soul. We must keep our eyes always on Our Divine Master, we must be silent at His feet. I will keep silence so that He may flow into me, take possession of me, giving full liberty to His grace and love to act in me. I delight in listening to Him. I love to meditate on the mystery of God dwelling within the Blessed Virgin, it seems to resemble my usual attitude of soul, and like Her I adore the hidden God within me. O how I desire my union with Him to be closer every day. I believe that the ideal life of the soul is reached by living in the supernatural, by realizing that God dwells within the depths of our soul, and do all things with Him; then nothing can be small, however common-place in itself, for we do not live in, but above, such things. A supernatural soul does not deal with secondary causes, but solely with God. It does not matter how He wishes me to employ myself, since He is always with me. Prayer and our interchange of love will never cease I feel so distinctly that He dwells in my soul. I have only to recollect myself to find Him within, which is the source of all my happiness. He has put into my heart a thirst for what is Infinite and a longing to love which He alone can satisfy. I go to Him like a little child to its mother, and ask Him what I long for and to take possession of me. How I love this saying of a 'Saint,' I have found my heaven on earth, since heaven is God and God is in my soul.

(Mother continues:)

Our Lord needs no Sacrament to come to us; we can communicate all day since He is living in our soul. O Thou 'Soul,' most beautiful of creatures, who so earnestly longest to know the place where Thy Beloved is, that thou may seek Him and be united Him. Thou are thyself that very Tabernacle where He dwells, the secret chamber of His retreat, where He is hidden. Rejoice therefore and be glad because all thy good, and all thy hope is so near thee, as to be within thee; yea rather rejoice that thou canst not be without it, for lo the kingdom of God is within you. We are told in the Gospel that when Our Lord was on earth, a secret virtue went out from Him, the sick recovered, the dead were raised to life when brought in contact with Him. Yet He is still living, in the Blessed Sacrament of the altar, in our own souls. He Himself has told us so, 'If any one love Me, he will keep my word, and My Father will love him, and We will come to him and make Our abode with him.' This Divine Union is wholly interior.

When I have the happiness of visiting my Jesus in the Blessed Sacrament I find myself mute and fascinated before Him Who looks at me from the interior of the Tabernacle. I could stay for hours in His Presence. It needs an effort of the will to tear myself away. In silence and recollection, one feels what one really is, and my soul is seized with a great longing after 'Perfection,' and complete union with God. I would so love to live a truly contemplative life and yet I feel in myself so little courage for that perfect abnegation which is so necessary for an interior life, then I try to retire into solitude of my own heart, and live retired in God. My constant care is to prevent myself from being carried away by my work from recollection and contemplation. I have been asking myself whether I ought not to put narrower limits to my activity for union with God is the sole condition for efficacious labor.

(Mother concludes:)

When we take the habit of living in the Presence of God, we soon learn to live retired interiorly in complete silence and abandonment. We feel moved by a mysterious action which directs, supports and influences us and makes us understand how God dwells in us. To dwell within our own soul is to have heaven on earth, to become the intimate companion of Jesus, and to contemplate the Blessed Trinity assiduously. I will banish all haste from my actions, for it destroys recollection and hinders love.[3]

Further Reflection

Beyond Mother M. Angeline Teresa's spirit and practice of prayer, scriptural, liturgical and contemplative, it would be a disservice to her not to comment on her rich devotional life. The Fathers of Vatican II carefully noted "that the spiritual life, is not limited solely to participation in the liturgy. The Christian is indeed called to pray with others, but he must also enter into his bedroom to pray to his Father in secret."[4] Moreover that "Popular devotions of the Christian people, provided they conform to the laws and norms of the Church, are to be highly recommended."[5]

She never forsook the name given her first in religion, Angeline. Her devotion to the Holy Angels became a lifelong practice. Above all was her tender devotion to the Blessed Virgin Mary. For some forty years she always sent out a circular letter to the members of her Congregation for the Feast of the Immaculate Conception. These form a treasury of her doctrine and devotion to Mary. Also was found her filial love for Our Lady of Mount Carmel with her specific practices in her honor for the devotional life of her Sisters. She wrote:

> When our Congregation was started I placed everything in the Hands of Our Lady. I do so now once again and ask her to watch over, guide and protect each and everyone of you.[6]

The Passion of Jesus with which she identified her own sufferings and those of her beloved "old people" became her own constant motivation to suffer in union with Him, for the Church and especially for priests. For her the story of the Passion showed the whole life of Christ.[7] From it she learned and taught the "poor Christ," the "obedient Christ" and the "gloriously risen Christ."[8] This same Passion devotion crystallized into her love for the Sacred Heart of Jesus, another recurrent theme in her instructions and letters. Moreover, with true Carmelite zeal, she placed her own needs and those of her religious family at the feet of Good St. Joseph.

Her most ardent fervor was directed toward Jesus in the most Blessed Sacrament of the altar. She spent hours before the tabernacle. She frequently announced new foundations simply as we have "opened another new Tabernacle for the Lord."[9] She introduced into Community devotion an ejaculatory prayer to be said at the end of every chapel function whether Mass, Office, meditation or devotion. she herself ever exemplified this with a firm and fervent proclamation still echoing as the decades pass:

> Loved, adored, praised and blessed be Our Lord Jesus Christ in Heaven and in the most holy Sacrament of the Altar.[10]

NOTES

[1] *Jerusalem Bible* Translation Mt.5:3. Also cf. J.B. Philips, *New Testament in Modern English*, London, 1958.

[2] cf. MT. 6, 10.

³ Exhibit D. Mother M. Angeline Teresa, O. Carm. *Diary*. pages February 2 through February 14. (sic) ca.1905.

⁴ *Sacrosanctum Concilium*, "The Constitution on the Sacred Liturgy," December 4, 1963 Vatican II, num. 12.

⁵ *Ibid*. num. 13.

⁶ *Circular Letters*, Letter 168, p. 5, Vol. IV.

⁷ *Op. cit*. Letter 86, p. 1.

⁸ *Ibid*. p. 2: Vol. II, Letter 96, and 97.

⁹ *Circular Letters*. Letter 54, Vol. I.

¹⁰ Community practice begun by Mother M. Angeline Teresa from the beginning and still in vigor.

MOUNT CALVARY

In one of her circular letters Mother M. Angeline Teresa wrote to the entire Congregation of her Carmelite Sisters,

> I assure you, the crown of thorns God asks you to wear now for His sake shall some day be replaced by a crown of unearthly splendor, your crown of eternal glory. What matter then the little aches and pains we must all bear; the sufferings of mind that sometimes come to torture us: loneliness, humiliation, fatigue or discouragement? If only we could grasp the true worth of the pearl of great price which we now possess, we would stop at nothing to make our religious lives all they should be.[1]

This simple instruction of Mother Angeline reflects the clear doctrine of Jesus found in St. Mark's Gospel: "He summoned the crowd with his disciples and said to them, If anyone wishes to come after me, he must deny his very self, take up his cross and follow in my steps" (Mk. 8.34). It is worthy of note that this injunction to take up the cross was not restricted to the disciples only, but also to the crowd. This then becomes the imperative for anyone who wishes to follow after Christ, as well as those whom he calls in a special way.

In the Letter to the Hebrews much is made of the fact that Jesus died outside the wall (Heb. 13:12). In this sense Christ was separated from his own people but by the same token opened up his redemption to all men. That Jesus voluntarily died outside the wall has another spiritual dimension, namely that if Jesus crucified on Mount Calvary is beyond the wall, there is no wall to keep those who love him from ascending Mount Calvary to come to him. There is also the other sad alternative: there is no wall to keep one there should they wish to leave. Mother Angeline Teresa made Calvary her lodestone. Not only was it embraced as a gift, a share in the mystery of the Passion of Christ, but even sought after.

The Reverend John Lamont, O.Carm., who was the long-time Chaplain for the entire Community at the Avila Motherhouse (1967–1978) and thereafter the personal chaplain for Mother Angeline in her declining years (1978–1984) was also Mother Angeline's spiritual director. He was asked to write a memoir about Mother Angeline for a book being prepared for the Fiftieth Anniversary of her Carmelite foundation. From personal experience he observed:

> Although Mother Angeline is deeply understanding and spiritual yet she carries her great gifts lightly, almost self effacingly. That is because she sees God in these gifts too and appreciates the fact that God is the author of these too! I can recall how when she told me once of the defection of one of her sisters who was more than close to her, and her reaction was to ask me to pray and thank God for the crosses He allows her. Think of it, she thanks God for His crosses while so many do not thank him for His gifts ever![2]

The first sharing in the sufferings of Jesus on Calvary came to Mother M. Angeline Teresa in her physical suffering. She was a tall, vigorous and active woman almost to the end of her ninety-one years. But this could not hide the fact that she did have physical pain.

Up until 1948 Mother Angeline Teresa enjoyed normally good health. Her first recorded illness was diagnosed by Doctor Stratford Wallace (1949) who found that Mother had an enlarged heart. He cautioned her against the frequent use of the stairs. At this time an "elevette" (a kind of mini-elevator) was installed in the Avila white house. He advised Mother to rest each afternoon. This experiment lasted only a short while as Mother felt she must be up and doing.[3]

After Doctor Wallace died, Doctor Ann Maloney, M.D. of New York became Mother's physician. She is still living at this writing and shared her memories of Mother.[4] Doctor Ann found Mother's blood pressure elevated and prescribed medication for that and another medicine for her heart. Later Mother suffered from a kidney condition. The sulpha drugs used to combat this caused side effects of swelling and discomfort until it was discovered to be the causal agent.

Over the years Mother Angeline suffered severe back pain. Her older sister Elizabeth also developed this same condition and it was thought to be hereditary. X-rays showed a progressive arthritic condition in the spine. This painful affliction stayed with her the rest of her life. Further x-rays done by Doctor Vincent Lynch of St. Joseph's Manor at Trumbull, Connecticut, indicated that Mother was also suffering from an inactive gallbladder. Surgery was not advised but a restrictive dietary regimen was imposed.

In 1968 Mother tripped over a desk chair in her office. She suffered facial contusions and sprained her wrist. She was taken for treatment at Northern Dutchess Hospital and x-rayed. The attending physician, Doctor David Block, was amazed at her vitality. She would not keep on the splint he gave her. Then he noted at a later visit that Mother was having fibrillations of the heart. In 1978 Doctor George Ward from Poughkeepsie was summoned as Mother was having continued back pain which he diagnosed as muscle spasms due to her back condition. This made travelling very difficult but she continued her visitations.

For the next few years Doctor Leo Guanzon, a local physician, came gladly whenever help was needed for Mother. When he went into the army, Doctor Milagros Gamoso, who was associated with the nearby Carmelite Sisters' Residence for the Aged in Ferncliff, N.Y., took over the regular care of Mother Angeline. This cultured and gentle woman doctor was beloved of Mother and in turn loved her. Mother was now suffering from severe anemia which was apparently irreversible. Because of this condition Mother's resistance was very poor. She came down with pneumonia several times during the four-year period of Doctor Gamoso's care. From 1981 onward she began to decline and need assistance.

Mother Angeline had a dread of medicine. When vitamins were prescribed she would give them away. She refused to take pain relievers until the pain was excruciating. She never complained but often belied her back pain by the way in which she would try to sit and a tense look on her usual calm countenance. Dr. Gamoso in a sworn testimonial expressed the opinion that the speech disorder suffered by Mother Angeline toward the end of her life was such that, in spite of it, Mother certainly could understand what was said to her; further, on occasion she could and did speak intelligibly. In her last days Mother Angeline suffered from upper respiratory infections, arteriosclerotic heart disease, mildly congestive heart failure and chronic anemia. It was Dr. Gamoso who signed Mother's death certificate at 2:00 p.m. on January 21, 1984. In her report Dr. Gamoso testified to the exquisite nursing care given to Mother Angeline Teresa by her Carmelite Sisters.[5]

After Mother Angeline Teresa's death, her statue of the little king, the Infant of Prague, towards whom she cherished a special Carmelite Devotion, contained a poignant disclosure. This particular image was dressed in the full brown Carmelite habit with its white mantle and hood. On the arm was a small purse made of brown cloth. A similar device is sometimes used by the credulous for coins. In Mother's case there was a small folded note in her own handwriting. "Dear little Infant of Prague, please preside at our General Chapter in March. Grant that the Bishop may be nice to us all and see our views for the good of the Community."[6] This might seem surprising that one who numbered so many of the hierarchy as close personal friends and open admirers should have at heart such anxiety. Yet she who had such outstanding respect for bishops was subject to misunderstandings with and from them.

Bishop Edmund Gibbons of Albany, a most firm supporter of the Carmelite Sisters, instrumental in the Community becoming pontifical and always so profoundly grateful for their work, had a strained relationship with Mother Angeline Teresa herself and more often than not gave her a hard time. One might expect that this arose from a personality clash. Yet this was not so. Many times he manifested pride in her accomplishments and an affection for her. One element of causality here is that she arrived on his doorstep, albeit at his invitation, with every canonical requirement fulfilled and with the highest recommendations from Cardinal Spellman, Archbishop McIntyre, who acted for Mother from the New York Chancery, and Father Francis Reh, later Bishop, who undertook so willingly and efficiently the multiple details of the orderly transfer. All this activity from his neighboring prestigious archdiocese moved him to demonstrate clearly the jurisdiction he now possessed. While fulsomely praising the Sisters' apostolate, the expansion at Avila and the remarkable increase in vocations, his attitude toward Mother Angeline remained subtly harsh. He delayed exasperatingly in giving her permission to make new foundations in prominent dioceses at the request of the most worthy prelates.[7] Perhaps his most violent reaction came when he discovered that the novice-mistress appointed by Mother Angeline, Mother M. Aloysius, O.Carm., was under age. Such an infraction whether accidental or intentional could easily have been corrected, as it was.[8] However, even in his petition to Rome for raising the Congregation of the Carmelite Sisters for the Aged and Infirm to pontifical status, accompanying favorable letters from some 10 other ordinaries, a Cardinal and an Archbishop included, he represented her, because of this, as having defied the Holy See.[9] Such an aspersion against Mother Angeline Teresa had to be unthinkable.

Then there was an unexpected and unfortunate dissension on the part of Bishop James E. Cassidy, D.D. of Fall River. He invited Mother Angeline to come into the diocese in 1937. He had visited Mother Angeline at St. Patrick's in the Bronx. He was a colorful but demanding man, yet he was charmed by Mother Angeline and impressed by the work of the Sisters. Mother agreed to staff two homes for him. One was the Catholic Memorial Home, a residence for elderly men and women. The second was a retirement home exclusively for priests. This specialized work was dear to the heart of Mother Angeline. This hostel for priests was among the first freestanding residences for ill and retired priests anywhere in the United

States.[10] Bishop Cassidy continued to expand these facilities. He demanded more Sisters frequently.[11] He was proud of the Carmelite Sisters and their work, and later on had Mother open a second home at Fairhaven. Despite his goodness he tended to regulate the lives of the Sisters. He did not want the Sisters to go in autos on Sundays, never in the company of a priest, and wanted them to use taxis.[12] He asked for the appointment of Superiors whom he chose, a practice with which Mother Angeline could not comply.[13] On October 23, 1946, because of the purchase of the new Motherhouse at Avila, Mother Angeline wrote to him, along with the other Bishops who had Sisters working in diocesan homes, for a salary increase of $5.00 per month.[14] At the time the Sisters were receiving $30.00 per month. On November 4, 1946 Bishop Cassidy sent a caustic letter in reply to Mother's request. He stated that he was most upset over this request for an increase in salary. He condemned Mother for ingratitude and avarice. He listed all his benefactions, commented on the excellence of the food he had been supplying the Sisters, their comfortable living quarters and now this ungrateful request.[15] Indeed the Bishop had overreacted but this was his response. In the light of so many concessions already made in his favor, this letter devastated Mother Angeline. He was the only prelate to react this way. Nevertheless, Mother Angeline overcame her own anquish at this defamation and in her own typical manner wrote back immediately on November 9, 1946, asking the Bishop to disregard her request, to forget the whole matter and to apologize for her "offence."[16] The bishop seems to have been insensitive to the hurt he had caused Mother. Shortly after he requested and got three Sisters for his summer house. He wrote congratulations to Mother on her re-election,[17] and on the occasion of the Silver Jubilee of the foundation of the Community wrote a letter of fulsome praise.

The volatility of this Bishop and at times others filled Mother Angeline's heart with anxiety about what might happen next despite the appreciative support of the overwhelming majority of the hierarchy.

In 1943 the late Bishop Gerard Shaughnessy, a Marist and the fourth Bishop of the Diocese of Seattle (now an Archdiocese), after some involved negotiations had Mother M. Angeline make a foundation at Centralia in the State of Washington. This home was called St. Luke's Infirmary and was opened on October 18, 1943. It was the farthest foundation from the New York Motherhouse. Almost from the beginning, instead of elderly residents he began to send them mentally disturbed people. The Sisters were not professionally trained to handle such cases. Despite Mother Angeline's protests the situation worsened and against his original agreement the Bishop persisted in his folly. The Sisters themselves could not cope with the situation over which they had lost control Finally there was only one solution and that was to bring the Sisters home. The effort to send the Sisters to such a great distance and then to have them suffer in this way was a great sadness for Mother.[18]

As Mother Angeline Teresa advanced in age there was no doubt that she became more precious in the eyes of her Sisters. In a certain sense this actually resulted in a situation which, instead of helping Mother Angeline, formed a wedge between her and the Community at large. Long before Mother really needed assistance of any kind some of the staff Sisters who served her with such love and devotion, with the best of intentions, began to become over-protective. They tried to shield her from anything which might cause her upset or anxiety. They monitored phone calls and correspondence, taking the messages, referring them to Mother and returning the answers themselves. This caused resentment among some of the Sisters who felt cut off and unable to get through to Mother personally. Subtle messages were sent out that Mother should not be called on such occasions as feast days, a custom long practiced by superiors of the houses. When Mother Angeline became aware of this, she was annoyed at being manipulated. The following first-hand report illustrates this point clearly:

MEMORANDUM

August 22, 1988

To: Father Jude Mead, C.P.
From: Sister Regina Carmel
Re: Mother Angeline Teresa

Some years ago, the Homes received a letter from the Motherhouse at Avila, requesting that we do not telephone to Mother Angeline Teresa on big Feast Days. No doubt, it was thought at Avila that such calls were tiring for Mother. The first Feast Day I would have phoned Mother after receiving this communication was the Feast of All Carmelite saints. I did not phone. That evening I received a telephone call. The first words I heard on the phone were, "My you are very stingy—not a word from you today." It was Mother Angeline Teresa. I was delighted to hear her voice. I told of the communication we had received, in regard to not calling her. She replied, "Do not pay any attention to them. I am entitled to speak with my friends or anyone else." We enjoyed a lovely, happy conversation. I never hesitated to call Mother after that.

Respectfully submitted,
/s/ Sister Regina Carmel[19]

On the other side of the coin there were some of the Sisters who felt that Mother had ruled the Congregation too long and that it was time to have or at least to seek a change. No one could honestly challenge Mother Angeline with misuse of authority or poor administration or not fulfilling the duties of her office competently, although some of these things were inferred. The approach was to rally around Mother's personal health and to represent her as losing her grip and unable to cope with responsibility because of senility. Mother Angeline Teresa was surely blessed with longevity but until the last few years of her life she was possessed of all her faculties. However, this campaign, which was rejected out of hand by the larger community, was successful in its impact on outsiders who accepted this rumor to be fact, especially because of the position of some of its disseminators.

This work of detraction culminated in the preparation for the Sixth General Chapter of 1972. In previous chapters Mother M. Angeline Teresa had been postulated. That means that although she was not able to be elected outright since her terms of office had exceeded the law, if the Community still wanted her in office they could postulate or request her re-election. This had to be done by a two-thirds majority within the first three ballots.

There were two ways of receiving the necessary permission from the Holy See for such a circumstance. The first, to make the petition during the Chapter itself. If this is done the Chapter must shut down until the confirmation is received. This happened at the Third General Chapter of 1954 when the work of the Chapter was suspended for some six weeks. The second approach was to notify the Roman authorities in advance, and to obtain beforehand the authorization for postulation when and if the prescriptions of law were fulfilled. Foundresses do not have the right to remain in office for life against particular and common law prohibiting reelection or limited terms.[20] Although since the Second Vatican Council postulation has become more rare, still the special eminence of being a foundress is yet an accepted reason along with others for postulation.

Both Terence Cardinal Cooke and Bishop Edwin Broderick were convinced that Mother M. Angeline should not be postulated again. In a special meeting held at the Astor Home for Children, a facility of the Archdiocese of New York at Rhinebeck, N.Y., on July 10, 1972, both the Cardinal and the Bishop informed Mother M. Brendan, O.Carm., of their negative decision to seek postulation.[21] Mother Brendan returned to Avila after this session "sad and disappointed."[22]

At this point, Mother M. Brendan, O.Carm. should be properly introduced. Although not one of the original six companions of Mother, she was one of the second group of the new Sisters to enter. Nora O'Shaughnessey, as she was known, was born in County Galway. As a young woman she came to the United States and was employed in a New York banking firm. She was the niece of Mother M. Leonie, a first companion. It was through her that she came to know the nascent Community. She was touched by their poverty and wanted to help. It is an oft-told story that when she came to visit the first convent in St. Elizabeth's Rectory, she would bring ice cream sodas as a treat. She entered the Community on September 29, 1931, and was professed on March 18, 1933. She became Mother Angeline's First Assistant and the first Treasurer. From the beginning her background and personal integrity made her very close to Mother Angeline. Over the years she was the first Assistant when Mother opened Mount Carmel Villa in Philadelphia in 1936. When another home was opened in Fall River again she was sent as first Assistant. Elected as Councillor General and Secretary General in the Chapter of 1948, she came to Avila and was a great support to Mother Angeline, frequently travelling with her on visitations. For years she was the Local Superior at the Avila Motherhouse until her death on February 9, 1976. She was loyalty personified and her untimely death was a great loss to the Foundress. This also explains her own personal pain when her petition was rebuffed by the prelates.

The reaction of the Carmelite Sisters was that both prelates had been misinformed. On July 15, 1972, a special petition was forwarded to Ildebrando Cardinal Antoniutti, Prefect of the Sacred Congregation for Religious, signed by the entire General Council and the Central Chapter Coordinating Committee for the upcoming Chapter for permission to postulate Mother M. Angeline Teresa, O.Carm., for another term as Superior General antecedently if such would be the choice of the Chapter. The reasons for such an action was Mother's work for and value to the Community. And secondly, that this was the mind and will of the Community. The petition attested that if the Holy See would forbid postulation it would be accepted. If not, then should Mother Angeline herself decline this would also be respected. The petition protested that the postulation of Mother would be declared unacceptable even before the Chapter began.[23] This petition was then submitted directly to Rome by the Sisters and expedited by John Cardinal Wright, a longtime supporter of the Sisters and a personal friend of Mother Angeline.

On September 8, 1972 Mother M. Angeline Teresa was postulated by a two-thirds majority on the first ballot under the presidency of

Bishop Broderick.[24] In this way both Mother Angeline and the larger Community were vindicated. The Bishop then recommended that a strong Vicar General or First Assistant would be elected. Subsequent events indicate that the new Vicar was expected to control more than to assist. In the person of Mother M. Michael Rosarie, O.Carm., the elected First Assistant, this unwarranted outside pressure was completely rejected. She performed her duties as prescribed in the Constitutions under the authority and directions of Mother Angeline, who continued to make every final and necessary decision according to law. When Mother M. Angeline's health was actually failing, she voluntarity withdrew from another term in office and Mother M. Michael Rosarie was duly elected her successor.

About a month after the Chapter, under date of November 19, 1972, Mother Angeline wrote to Bishop Edwin Broderick the following letter. Clearly she was neither in her dotage, nor unable to cope with a situation, nor was she intransigent offering options to others and choosing one for herself.

J.M.J.T.

November 19, 1972

Most Reverend Edwin B. Broderick, D.D.
Bishop of Albany
465 State Street
Albany, New York 12206

Your Excellency,

I trust this letter finds you well and am sure very busy. The reason I am writing is because it has come to me indirectly that complaints have reached you because we have not implemented the decision regarding the change of Veil and Habit.

At the General Chapter I told the delegates that I did not mind if they changed the veil and they could take out some of the material from the Habit and shorten it. I also was very honest in telling them that no matter what change was made, I would continue to wear the present Habit and Veil, and I felt that no Sister should be forced to change. In fact a proposal was made that the Habit should be a unifying force and choice of the individual in this matter should be respected. It was voted on unanimously. I did not in any way prevent the delegates from voting on a change but I did insist that the choice of changing was to be optional and this was also put to a vote and passed unanimously.

My intention was to wait until the Interim Directives were printed which should have been on November 15th and then to promulgate the Acts of the Chapter. However, there has been a delay in the printing, and instead I have sent a card with the Annual Circular Letter for December 8th telling the Sisters they may order the new veils and alter the present habit as voted on. I do not feel it is right to order new habits made up when we have hundreds of others that can easily be altered. This would be a financial burden on the houses.

I regret that there are Sisters who are still complaining. We have tried so hard to please them, and this most recent complaint regarding the Habit is very unfair for we have not even been given the chance to go ahead with our plans. Even the Companies that are making up the Veils will not be able to do so at a moment's notice. I also feel that those who are complaining about these matters, will find something else wrong once this is settled.

Over and above this, there are sisters who have left the Community who are sending letters to create dissension among us. If this is being done to us, it is very possible that they are also writing to various Bishops.

I appreciate Your Excellency's concern in the matter, and assure you that the decision of the Chapter is being carried out.

Be assured of our prayers for you and may God bless all your undertakings. Asking Your Excellency's blessing, I am,

Most respectfully yours in Carmel,

Mother M. Angeline Teresa, O.Carm.[25]

In the return mail the Bishop responded as follows:

November 21, 1972

Mother M. Angeline Teresa, O.Carm.
St. Teresa's Motherhouse
Avila on the Hudson
Germantown, New York 12526

Dear Mother Angeline:

I am grateful to you for sharing with me the information about the modification of the Habit.

I spoke to Mother Brendan about the number of letters that Cardinal Cooke and I have received concerning this matter and I merely passed this information on to her.

I am pleased that the decisions of the Chapter are being carried out. I look forward to seeing you on December 8.

My blessings and personal good wishes.

Sincerely yours,

+Edwin B. Broderick
Bishop of Albany[26]

Let this suffice to show that the detractors of Mother M. Angeline Teresa who deceived personages outside the Community, acted at least in error if not in malice.

Not only do we have incidents of petty persecution but also there is evidence of proffered consolation being deprived in the case of Mother Angeline Teresa. One such instance, not known until the intense research for this book, was revealed during the memorable visit to the General Motherhouse of the Little Sisters of the Poor at La Tour St. Joseph, France, on October 7th, 1987. After being received with gracious hospitality and privileged to celebrate Holy Mass at the tomb of Blessed Jeanne Jugan, the foundress, there followed an informatory session with Mother Marie Antoinette, L.S.P., the Superior General, and members of the General Council The material I had requested in advance was presented to me in perfect order. In an on-going discussion which followed, Mother Marie Antoinette told me of her effort to have a visit with Mother Angeline Teresa. She wanted to reach out to her and heal any misunderstandings left from the past. In her own words she just wanted to say, "All is forgiven, die in peace."[27]

This was during her visit to the United States as Superior General March-April of 1970. When her secretary approached one of the New York Carmelite Homes she was told that Mother Angeline was unable to receive visitors. The obvious implication was not a temporary condition, as for example a cold, which surely in a two-month period could have been remedied, but rather to some extended incapacity. At the time, Mother Angeline was not only well but able to come down to the city from Avila.

It would be hard to imagine the joy and peace that the proposed visit of the two Superior Generals would have brought, mutually indeed, but personally to Mother Angeline. On the other hand the insensitivity of preventing such a reunion must be seen as a grave responsibility. The last few remaining years of Mother Angeline were deliberately denied a symbolic reconciliation which would have been so gratifying to her.

The greatness of a person may frequently be judged by the way others magnify their petty faults. Mother Angeline Teresa was no exception to this rule, which in turn added to her sufferings. In the file containing the records of the Carmelite Sisters for the Aged and

Infirm at the Congregation for Institutes of Consecrated Life and Societies of Apostolic Life (formerly called the Congregation for Religious and Secular Institutes) at Rome along with many documents of import such as Constitutions and the Decree of Praise erecting the Congregation as Pontifical Rite, there is found a series of complaints about Mother Angeline.[28] On most of them no action at all was ever taken. The most serious was that in appointing Mother M. Aloysius as novice mistress, as she was defying the Holy See. This matter was immediately remedied as noted before and was one in which there was obviously no malice.

Others complained that she spent too much money on vestments and on flowers. That same complaint was made publicly against her in the Motherhouse Chapel at Avila by a missionary bishop who had received tremendous alms from Mother for his missions. More often than not these very items were gifts. Mother had a tremendous spirit of poverty and wanted nothing for herself, in fact usually giving things away to others she felt needed them more. Hence the houses sent vestments which would enhance the liturgical celebrations. Vestments were also bought by Mother Angeline to support cloistered Carmelite Nuns. The Cloistered Carmelite Nuns of the Ancient Observance made their first American Foundation on May 22, 1931 at Larnack Manor, near Allentown, Pa. They called their new home "St. Therese's Valley." Among the first to present themselves was Mother M. Angeline Teresa. The saintly foundress, Mother Therese of Jesus, O.Carm. wrote:

> Mother Angeline Teresa's limitless kindness and interest in the Allentown Carmel were a source of encouragement and help to the young Community. And, remarkable to relate, her own great work of establishing a Religious Institute commenced about the same time as the Allentown foundation began, and like its Sister Carmel, under the Divine Dew of God's Blessing, continues to prosper. Mother Angeline Teresa enjoyed the friendship of the two foundresses.[29]

On my visit to the Allentown Carmel the Sisters said that Mother Angeline was like a second foundress, and that she not only gave material help but would frequently arrive with sweets and delicacies which the poor Nuns could not afford but which lifted not only their bodies but also the spirits.

Mother always loved flowers and in her youth decorated the altar in her parish church under the direction of her pastor. Gifts of flowers received by her were sent down to the chapel at once. It was her delight on feast days to arrange the flowers herself. Yet this zeal for the beauty of the house of the Lord was turned against her, and criticism of such sent even to Rome.

Again she was unjustly criticized for not being economical. This complaint is beyond belief. In a time of world-wide economic depression, she paid all her debts on time and fully. Cardinal Hayes was amazed at her ability to expand and open new facilities, paying off indebtedness even before time.

Her great love and concern for priests also came under fire.[30] She was accused of being too generous to priests. She looked well after priests whom she thought were being neglected. In the time of economic hardship she would invite priests to the Home to make sure they had a good meal and enjoyed clerical association. Many a religious priest who came to give the spiritual exercises found his clothing not only cleaned and repaired but even replaced with something new. She was censured because she had priests eat with the Sisters on occasion even though not at the same table, her fault-finder wrote, but in the same room![31]

Her prudence regarding the formation of her young Sisters was also questioned. She kept the novitiate at the busiest house of the order, St. Patrick's. Yet where else could they go? On the fiftieth anniversary of the founding of the same St. Patrick's, Mother Angeline fondly recalled its significance:

> St. Patrick's was our first permanent home, and it included our Motherhouse and Novitiate. It was there we were able to introduce some new concepts of care for the elderly. St. Patrick's has been the stepping stone to progressive care for the aging and has served as a model for all our future homes.[32]

She was condemned for having too many parties for the novices. She even gave them wine. It is to be noted that she never forced anyone to take it.

Finally, she sent the young Sisters out begging. Indeed she did; in the early days this was a principal means of income, but never by themselves, only with older and wiser Sisters.

Closer to home some of the Sisters and some clergy complained that Mother had too big a car. Her first automobile was a second-hand, Model T Ford. Sometime later when Bishop John J. Dunn died his car, which was a Cadillac, was given to the Sisters. It had a vanity license plate, 2U-7, which Mother kept. Some tried to interpret this as a gift symbol which it was not. One of these plates is conserved in the Heritage Room. From then on, the Sisters insisted on a large car. In a sense, Mother had nothing to do with it. Travelling was difficult for her. The car meant that she could travel whenever she was ready and pace herself between arriving at the various homes. The Sisters wanted her to travel all those miles safely.

Another source of complaint by some of the Sisters was that Mother kept a collie dog, sometime two, with her at the Motherhouse. In answer to such a complaint Mother had her own answer. "In all these years at Avila, we have never had a break-in nor needed to hire a watchman."[33] Sometimes the dogs performed too well, once biting a visiting bishop!

When some ten years after her physical deterioration led to complete dependence on the loving care of the Sisters, she was an example of perfect resignation to God's will. Her speech had become impaired, but when she spoke with difficulty it was: "I'll do anything you want me to do." And often, "Thank God I have my own Sisters with me."[34]

This period is beautifully described as follows: "Now in her late eighties Mother is still able to be up each day and assist at Mass in her little private chapel, which is on the same floor as her living quarters. If she is unable at times to get to the chapel, Mass is offered in her room. Mother is always pleased to see the Sisters, especially the Novices, and her presence, even now with her frail health, means so much to each Carmelite Sister."[35]

In the warm evenings Mother would sit out on the porch of the great white house, the original Avila. So often the Sisters on retreat or the Motherhouse Sisters out for a stroll would come up and sit around her. She would frequently ask them to sing for her. In these idyllic times she would ask for her favorite:

Will Ye No Come Back Again?

Bonnie Charlie's noo awa'
Safely owre the friendly main,
Mony a heart will break in twa,
Should he ne'er come back again.

Will ye no come back again?
Will ye no come back again?
Better loved ye canna be,
Will ye no come back again?

Ye trusted in your Hieland men;
They trusted you, dear Charlie;
They kent your hiding in the glen,
Death or exile braving.

Sweet's the lavrock's note and lang,
Liltin' wildly up the glen,
But aye to me he sings ae sang,
'Will ye no come back again?'[36]

NOTES

[1] *Circular Letters.* Letter 70, Vol. II p.1 December, 1956.

[2] Lamont, O.Carm. John. Extract from "Impressions," AVGA Vertical File #1.

[3] Sister M. Gabriel Reis, O.Carm.,B.S.N., *Summary of the Medical History,* Mother M. Angeline Teresa, O.Carm., July 16, 1989. Avila Motherhouse.

[4] Letter to Mother Angeline. Ann J. Maloney, M.D. 1 West 86th St. New York 24, N.Y. under date of January 17, 1962. "Medical Report." 1. Bilateral moderately severe varicose veins. 2. Minimal hardening of blood vessels with fluctuating blood pressure. 3. Sensitivity of back muscles. 4. Excessive weight with dietary regimen. 5. Recurrent allergic reaction of skin.

[5] Dr. Milagros Gamoso, M.D., Rhinebeck, N.Y. Notarized author's interview, April 25, 1989.

[6] This statue, with the note still appended, preserved in the HERITAGE ROOM, Avila Motherhouse.

[7] ADCV. Correspondence: Bishop William T. Mulloy, Bishop of Covington KY with Bishop Michael J. Ready, of Columbus OH, Bishop William A. Scully, Coadjutor of Albany, and Mother M. Angeline Teresa, O.Carm. concerning the foundation in Covington, with or about Bishop Edmund F. Gibbons. 12 letters between January 14 and June 12, 1949. Response of Bishop Gibbons January 28, 1949 to Bishop Mulloy to be patient he would let them know. Bishop Mulloy wrote to Mother M. Angeline Teresa, O.Carm., February 12, 1949 that he had a novena of Masses offered to get Bishop Gibbons to give his permission and had also recommended it as a special intention to "our dear good Passionist Nuns." (Erlanger KY Monastery) Not until six months later was permission given. Chancery Archives, Diocese of Covington. Foler, *Carmelite Sisters.*

[8] ADAL. *Carmelite Sisters,* Folder #2. Letter to Mother M. Angeline Teresa, O.Carm. May 1, 1948. *Sanatio* for Mother M. Aloysius, O.Carm. for defect of age. Tax $10.00.

[9] SCRIS. Archives at Congregation for Religious, Rome. Folder N. 29.

[10] Wisely, O.Carm. *op. cit.* p. 290.

[11] ADFR. *Carmelite Sisters' File*: Correspondence with Mother M. Angeline Teresa, O.Carm. May 13, 1948, February 9, 1949, January 21, 1951.

[12] *Op. cit.* To Mother M. Angeline Teresa, O.Carm. June 7, 1939.

[13] *Ibid.* Letter from Mother M. Angeline Teresa, O.Carm. October 23, 1946.

[14] ADFR. Bishop Cassidy's letter to Mother M. Angeline Teresa, O.Carm. November 4, 1946.

[15] *Ibid.*

[16] *Ibid.* Letter from Mother M. Angeline Teresa, O.Carm. to Bishop Cassidy. November 9, 1946.

[17] *Ibid.* Letter of Bishop Cassidy to Mother M. Angeline Teresa, O.Carm. December 16, 1948.

[18] AASE. No record exists in the Chancery regarding this disappointing venture. Cf. Collection of Correspondence, Sister Assumpta Marie, O.Carm. n.6. Also testimony of Sister Maria Paul, O.Carm., member of Centralia Community.

[19] Sister M. Regina Carmel, O.Carm. Teresian House, 200 Washington Ave. Extension. Albany, N.Y. dated August 22, 1988. Letter requested by the author.

[20] Gallen, S.J., Joseph F., *Canon Law for Religious* Alba House, New York, 1983, p. 62.

[21] AVGA Drawer 1972 General Chapter.

[22] *Ibid.* Note from Mother M. Brendan, O.Carm.

[23] *Ibid.* Copy of Special Petition to Scris July 15, 1972.

[24] *Ibid. Acts of the VI General Chapter.*

[25] AVGA Drawer 1972 Chapter, September 8, 1972.

[26] *Ibid.*

[27] Mother Marie Antoinette, L.S.P. Author's personal interview La Tour, France, October 7, 1987.

[28] SCRIS Archives, steel folder, N 62 1.

[29] A Sister of Allentown Carmel. Mother Therese and the Carmel of Allentown, Jeffries and Manz, Philadelphia, 1949. pp. 142, 143.

[30] SCRIS Archives, steel folder, N 62 2.

[31] *Ibid.*

[32] Mother M. Angeline Teresa, O.Carm. cited in *The Catholic News*, October 27, 1956.

[33] Sister M. Gabriel Reis, O.Carm. Author's personal interview, June 11, 1989.

[34] Sister M. Gabriel Reis, O.Carm. Monograph. *Mother Angeline Teresa's Last Years* pro manuscripto, Avila, 1984. Here are listed the Sisters provided to care for Mother M. Angeline full or part time:
Sister Daniel Marie, Sister Mary Gabriel, Sister Matthew James, Sister Louise Joseph, Sister Agnes Patricia, Sister Mary Ann, Sister Celine Patricia, Sister Kathleen Immaculate, Sister Veronica Robert, Sister Stephanie, Sister Elias, Sister Magdalen Joseph, Sister Clare and Sister Constance. Others frequently called upon to assist in lifting Mother were Mother Michael Rosarie, Sister Patrick Michael, Sister Therese Regina, and Sister Rosemary Ann.

[35] Sister M. Bernadette de Lourdes Wisely, O.Carm. Monograph. *The Heart of Avila*, pro manuscripto. Avila, 1982.

[36] Song: "Will Ye No Come Back Again?" Baroness Nairne. *Scottish Songs*. Bayley & Ferguson, Limited, London and Glasgow.

MOUNT TABOR

Saturday, January 21, 1984 seemed to dawn begrudgingly. It was typical of what Hudson Valley dwellers call the January thaw. The turgid Hudson River swirled its way to the sea between its ice bound shores with their frozen coves and inlets. The sudden warmth had turned roads into shiny black ribbons and sullied the once white snow fields. The bare trees glistened with moisture and vestigial ice fell to the ground with a crack. Yet there was half a promise of spring in this mid-winter spell.

It was the feast of St. Agnes, the Roman child martyr. It was also the 91st birthday of Mother M. Angeline Teresa, O.Carm. The Avila Motherhouse and its Carmelite Sisters had not planned any special celebration because the word had been quietly circulated that the Foundress was far from well.

Sister Agnes Patricia, R.N. came off duty at 7:00 a.m. Her last notes on Mother's chart stated that Mother had had a restful night but was still very weak. Mother had coughed just before she left and prayed, "Infant Jesus, where are You?"[1]

Mother Gabriel and Sister Matthew James came together into Mother's room at 8:20. She had gone back to sleep but awakened as they wished her a happy birthday and gave her a hot drink with her vitamins.[2] Mother Michael Rosarie slipped in briefly to sing "Happy Birthday" and embrace Mother on her 91st birthday. The Sisters then made Mother Angeline comfortable, gave her a light breakfast eaten only sparingly and prepared her for Mass.[3]

Mother Gabriel was distressed by Mother Angeline's evident weakness so at 9:30 a.m. she telephoned Doctor Milagros Gamoso, M.D., Mother's personal physician in nearby Rhinebeck, N.Y. The doctor gave instructions to get Mother to sit up for an hour or two and try to have her take fluids and some food.[4]

Father John Lamont, O.Carm. Mother Angeline's faithful friend and devoted chaplain had been saying Mass daily for her. On days when Mother could not rise he would celebrate Mass in her office at the bedroom door. The Sisters would turn her bed so she was able to look straight ahead and participate with greater ease. During her last illness she would receive only the Precious Blood as she had difficulty in swallowing. On this day Father graciously postponed the celebration of Mass until a little before 10:00.[5] Unknowingly, this Communion would also be her Viaticum.

After Mass Mother Michael Rosarie returned with more birthday gifts. Sister Matthew and Sister Patrick Michael assisted Mother Angeline to put on her habit, scapular, headdress, and veil which Mother insisted on wearing. They helped her into the wheel chair and seated her at her desk.[6] Around the room were numerous birthday cards festooned around her door and window frames. In the adjoining office exquisitely wrapped gifts were piled up. These had been previously shown to Mother Angeline who smiled radiantly over such a tribute of love and affection from her Sisters. Suddenly the sun had come out in all its glory.

Meanwhile some thirty Sisters from the missions were assembled at Avila to begin their annual retreat that evening under the direction of the Very Reverend Thomas McGinnis, O.Carm., Provincial of the Carmelite Fathers, St. Elias Province of New York.[7]

Sister Kathleen Immaculate as usual prepared Mother's lunch to be served her on a tray at the desk. The little group once more sang "Happy Birthday" to Mother and then left her so she could have privacy and peace. Sister Teresa Kathleen, O.Carm. one of the retreatants and herself a nurse unobtrusively came up to see if she might greet Mother who had already retired when she had arrived the night before. Mother Gabriel invited her in and each of them sat on either side of Mother. Sister wrote:

> When I arrived upstairs in Mother's room, Sister Patrick Michael, Sister Matthew and Sister Kathleen were all helping to get Mother ready for her lunch. Mother Gabriel told me to wait a minute. The Sisters left and Mother Gabriel put Mother Angeline's tray in front of Mother who was sitting up in her wheelchair by her desk. Mother Gabriel was on the right side of Mother and I sat on her left and just held her hand. Mother Gabriel was being very careful to give Mother Angeline small amounts of puree food at a time as she knew Mother was still not feeling well and having some problems with swallowing. Mother Angeline seemed to me to be very content and happy. Surrounding her were flowers and cards and Mother Gabriel was telling me how she had read each one to Mother. Suddenly Mother (Angeline) started to cough and could not get her breath. Mother Gabriel grabbed the suction and we both tried to see if there was anything obstructing Mother's airway but there was nothing there. Mother started to turn blue.[8]

Quickly, Sister Kathleen Immaculate summoned the priests and called Mother Michael Rosarie to come at once. Meanwhile Sister

Teresa Kathleen tipped the wheelchair to put Mother's head back and wheeled her to her bed. Sister Matthew came running and helped lift Mother onto the bed. Mother Michael Rosarie arrived and assisted in getting oxygen on Mother Angeline and got her into a better position in bed holding her in her arms. Typically it was she who restored calm by telling the Sisters to pray. The priests rushed in. Father Eugene anointed Mother's forehead for the Sacrament of the Anointing of the Sick using the short emergency formula. Mother's color improved but it was obvious to all she was dying. Mother Angeline did not fight the death of the body. She struggled only for enough breath for Mother Michael Rosarie, Mother Bernadette and her devoted priests to be at her side.

Mother Michael Rosarie quietly announced, "She's gone!" Sister Teresa Kathleen on Mother Angeline's other side responded, "I know."[9] Each of the three Fathers gave her a final blessing.

All that could have been done for their aged and beloved Mother Foundress had been done. From the loving hands of her successor and her other Carmelite daughters she passed gently into the loving hands of the Father, God. It was 12:45 p.m.[10]

The official report records those present around the death bed of Mother M. Angeline Teresa, O.Carm. Foundress of the Carmelite Sisters for the Aged and Infirm: "Father Lamont, Father McGinnis, Father Eugene. Mother Michael, Mother Bernadette, Mother Gabriel, Sister Mary Ann, Sister Kathleen Immaculate, Sister Matthew James, Sister Teresa Kathleen (with Mother when she had seizure) and Sister Mary Perpetua (RSM)."[11]

Mother Michael Rosarie asked all to leave the room. They joined with the Sisters, who having been notified of the imminence of the Foundress' death, had gathered in the chapel. The rosary was recited by all. The deeply respected body of the deceased Mother Foundress having been reverently composed on her bed, Mother Michael invited all to return to pay their respects. Doctor Gamoso was summoned. She rushed to the Motherhouse and officially declared Mother Angeline dead at 2:00 p.m. This was the last entry on the medical chart of Mother M. Angeline Teresa, O.Carm. except for the touching insertion: "May she rest in Peace."[13]

The day before Mother Angeline's birthday Irene McCrory, the wife of Mother Angeline's nephew John, called Avila and said that "Mother", Mrs. Katherine McCrory, her mother-in-law, was anxious about Mother Angeline Teresa and could John and Irene come up to make a birthday visit. Mother Gabriel who had received the phone call gladly invited them to come. It was suggested they wait until afternoon to come since Mother's mornings were sometimes difficult.[14] Expecting them to arrive Mother Michael Rosarie would not release the Foundress' body to leave Avila until her loving relatives would be able to pay their last respects. When they arrived and saw a hearse waiting their anxieties became realities. When ushered to Mother's bedside their own sorrow was eased by the presence of so many Sisters on their knees praying with such sincere love for this wonderful woman tied to them in spirit as the McCrorys were in flesh.

When this last tribute had been allowed the body of Mother Angeline was handed over to Mr. Fred McDonald, the funeral director from Hudson, who had given most respectful service to the Carmelite Sisters over many years. This was Saturday afternoon. On Sunday morning, January 22nd, the undertaker called the Avila Motherhouse to invite the Sisters to come down to his mortuary to clothe Mother M. Angeline's body in her full habit. Mother Michael Rosarie sent Mother Gabriel and Sister Matthew James to fulfill this loving service.[15] For these two devoted daughters who had so often dressed Mother in life it was a final fidelity but nonetheless a deeply painful one.

Meanwhile the Avila Motherhouse was a bee hive of activity. All the houses of the Congregation and all the Sisters had to be informed, the Cardinals, Archbishops and Bishops of dioceses where there were foundations, the Carmelite Prior General in Rome and the American Provincial, all Mother's family and relatives in the United States and abroad, her countless friends in the hierarchy, the priesthood, other women religious, and so many generous and faithful men and women whose lives she had touched.[16] A Mass was offered for the repose of Mother's dear soul that very Saturday afternoon, so that in the midst of notifying so many others, she would be prayerfully remembered by those who were closest to her when she died.

The Gospel points out that in preparation for their share in the Passion, Jesus took Peter, James and John up into a high mountain (Tabor) and was transfigured before them. (MK. 9, 1–8) The holy prophets Elias and Moses also appeared speaking with Jesus about His impending death. (Lk. 9, 30–31) Thus Tabor was the means for disposing the disciples for their share in the Passion of Jesus, beginning in the garden of the Mount of Olives. On the other hand, it would seem that Mother Angeline first embraced Mount Calvary. She had a life of interior sufferings with Christ of misunderstandings, contradictions, betrayals, disloyalties and desertions. She endured spiritual sufferings, manifested in her deep life of prayer in God and her battles against self to always put God first and His work above herself. She bore physical sufferings of many and grievous afflictions, often secreted even from medical help. Finally, the crippling effects of old age with its impediments of locomotion and locution, all of which Mother accepted with equanimity, patience and loving trust. Through these totally and lovingly accepted crosses Mother ascended not only Mount Carmel but even more demonstrably Mount Calvary. For this lifelong fidelity to God, the Church, her own Congregation as well as to God's aged and infirm, on the day of her holy death, God rewarded her with the transfiguration of all her suffering into His own, as He had done in anticipation for His disciples on Mount Tabor.

Sunday, at one in the afternoon, the body of Mother M. Angeline Teresa was returned to the chapel of the Motherhouse, which she herself had constructed as a tabernacle for the Most High; to a great company of her spiritual daughters, the Carmelite Sisters for the Aged and Infirm, whom she had founded; and to her beloved priest friends who met the body at the portals of the Chapel. In procession the remains were borne into the sanctuary and placed in the side chapel of the Blessed Virgin Mary, Our Lady of Lourdes, to whom Mother had had such personal devotion. The casket was open for all to view. Her head was circled with a crown of white roses, the autographed formula of her vows cherished in her right hand, clothed in her full Carmelite habit, with brown scapular, leathern belt and side rosary, her white mantle, guimpe and black veil. It was as she had always presented her witness in life, and even now gave the illusion she was still with her devoted Sisters. Holy Mass was celebrated by Father John Lamont, O.Carm., with Fathers Thomas McGinnis, O.Carm. and Eugene Robitaille, SS.CC., homilist. Then there began an almost continuous succession of mourners. Not a few lovingly touched their rosaries or other articles to Mother's body as they passed her coffin—a silent witness to their conviction of her holiness of life and deep personal sanctity.[18]

At four in the afternoon Holy Mass was again offered in the chapel. This time it was Mother's loyal friend, Father Richard A. Nagle, O.Carm., former Provincial of the Carmelite Fathers. In his homily he attested to Mother Angeline's devotion to the aged and infirm and her charismatic foundation of the Carmelite Sisters. Father John Lamont, O.Carm. and Father Eugene Robitaille, SS.CC. were assistant celebrants.

Again the procession of mourners was interrupted this time for a 9:00 p.m.Vigil Service celebrating the Word of God and presided over by Father Eugene who gave a reflection on Mother's life-long zeal.

On Monday, January 23rd, while messages of condolences flooded in from Rome, Ireland, Scotland, England, almost every state in the United States, South America and far-off Africa, an endless line of visitors passed through the Chapel; members of the hierarchy, clergy, Carmelite Sisters, religious and loving layfolk, both young and old, many of whom had never met Mother Angeline in her life but had come to know and love her for her service to the Church in her apostolate for the aged. At four o'clock in the afternoon the Most Reverend Donal R. Lamont, O.Carm., retired Bishop of Umtali, Africa, and blood brother of Father John Lamont, O.Carm. offered a Pontifical Eucharist in the Chapel. Concelebrating with him were: Monsignor John Gillespie, V.G. representing Most Reverend Thomas J. Winning, Archbishop of Glasgow, Scotland, Fathers John Lamont, O.Carm., Richard Nagle, O.Carm., Albert Daly, O.Carm., Thomas McGinnis, O.Carm., and Eugene Robitaille, SS.CC. who preached a touching homily.

Tuesday, January 24th. In order to accommodate the scores of Carmelite Sisters for the Aged and Infirm coming to Avila to honor their Foundress who could not be expected to have a place in the chapel at the final ceremonies, Father Eugene Robitaille, SS.CC. offered a Memorial Mass at two o'clock in the afternoon.

At four o'clock the Most Reverend Walter Curtis, S.T.D., Bishop of Bridgeport, Connecticut, offered a concelebrated liturgy. With him were Most Reverend Donal Lamont, O.Carm., Msgr. John Gillespie, V.G., Fathers Thomas McGinnis, William Mel Daly, John Lamont, Richard Nagle, Gerald McGovern, Gary O'Brien, Francis Donohue, Robert Hulse, Denis Graviss, and Augustine Graap, all Carmelites, Eugene Robitaille, SS.CC. and Edwin Milne, of the Diocese of Manchester, the Chaplain of the Carmelite Sisters' St. Francis Home at Laconia, New Hampshire. Father William Mel Daly, O.Carm. devoted friend of Mother Angeline preached. After the Communion of the Mass, the celebrant, Bishop Curtis, gave a few reflections of his own in which he remarked how privileged those present were to have known Mother Angeline Teresa, "a person who as Foundress would most likely one day be a canonized saint."[19]. Because of the many Masses practically every Carmelite Sister was able to participate at the Motherhouse during those days. In the evening at nine o'clock the paraliturgical wake service was presented by Father Eugene Robitaille, SS.CC. while Msgr. Gillespie gave the homily.

On Wednesday, January 25th, the Mass of Christian Burial was held for Mother M. Angeline Teresa, O.Carm., followed by her internment in the Queen of Carmel Cemetery on the grounds of St.

Teresa's Motherhouse at Avila on Hudson, Germantown, New York. That there would be so many archbishops, bishops, priests, religious of other Communities and a host of men and women from distant places united with the Carmelite Sisters for the Aged and Infirm is extraordinary in itself. Geographically, the Avila Motherhouse is remote. It is the southernmost area in the Diocese of Albany. It is three miles from the northernmost border of the Archdiocese of New York. It is 14 miles from a railroad stop and 20 miles from the nearest bus station across the river. It is about 60 miles from Albany airport and 120 some miles from the New York metropolitan airports. On that Wednesday all the roads were covered with an ice slick. Yet every place in the chapel and sanctuary was taken and the crowds stood around the walls and overflowed onto the porch. A gracious touch was the presence in the first row of two Little Sisters of the Poor, Sister Mary Vincent Mannion, L.S.P., Administrator, Our Lady of Hope Residence, Latham, New York and Sister Mary Celestine Meade, L.S.P. Symbolically Mother's beginning was recalled at her consummation.

The Most Reverend Howard Hubbard, D.D., Bishop of Albany, was the principal celebrant. On his arrival he had visited Mother's body and gave her his blessing. In the solemn procession to the altar were over sixty priests. Episcopal concelebrants were: Archbishop Joseph T. Ryan, D.D., Coadjutor Military Vicar for the United States Armed Forces; Most Reverend Edward J. Maginn, D.D., Auxiliary Bishop of Albany, a lifelong family friend of Mother Angeline; Most Reverend Odore J. Gendron, D.D., Bishop of Manchester; Most Reverend Daniel A. Cronin, S.T.D., Bishop of Fall River; Most Reverend Thomas V. Daily, D.D., Administrator of the Archdiocese of Boston; Most Reverend Donal Lamont, O.Carm., retired Bishop of Umtali, Africa; Most Reverend James P. Mahony, D.D., Auxiliary Bishop of New York; Most Reverend Anthony Mestice, D.D., Auxiliary Bishop of New York; Most Reverend Patrick V. Ahern, D.D., Auxiliary Bishop of New York; Most Reverend Austin B. Vaughan, D.D., Auxiliary Bishop of New York; and Most Reverend Robert E. Mulvee, J.C.D., Auxiliary Bishop of Manchester. Monsignor James J. Murray, Executive Director of the Catholic Charities of the Archdiocese of New York preached the eulogy. He drew from his many experiences working with Mother, both personally and officially, as he reviewed her life and work, particularly her contribution to the care of the aged. Very Reverend Thomas McGinnis, O.Carm., Provincial, represented the Carmelite presence in the sanctuary. At the end of the solemnly sung liturgy, Bishop Howard Hubbard expressed his gratitude for all that Mother M. Angeline Teresa had contributed to the Diocese and extended his personal sympathy to the Carmelite Sisters, Mother's family members present and to all those who had come to the obsequies.

Following the solemn rites of Mother's funeral liturgy a hushed file of mourners gingerly picked their way down the still-slippery roadway to the Motherhouse cemetery. A tent had been erected as a shelter at the graveside. Once more Bishop Hubbard presided now at the final commendation and last farewell, assisted by Father Eugene Robitaille, SS.CC.[20] who had also been Master of Ceremonies in the chapel. He prayed,

> Father, into Your Hands we commend our beloved Mother Mary Angeline Teresa whom You chose to be an instrument of Your love for the Aged and Infirm. We thank You for all the blessings You gave her in this life. Lord, hear our prayer; welcome Mother Mary Angeline Teresa to Paradise and help us to comfort each other with the assurance of our Faith that we will all be united in eternal life one day. We make our prayer through Christ our Lord.

Then according to an ancient practice among the Carmelites the antiphon *Salve Regina* was sung in sonorous Latin. In the cold dampness there was hardly a dry eye. Almost as if unwilling to leave Mother even in these hallowed precincts the various groups slowly departed. Later there would be a simple monument reading:

Our Beloved Foundress
Mother M. Angeline Teresa, O.Carm.

Entered Life	January 21, 1893
Entered Religious Life	February 2, 1912
Professed Vows	March 19, 1915
Founded Community	August 5, 1929
Entered Eternity	January 21, 1984

On earth there now remains only a memory, albeit vivid and unforgettable. A faithful daughter of Carmel. An embracing mother to the Aged and Infirm whether poor or rich, who in her own lifetime opened 59 Homes for the Aged from the Atlantic (New York) to the Pacific (Seattle): two further also in Dublin, Ireland and Dunoon, Scotland, and received into her new American Carmelite Congregation over 500 Sisters.

NOTES

[1] *Medical Nursing Record Book*, Mother M. Angeline Teresa. February 13, 1983–January 21, 1984. *Night Report*, 265 pages. AVGA Final entry p. 265 Nurses on duty: Sister M. Louise Joseph, O.Carm., Sister M. Agnes Patricia, O.Carm.

[2] Sister M. Gabriel, personal interview with author, September 26, 1988.

[3] Sister M. Matthew James, personal interview with author, September 30, 1988.

[4] *Medical Nursing Record Book*, Mother M. Angeline Teresa. December 6, 1983–January 21, 1984. *Day Report*. 29 pages. AVGA Final Entry p. 29. Nurse on duty: Mother M. Gabriel, O.Carm., B.S.N. Nursing care: Sisters M. Matthew James, Kathleen Immaculate, Constance, Celine, Brenda, Clare, Mary Ann, Veronica.

[5] *Ibid.*

[6] Sister M. Patrick Michael, personal interview with author, September 29, 1988.

[7] Reverend Thomas McGinnis, O.Carm., personal interview with author, September 29, 1988.

[8] Sister M. Teresa Kathleen, O.Carm., Testimony in a letter at author's request dated September 24, 1987, Kahl Home for the Aged and Infirm, 1101 West 9th Street, Davenport, Iowa 52304.

[9] *Ibid.*

[10] *Day Book Nursing Record, op. cit.*, page 9.

[11] *Ibid.*

[12] *Ibid.*

[13] *Ibid.*

[14] Sister M. Gabriel, cf. note 2.

[15] Sister M. Gabriel, O.Carm., personal interview with author, September 26, 1988.

[16] *Author's note.* It took Father Eugene Robitaille, SS.CC. eight hours to get a telephone call through to Father Jude, C.P. who was teaching a summer school of Spiritual Theology for the Sisters, Servants of the Immaculate Heart of Mary from Philadelphia at Villa Maria, La Planicie, a suburb of Lima, Peru. Another three hours to return the call. Unable to come a Memorial Mass was offered there immediately.

[17] The exact chronology of the last hours and death of Mother M.

Angeline Teresa, O.Carm. established from documentary and personal testimony was carefully verified in detail by Mother M. Michael Rosarie, Sister M. Patrick Michael, Sister M. Gabriel, Sister M. Bernadette de Lourdes and Sister M. Matthew James at a fact-finding panel with the author October 6, 1988.

[18] Reverend Eugene Robitaille, SS.CC. conversation with the author, December 7, 1987.

[19] Cited. Wisely, *Epilogue*, p. 497.

[20] Reverend Eugene Robitaille, SS.CC. (1920–1988) was a devoted friend of Mother M. Angeline Teresa. He served as chaplain to the Carmelite Sisters at the Avila Motherhouse for almost 20 years. He died on May 15, 1988.

MOUNT ZION

The death of the body as a natural and supernatural reality was never far from the experience of Mother Angeline Teresa. This final certainty had insinuated itself early into her family life through her grandparents, a baby sister and later a loving teen-age brother. The cruelest blow had been the premature and traumatic death of her beloved father. In her concerned and compassionate care of the elderly she had prayed with countless old people as a mother might in their death agonies and had closed their eyes in peace. Because of her own deep faith in each of these many encounters, she saw the peaceful reward of long lives, the serenity of surrender after the encroachments of old age, immobility, deprivation of eyesight and hearing, and the loneliness of being the ultimate survivor culminate into a longed-for and gentle release. For her and her religious daughters, their homes became veritable "vestibules to heaven" where death had indeed lost its sting.[1] Before her eyes so often the exquisite profession of Faith found in the Preface of the Mass for the Dead was fulfilled:

> Lord, for your faithful people life
> is changed, not ended.
> When the body of our earthly dwelling
> lies in death we gain an everlasting
> dwelling place in heaven.[2]

As she advanced in years Mother Angeline Teresa was well aware of her own human frailty and inevitable death. She faced this reality without fear and often spoke of her death not so much as a release from this life but rather as a fulfillment of her life, a dream come true, of going home, of seeing God, of beholding Jesus Himself, and of encountering the Blessed Virgin Mary, the Queen of Carmel, in whose blessed scapular she had been so long so securely embraced.

In her very self now were accomplished the words from the Epistle to the Hebrews:

> But you have come to Mount Zion and to the
> city of the living God, the heavenly Jerusalem
> (Heb. 12, 22).

This uniquely Pauline concept conjures up Mount Zion itself as a salvation history event. Originally Zion was the Jebusite fortress[3] at Jerusalem which David had captured and then named the city after himself. Later Zion was extended to embrace the entire temple area. Early Christian tradition placed the Cenacle of Jesus, the upper room of the Last Supper, the Resurrection manifestation to the Apostles and the place where the Holy Spirit descended on the Blessed Virgin Mary and the Apostles, all on Mount Zion. For this cause Bishop John of Jerusalem in the fourth century erected a commemorative Basilica under the title *Sancta Sion* on Mount Zion. In Christian spirituality Zion is again delineated as supplanting Mount Sinai, the site where God's first Covenant of the Old Testament was received, now by the final and perfect New Covenant, the sacrificial death of Jesus at the place of Calvary on Mount Zion.

After many trying Calvaries lovingly endured in this life, Mother M. Angeline Teresa, O.Carm., had reached the final ascent of Mount Carmel and quickly, with hardly a struggle, had come upon Mount Zion surrounded by her loving daughters on earth, and awaited with out-stretched arms by her first six treasured companions, and the fourscore spiritual daughters who had preceded her into the city of the living God, the new Jerusalem.

In the short five years since Mother M. Angeline Teresa, O.Carm. left this world ringed by her spiritual daughters, the memory of her holiness and good works has not been allowed to diminish. Instead, her example and teaching have been spread far and wide living in the minds and hearts of countless men and women worldwide and even memorialized in wood and stone.

One example of such spontaneous recognition of Mother M. Angeline Teresa's holy life and work took place on the very day of her funeral. The Reverend Monsignor John J. McClafferty presented Mother M. Michael Rosarie, O.Carm. with a generous check instructing her "to use this as an offering toward the Cause of canonization of Mother Angeline."[4] This even before the Mass and interment of Mother's last remains.

On February 18, 1984, a Month's Mind Memorial Mass was celebrated at St. Patrick's Cathedral on Fifth Avenue in the heart of New York City. It was expected that the Carmelite Sisters would want to remember the passing of their Mother Foundress. It was hoped that by having this memorial in the city some who could not attend her Funeral Mass and burial at the distant Motherhouse might also have an opportunity to pay their respects to her memory. The result was a never-to-be forgotten outpouring of pure love, remembrance and appreciation.

Seldom is the vast nave of that great Gothic structure fully occupied. However, long before the 11:00 a.m. hour for the Memorial Mass for Mother Angeline Teresa, it was filled to capacity. Hundreds of Carmelite Sisters, delegations from the aged residents of almost all their homes, employees and friends of the Sisters, representatives of other orders of women and men religious were present. Doctors, lawyers and businessmen who knew Mother, groups from various charitable and professional services, and so many ordinary people who had been inspired by the flame which had consumed this true Carmelite nun, filled up the Cathedral precincts. Nor was the *presbyterium* between the pulpit and altar less congested. Ten bishops, scores of monsignori and priests occupied the oak choir stalls. The principal celebrant for this memorial Mass was the Most Reverend Joseph T. O'Keefe, D.D., Auxiliary Bishop of New York and Vicar General of the Archdiocese. At the time His Excellency, Most Reverend John J. O'Connor, now Cardinal, had been appointed as the new Archbishop but not yet installed so he sent the following announcement to be read to all present at the Mass:

STATEMENT OF HIS EXCELLENCY, MOST REVEREND
JOHN J. O'CONNOR, ARCHBISHOP OF NEW YORK
ON THE OCCASION OF THE MEMORIAL MASS FOR
MOTHER M. ANGELINE TERESA, O.CARM.
ST. PATRICK'S CATHEDRAL, NEW YORK
SATURDAY, FEBRUARY 18, 1984

While I am unable to be with you today, I am nevertheless pleased to join my prayers with all of yours in the celebration of this liturgy as a memorial to Mother Angeline Teresa, the Foundress of the Carmelite Sisters for the Aged and Infirm.

Since the beginning of the community in 1929, Mother Angeline exhibited vision and courage in pioneering new methods in the care of our beloved aging. She has already become a legend as a result of her never failing faith in Our Lord and His Blessed Mother. The difficult apostolate Mother Angeline undertook more than fifty years ago continues in its innovative way in a manner which can be traced only to the blessing of Almighty God.

To all the Carmelite Sisters, true daughters of Mother Angeline and of Carmel; to the thousands of residents in their care; to all who work for and care for them; to the countless volunteers who are dedicated to their care; to the families and friends of the residents—to all I extend my greetings and blessings.

I pray that, with Mother Angeline as their model, others will emerge to take up her mantle of service and lead perhaps to as yet unenvisioned ways to promote the welfare and dignity of all of our elderly population regardless of their state in life.

May God bless you all.

+John J. O'Connor
Archbishop-designate of New York[5]

Occasioned likewise by the inability of Archbishop O'Connor to be present was another delightful vignette. The Carmelite Sisters had brought to the Cathedral a large oil painting of Mother Angeline Teresa for display during the memorial liturgy. Because of the numerous clergy, a proper place could not be found to exhibit it. The Master of Ceremonies ultimately placed it on the Cardinal's throne! Mother Angeline Teresa, who all her life was filled with awe of bishops, on this day looked down on all assembled from the episcopal throne.

During the Liturgy the first reading was done by Mother M. Michael Rosarie, O.Carm., Superior General and Mother Angeline's first successor. The second reading was done by Mother M. Bernadette de Lourdes, O.Carm. The Gospel was proclaimed by Deacon Art Eccleston. The Petitions for the Prayer of the Faithful were delivered by Mr. John McCrory, the nephew of Mother Angeline. Representatives from the Carmelite Sisters, relatives of the McCrory family, residents and workers from the Homes brought up the Offertory gifts.

The eloquent speaker of the day was the Most Reverend Edward D. Head, D.D., Bishop of Buffalo, who had known Mother M. Angeline personally and had worked with her through Catholic Charities in the Archdiocese of New York. The following are some excerpts from his eulogy:

Yours was the first modern American Congregation for the aging and infirm. Your Order always had a special American insight and lively spirit. Its special genius was the manner in which it challenged women and men to live their later years in dignity and in independence. From the beginning, its goal was to encourage and enhance that sense of personal worth that comes to those who are at peace in their hearts. From the very beginning years at St. Patrick's Home—Mother Angeline led her Sisters as trail-blazing pioneers in the field of modern geriatrics. Now in your young—yet golden years—you are singularly recognized as a model in this great professional religious apostolate. Under the leadership of your Mother, you have reached the very zenith of professional expertise and skill.[6]

There was a traffic jam as great as any ever seen before in New York City when these multiple mourners lifted up by such a thrilling tribute poured out of the Cathedral seeking their cars, buses and limousines.

On March 9, 1984 hardly two months after Mother M. Angeline Teresa's death, the room in which she gave forth her dear soul to God was blessed as a Chapel dedicated to Our Lady, Queen of Carmel. A small chapel on the second floor had some years back been available to Mother as her health failed. This was removed and the area of her bedroom was converted into a new chapel. It was dedicated at 4:30 p.m. and every Sister at Avila crowded into the small area for the Blessing and Holy Mass by Father Eugene Robitaille, SS.CC., the chaplain. There is a carved wooden altar of sacrifice and a matching altar of repose for the Blessed Sacrament. The Way of the Cross from Mother's original chapel of ease covers one wall. Carved wood statues of Our Lady, St. Joseph and the Infant of Prague, a Carmelite devotion and one of Mother's favorites, are fittingly placed along the opposite wall. Two delicate stained glass windows were also installed. The memorial plaque on the door reads:

> MOTHER M. ANGELINE TERESA
> FOUNDRESS OF THE CARMELITE SISTERS
> FOR THE AGED AND INFIRM
> DIED IN THIS ROOM ON JANUARY 21, 1984[7]

Holy Mass is offered here frequently to renew the Sacred Species and to accommodate special groups.

Immediately following the death of Mother M. Angeline Teresa, the library of the original manor house, which had also served as the first chapel at Avila, was turned into a repository for all kinds of mementos of Mother. In the glass-paneled, hand-carved wooden book cases are such personal artifacts as her habit, scapular, mantle and veil; the formula of her hand-written vows; gifts and relics given to her; her devotional articles; a collection of pictures and photos displaying her work from the beginning and up to her death; her papal awards and academic degrees; her own books of devotion and other books inscribed to her by outstanding authors. In this pot-pourri a panorama of her life and work is made palpably present. The heritage room, opened March 25, 1984,[8] has become a place of pilgrimage for the Carmelite Sisters, their families and friends.

Early in February, 1987, with the permission of Bishop Howard J. Hubbard of Albany, the Teresian Society was established. It consists of an association of clergy, religious and laity formed to spread the knowledge of the life, work and holiness of Mother M. Angeline Teresa. In a sense this is a LIVING MEMORIAL to her memory rather than a material object. The members pass out information and offer prayers and sacrifices with the hope that one day in the Providence of God the Cause for Mother M. Angeline Teresa's recognition by the Church may be officially undertaken. Since Autumn-Winter of 1987 they have a bi-annual Bulletin. They sponsor an annual Novena of Masses in all the Carmelite Homes recalling both Mother Angeline's birthday and anniversary of her death. In some cases they act as monthly prayer groups. The last mailing numbered some 3000 members. Through them special favors received through the intercession of Mother M. Angeline Teresa are recorded, such as improved health, employment obtained and return to the sacraments. Sister Raphael Peregrine, O.Carm. wrote to Mother Michael Rosarie, the Sisters of St. Margaret Hall where she is missioned, and to the members of the Carmelite Community a message of gratitude for their prayers and cooperation in a novena in which all had shared for the recovery of her father. He had a progressive deterioration of the liver and was diagnosed as incurable with no more than six months to live. In their distress the whole family and the Carmelite Sisters participated in a novena of prayer asking God through the intercession of Mother M. Angeline Teresa to give him strength in his terminal ordeal and if possible a cure. In mid July 1989, the physician made a periodical evaluation only to discover that his liver had suddenly returned to normal function. The doctor was amazed and the family delighted. Her father, Anthony Eugene Schmitz, and family credit this remarkable cure to the prayers and intercession of Mother Angeline and all join in expressing gratitude to God and to those who joined in this prayer to the Servant of God.[9]

Interestingly enough, the claim of Rita Marsh of Schenectady incited a deluge of response in the press, radio and television because of her declaration of a cure through the intercession of Mother M. Angeline Teresa. She stated,

> I was on the verge of suicide from a form of cystitis, a disease which had kept me in agony for over a year. Suddenly I got a picture of Mother Angeline into my mind and I couldn't figure out why. One night when I was walking the floor screaming in pain when she (Mother Angeline Teresa) came to mind again, and I started praying to her, I said, 'Bring my symptoms under control. Don't cure me because if I am cured I can't

help others.' I experienced significant relief of my pain and have begun helping others with the affliction.[10]

The continuing loving service and care of the Aged in their twenty-eight thriving Homes in eleven states and Ireland physically evidence how well the Sisters and their apostolate established by Mother M. Angeline Teresa are received today. The following is the documentation by way of a Mission Statement from the Eighth General Chapter of the Carmelite Sisters for the Aged and Infirm in 1984:

> We, the Carmelite Sisters for the Aged and Infirm, as women of the Church inspired by Mother M. Angeline Teresa, respond with faith, courage and love to the healing ministry of Christ. Our philosophy is steeped in her words:
>
>> "Our apostolate is not only to staff and operate up-to-date homes for the aged, but as religious it is to bring Christ to every old person under our care. Bringing Christ means giving them His compassion, His interest, His loving care, His warmth—morning, noon and night. It means inspiring the lay people who work with us, to give the same type of loving care."
>
> Our mission is reflected in the philosophy of care inherent in all policies and practices promulgated within the health care facilities under our supervision, thereby charging the administration, boards of directors and medical staff with promoting the Christian mission of healing and care.
>
> We, the Carmelite Sisters for the Aged and Infirm, affirm our philosophy of care and mission in the Church. As vowed religious, nourished and sustained by prayer, strengthened by community and committed to the Legacy of our Foundress, Mother M. Angeline Teresa, we seek to witness the healing ministry of Christ to all those entrusted to us.[11]

History, by its definition and nature, narrates confirmed dates and events without embellishment. On the other hand, biography bases its narration on dates and events but goes further to show the influence of these same sources on the life, personality and development of the individual whose life story is being related. Mother M. Angeline Teresa, O.Carm., steps forth from our manuscript as a vital, vigorous and alive personality. This radiates from her own inner gifts but also in the way in which she used these powers to advance her charism in the care of the elderly and perhaps even more her persuasive powers for good affecting so many other people who came in contact with her. Her prayer life was elevated but did not ever prevent her from action. The witness of so many people, her own relatives, her spiritual daughters the Carmelite Sisters, all ranks of the hierarchy and clergy, and so many others who came to be associated with her, is that Mother Angeline Teresa was a saintly person. She was not perfect. But she was aware of her faults, mostly those of temperament, and 'till the day of her death she made a valiant effort to overcome them. For faults of impatience or insensitivity she was the first to regret them and apologize. She readily forgave but was not always forgiven as readily herself. She was, on the other hand, a woman taken up with God. She is a model of the *always* prayer of Jesus.[12] She was the first in the chapel for Holy Mass and Office as well as the prescribed periods of meditation. In her busy schedule she found time to visit the eucharistic Jesus. Whenever she travelled she kept up the rosary, mental prayer and oftentimes even her spiritual reading. Her entire life, action, mission and charism were God-centered. All were to see Jesus in each aged person.[13]

It was her innate goodness, both natural and supernatural, which made her so easy to follow. Especially among the first young women who came to the Community, it was Mother's presence which at once drew them.[14] Her presence radiated dignity, humility, gentleness and joy. Her counsels were always uplifting and inspiring.[15] Even in a crowd, she who was both timid and shy, stood out among the rest. Although totally dedicated to her "dear old people"[16] she had a great love for children who in turn were drawn to her as to a magnet. She certainly by nature and by grace was a universal woman. Above all her love for God manifested itself in her reverential love for priests. Nothing was too good for the priest. Whether he was old or young, strong or weak, friendly or unfriendly, every priest was God's priest and in her reverential charity every priest was "her" priest.

When Mother Angeline Teresa visited the great Marian Shrine at Lourdes in August 1950 her lifelong devotion to the Blessed Virgin Mary under the title of the Immaculate Conception emotionally reached new heights and spiritually plumbed to even greater depths. The massive grotto of the Apparition, the towering Basilica with its vast immense courtyard, along with the surging multitude of the devout pilgrims gave her a renewal of courage and purpose as she placed her own life and the life of her new Community in the hands of Mary. it was not surprising then that she crossed the footbridge over the torrents of the River Gave to visit the adjacent monastery of the Discalced Carmelite Nuns nestled as it were at the foot of the overshadowing terraces and buildings of the Lourdes precincts. She came as a pilgrim seeking the prayers of these nuns for herself and her Carmelite Congregation.

When Mother Marguerite Marie of the Sacred Heart, O.C.D. the Prioress, and the Sisters met Mother Angeline at the grille for the first time it was an unforgettable moment. At once they recognized in Mother a greatness both human and supernatural. They were amazed at the rapid expansion of this new Carmelite Community. The foundress' humility, candor and spiritual depth came through more powerfully than her words. Mother Angeline told them that "She had done nothing but Our Lady of Mount Carmel had done all for her."[17] The nuns promised their prayerful support and Mother Angeline became their benefactor. When Mother visited them on other occasions they always made a fuss over her even opening the cloister door so they could embrace. Indeed, so impressed were these Carmelite Nuns that they kept a special folder on her. Every visit, every letter she wrote, each gift that she gave, every communication. All this because they recognized her as something special in God's eyes as well as their own. Years afterwards the nuns who met Mother the first time have never forgotten their impression of Mother Angeline. Acquaintance grew to knowledge to love and gratitude. Mother herself felt that her ongoing material support of this powerhouse of prayer next to the Lourdes Grotto was returned far more than a hundredfold by their spiritual assistance to her.

Upon learning of her death they exclaimed "Like the disciples on the way to Emmaus we know holiness better when it is no longer with us."[18] With that innocent candor so characteristic of cloistered nuns, yet without any appearance of judgment, they observed that other Carmelite Sisters for the Aged and Infirm continued to visit them over the years but none were ever like Mother M. Angeline, O. Carm. herself.

All these facets come together in her life as pieces in a mosaic, some outstandingly striking, others filling out the vast design. And the design which portrays the holy life, inspired vocation and specialized charism of this memorable religious woman coalesces in the title of this book:

THE SERVANT OF GOD

MOTHER M. ANGELINE TERESA, O.CARM.,

DAUGHTER OF CARMEL   and   MOTHER TO THE AGED

NOTES

[1] Cf. I Cor. 15, 55

[2] Preface for Christian Death I, P 77. *Sacramentary*, The Roman Missal. Catholic Book Publishing Company, New York, 1955, p. 527.

[3] Cf. 2 Samuel 5, 7.

[4] Author's Interview. Mother M. Michael Rosarie, (Devaney) O.Carm. June 11, 1989 at Avila.

[5] AVGA Archives Box #1

[6] *Ibid.*

[7] *Newsletter*, St. Teresa's Motherhouse, Avila, March 1984.

[8] AVGA ARCHIVES BOX #1

[9] Letter from Sister Raphael Peregrine, O.Carm. July 25, 1989, Promoter's File, AVGA

[10] Interview, Jane Gottlieb, *The Times Union*, Albany, NY August 11, 1989

[11] *CONSUMING ZEAL*, Constitutions of the Carmelite Sisters for the Aged and Infirm, Approved December 8, 1986, p. 94

[12] Cf. Lk. 18, 1

[13] "She saw 'the person of Christ in each and every old person.'" Mother M. Bernadette de Lourdes (Wisely) O.Carm. *op. cit.* p. 17

[14] *Recollections of the First Decade* (1929–1939) cf. Chapter V, note 1

[15] *Ibid.*

[16] EXHIBIT C, "Foundation" p. 11 line C.

[17] Author's personal visit to the Lourdes Carmel, 17 Route de Pau, 65100, Lourdes. October 11, 1987.

[18] Interview with Soeur Dominique, O.C.D. an Irish Nun, English Secretary for the Monastery for 40 years,. On above occasion.

EPILOGUE

On May 1, 1989 Mother M. Michael Rosarie, O.Carm., Sister M. Kathleen Rosarie, O.Carm., and Father Jude Mead, C.P., who became the Promoter for the introduction of the Cause of Beatification of Mother M. Angeline Teresa, O.Carm., upon the death of Father Eugene Robitaille, SS.CC., presented the Most Reverend Howard J. Hubbard, D.D., Bishop of Albany, with a petition. In this petition, along with a brief biography of Mother Angeline, they requested the Bishop to take the first preliminary formal step toward Mother Angeline Teresa's Cause, namely, a declaration from the Congregation of Sainthood Causes that there were no objections on its part to beginning the process. The very next day Bishop Hubbard sent the request to Rome. Under date of June 4, 1989 the following affirmative response was received. Now Mother M. Angeline Teresa may be addressed as SERVANT OF GOD.

Congregazione
Per Le Cause Dei Santi   Roma, li June 1, 1989

Prot. N. 1676–1/89

Your Excellency,

In your letter of May 2nd of this year, you have asked whether there be any objection on the part of the Holy See which might impede the Cause of Canonization of the Servant of God Mother Mary Angeline Teresa (Bridget Teresa McCrory), O.Carm., foundress of the Carmelite Sisters for the Aged and Infirm, who died with a reputation of sanctity on January 21, 1984.

In accordance with 'The Norms to be Observed in Inquiries made by Bishops in the Causes of the Saints', promulgated on February 7, 1983, I am pleased to inform you that, on the part of the Holy See, there are NO OBJECTIONS that the Cause of Canonization of the Servant of God Mother Mary Angeline Teresa McCrory proceed according to existing legislation.

I wish to take this opportunity to wish upon you and the people of Albany the choicest of God's blessings.

Fraternally in Christ,

Angelo Card. Felici
Prefect

APPENDICES

Facsimile of Mother M. Angeline Teresa's Autograph RESUME cf p. 190

J. M. J. A.

1 What was your full name in the world,
  Bridget Teresa McElroy, Name in L.S. M. Angeline de Ste Agathe.
2 M. Angeline Teresa.

  January 21, 1894
3 Date + place of birth, Mountjoy, Co. Tyrone, Ireland,
  Place of Baptism. Roman Catholic Chapel of Mountjoy Co Tyrone, Ireland
  Baptised by Rev. Fr. Keane Jan. 22, 1894.
  Attended School from 5 yrs of age to seven in Mf. Ireland.
  Continued education at St. Francis Xavier's Carfin S. Holy Family Mossend S
  Elmwood Convent, Bothwell, Scotland 6 yrs High School.
  Left school Jan 1912, Entered L.S. in Glasgow Feb 2, 1912
  Sent to Paris to St. Lawrence Home to study French Aug: 11, 1912
  Went to Nov. Feb. 14th. 1913, Recd. Habit Sept 8, 1913
  Professed March 19th. 1915; at La Tour St. Joseph. St. Pern France
  Remained at Motherhouse until Oct. 15, 1915;
  Arrived in America Oct 31, 1915, First Mission Brooklyn, N.Y.
  Was named Councillor by Supr. Gen: in Nov. 1919.
  Returned to France to make F.D. Sept. 1924
  Made Final Vows April 21, 1925.
  Named Assistant at Pittsburgh in May 1925,
  Appointed by the Supr. Gen. L.S. of Home in Bronx, N.Y. in Oct 1, 1926. 230 old people; 18 Sisters
  Remained there as Sup. until day we left August 11th 1929,
4 No extraordinary occurrances, no visions.
5 Contemplated change during Annual Retreat 1929. Consulted our Pastor + Confessor
  Fr. Sinnott. Msgr. Breslin Dean of Bronx, Fr. Flanagan Prov. of Carmelites
        over

Msgr. Breslin made first appointment for us with Cardinal Hayes.
We had several Conferences with H.E. many with Aux. Bishop Dunn.
We followed their advice faithfully step by step,
Received Dis. from Rome Aug: 9th 1929. Left in Habit Aug 11, 1929
Spent three weeks in St. Martins Dominican Convent, Bronx.
Moved to old St. Elizabeth Rectory, which we used as Convent
from Sep 3, 1929 until Sept 29, 1931 when we moved to St. P

Bishop Dunn named me Local Supr. of new group Sept: 3, 1929.
We made Retreat & Vows Oct. 9, 1929.
The first seven, two were American, two Irish, two Canadian
one Belgium
You can vie sketch of other six beginning with M. Louise
M. Leonie, M.M. Teresa, M. Colette, M. Alodia, M. Alexis.

Catholic Charities of the A.D. of NY. sent us a monthly check during
the two years 1929-1931 & gave us generously more than we needed.
C.H. gave us 50 thousand as first payment on St. Patricks. He also
signed all notes for loan in Central Hanover Bank & Trust Co,

N.2384=47

Rome   5 February 1947

Most Reverend and Most Eminent Lord

The Superioress General of the Carmelite Sisters "for assisting the Aged and Infirm" (New York City 66 Van Cortlandt Park South) has petitioned that a decree of praise and a first approval of the Constitutions for her Institute be granted by this Sacred Congregation for Religious.

Before this same Sacred Congregation judges this matter it asks the Most Eminent and Most Reverend (Lord) that he send certain records, namely:

a) To make note of the name and family name in the world and in religion of the Founder or Foundress as well as that of the first Superior General with a brief curriculum of their life;

b) To discover whether in the foundation or timely progress there may have taken place any extraordinary events, such as visions or the like, along with what special devotions or characteristic exercises of piety are preferred;

c) To send on a copy of the book of prayers if there be a special one in use among the members;

d) To give notice of how many members there are and how many houses of the Institute distributed in how many dioceses, and also what the work is along with commendatory letters of the Most Reverend Ordinaries having them, and an historical-juridical account of the Institute from its beginning to the present day;

e) To determine whether or not there may be in the Archdiocese another Institute with the same specific end.

Most Eminent and Reverend

Cardinal Francis Spellman

Archbishop of New York

concordat cum originali

(signature of Father Jude Mead, C.P.)
17.XI.88

Original Document   Recently discovered questionnaire
SCRIS ARCHIVES, ROME   for which Mother Angeline Teresa
FILE N 62 n.1   wrote her RESUME.

DECRETUM UNIVERSALE AGNITIONIS

DECRETUM UNIVERSALE AGNITIONIS
UNIVERSAL DECREE OF RECOGNITION

To the Reverend Mother M. Angeline Teresa, O.Carm.
and to all who view these present letters:

Be it known that the FIRST ACT of the Seventh General Chapter of the Carmelite Sisters for the Aged and Infirm held at St. Teresa's Motherhouse, Avila-on-Hudson, Germantown, New York, is to decree and declare for all time, that Mother M. Angeline Teresa, O.Carm. is forever their *Superior General Emerita*, with every right and privilege of that office, and is acclaimed throughout the whole Church, as the true and only Foundress of the Congregation after God and Our Lady of Mount Carmel.

Given at Avila-on-Hudson, this eighth day of September in the year 1978, the sixty-fifth year of her Religious Profession and the fiftieth year of her maternal and ecclesial leadership and founding charism.

Signed by all the Capitulars *ex-officio* and delegates and the presiding Ordinary:

PRO ECCLESIA ET PONTIFICE

PAPAL AWARD
OBTAINED BY FRANCIS CARDINAL SPELLMAN
MEDAL AND ACCOMPANYING CITATION

"Pope John XXIII, Supreme Pontiff, signed under the August Cross, the Reverend Mother Mary Angeline Teresa, Superior General of the Carmelite Sisters for the Aged and Infirm was chosen especially for performing outstanding work merits and deserves the PRO ECCLESIA ET PONTIFICE AWARD and may display this medal publicly."

Presented to Mother M. Angeline Teresa, O.Carm. Saturday morning, July 1, 1961 by Francis Cardinal Spellman in the Archbishop's House Madison Avenue New York. Recorded in *Catholic News* July 8, 1961.

BENEMERENTI

PAPAL AWARD
OBTAINED BY TERENCE CARDINAL COOKE
MEDAL AND ACCOMPANYING CITATION

"POPE PAUL VI, SUPREME PONTIFF RECOGNIZING THE SIN-GULAR CHRISTIAN CHARACTER OF THE WELL-DESERVING MOTHER M. ANGELINE TERESA, O.CARM. FINDS HER MOST WORTHY AND HAPPILY BESTOWS ON HER THIS GOLDEN MEDAL AND EXTENDS TO HER THE RIGHT OF PUBLICLY DIS-PLAYING THIS PAPAL DECORATION."

Presented to Mother M. Angeline Teresa, O.Carm. in the name of Cardinal Cooke, September 10, 1978 at Avila by Monsignor James J. Murray, Dirctor of Catholic Charities of the Archdiocese of New York.

NATIONAL AWARD OF HONOR
PRESENTED BY THE AMERICAN ASSOCIATION
OF HOMES FOR THE AGING
8TH ANNUAL CONVENTION IN ST. LOUIS 1969

"This year, we of AAHA are proud to pay tribute to a pioneer in the field of caring for the aged, Reverend Mother M. Angeline Teresa, Mother General and Foundress of the Carmelite Sisters for the Aged and Infirm, whose inspired leadership had made history in establishing a philosophy of care 40 years ago which was so modern and comprehensive that it could serve as the goal of any Home today. In 1929 Mother Angeline was inspired by our American way of life, its spirit of independence and personal dignity, to begin an Order which would exclusively care for the aged and which would stress these values. The Carmelite philosophy, comprised of respect for the privacy, dignity, and independence of the individual, has become recognized as one of the most effective and modern in this country. The 33 Homes across the United States and two in Europe which were founded under the leadership of Mother Angeline, are each a gratifying example of this philosophy put into action. Carmelite care has become synonymous with the finest care."

HONORARY DEGREE PRESENTED BY SIENA COLLEGE
LOUDONVILLE, NEW YORK

On May 31, 1970, Mother M. Angeline Teresa, O.Carm. received an HONORARY DEGREE OF HUMANE LETTERS from Siena College, Loudonville, New York, presented to her by the Reverend Brian Duffy, O.F.M. The Citation read:

"Pope Pius XII, of happy memory, once made this wise and felicitous observation: 'True religion and profound humaneness are not rivals. They are sisters.' This quotation can indeed serve as a brief summary of the many years of Christlike labor which Reverend Mother M. Angeline Teresa has devoted to the love and care of neighbor. Before pronouncing her vows as a religious of the Carmelite Order, she had pursued her studies in her native Ireland, and subsequently in Scotland and France. Then, as a Carmelite nun, in our own United States she founded the Congregation of the Carmelite Sisters for the Aged and Infirm. Today her Congregation consists of almost five hundred religious who staff thirty-three homes, some of which are in locations as distant as Iowa and Florida, Ireland and Scotland. But the guiding principle inspiring this work of Christian love is not numerical growth but rather the God-given dignity of the individual person, aged or infirm, regardless of race, color, or creed. This noble apostolate has gained the approval of Popes Pius XII, and Paul VI; and in the year 1961, Reverend Mother was awarded by Pope John XXIII the medal PRO ECCLESIA ET PONTIFICE. Within the past year (1970), the Church has seen fit to confer upon Saint Teresa of Avila, the great reformer and mystic of the Carmelite Order, the title of Doctor of the Church. And so, Reverend President, Siena College can feel honored in conferring upon this daughter of Carmel the degree of Doctor of Humane Letters, honoris causa."

HONORARY DEGREE PRESENTED BY
MANHATTAN COLLEGE
NEW YORK, NEW YORK

Manhattan College, Riverdale, New York, presented Mother M. Angeline Teresa, O.Carm. with an HONORARY DEGREE OF HUMANE LETTERS on October 18, 1970. The Citation read:

"All too frequently the charity that begins at home—and stays there—burns out into cold gray ashes. The blazing flame of Christian charity that leaps the borders of homeland to warm and enlighten the people of other lands burns with an everlasting flame. And so, Mother M. Angeline Teresa, who came to our shores during World War I, a wandering apostle like so many of her Irish forebears during the dark ages of Europe, came to us from Ireland by way of France. In 1929, in the depth of depression, Mother M. Angeline Teresa, in concert with Manhattan's alumnus, Patrick Cardinal Hayes, founded the Congregation of the Carmelite Sisters for the Aged and Infirm. From its original seven members the Congregation has grown to 500 religious and is serving the aged and infirm as far South as Florida and as far West as Davenport, Iowa in some 36 homes.

"Some of our Christian heroes and heroines, in the face of the anguish of human existence, have dedicated themselves to the poor; others to the vibrant young; it is of the fiber of Mother M. Angeline Teresa's vocation to confront the so-called 'absurdity' of human decline and death and to transmute it into charity. If we might paraphrase an encomium of one of her countrymen: 'In the realms of suffering her charitable work rises like a Te Deum, its outpouring major key sounding liberation to the dying and comfort to those in need'. Plunging her charity into its eternal roots, she has kept it clean of all debasement. She has ever kept the delicate balance between the individual and the person, so that today in all her homes an environment has been created to preserve both individualism and personalism. In recognition of her great work, Manhattan deems it an honor to confer on Mother M. Angeline Teresa the Degree of DOCTOR OF HUMANE LETTERS."

Typical Letter from Mother Angeline Teresa to Author.

ST. TERESA'S MOTHERHOUSE
AVILA ON THE HUDSON
GERMANTOWN, NEW YORK 12526

J.M.J.T.

September 19, 1972

Reverend and dear Father Jude,

How could I ever thank you for all you have
done for us this past year, and in a special way,
this past month? No one will ever know how
apprehensive I was before we held our Sixth General
Chapter, and I honestly feel that all the Masses
that have been said were responsible for the way
things turned out. Through those prayers, God
sent you to us -- and He could not have sent us a
better assurance of His loving care and solicitude.

Thank you from the bottom of my heart for
all your wise advice since the beginning of 1972.
For all the help you gave us in planning, and
organizing our Chapter. I never believed that the
Meetings could go so smoothly and well, and appreciated your quick course in Parliamentary Law!
You have helped to make things so easy to understand, and I pray that all the hard work will
produce rich fruits of holiness in the entire
Congregation.

In a special way, I thank you for the work
of the past few days. I thought we might be able
to give you a little rest after your busy Summer,
but I think you worked harder on Saturday, Sunday
and Monday than all the Committees put together.
For all your time, your wisdom, your deep concern
and your eagerness to share your wealth of knowledge with us, I say a very big thank you! May
God reward you, for we could never repay your
goodness. Each time we see the new Directive,
we will certainly remember the Passionist Father
who was truly "Consumed with Zeal". Thank you,
and please keep me in your prayers. Assuring
you of mine, I am,

Very sincerely yours in Carmel,

Mother M. Angeline Teresa
Mother M. Angeline Teresa, O.Carm.

SOURCES AND BIBLIOGRAPHY
UNPUBLISHED

Primary sources in Mother M. Angeline Teresa's Own Handwriting.

EXHIBIT "A":
RESUME: One sheet unlined paper
11 x 8–1/2
Written on both sides—Blue ink.
J.M.J.T. (Devotional Heading)
Date: Manuscript undated—
MATERIAL: In form of a questionnaire.
Mother Angeline Teresa's response in own hand.

Personal information:

Her name: Bridget Teresa McCrory; date of birth (January 21, 1894).
Place of birth, place and date of Baptism (January 22, 1894)
Education: Primary, elementary, High School.

Religious Life:
Entered Little Sisters in Glasgow Feb. 2, 1912.
Religious name: M. Angeline de Ste. Agathe.
Received Habit Sept. 8, 1913
1st Profession March 19, 1915
Final Profession April 21, 1925

Assignments:
Motherhouse, St. Pern, France
1st mission: Brooklyn N.Y. 1915
   Councillor
2nd mission: Pittsburgh 1925
   Assistant

3rd mission: Bronx, N.Y. 1926
Superior

Foundress:
No extraordinary occurrances, no visions.
Consultation with Cardinal Hayes
Many sessions with Auxiliary Bishop Dunn
Received dispensation from Rome, Aug. 9, 1929
Left in her habit Aug. 11, 1929
Stayed 3 weeks with Dominican Sisters at St. Martin Convent, Bronx.
Moved to St. Elizabeth Rectory 1929–1931
Named local superior Sept. 3, 1929
Retreat and profession of vows Oct. 7, 1929
Names of six first companions.

Cardial Hayes gave $50,000.00 for 1st payment on St. Patrick's Home. Catholic Charities gave a monthly check 1929–1931
(No mention of actual move to St. Patrick's Home Bronx, N.Y.)

IMPORTANCE: In her own hand problems regarding date of birth, spelling of name BRIDGET, are settled once and for all.

PURPOSE OF RESUME: A response for information requested by Church authority. Occasion and date unkown until author's visit to Congregation for Institutes of Consecrated Life and Societies of Apostolic Life at Rome. The original questionnaire in Latin was actually addressed to Francis Cardinal Spellman under date of February 5, 1957. N. 2384=47. This was in preparation for the Decree of Praise. An English translation is found in Appendix B.

Document preserved in a plastic sleeve, at the Motherhouse Avila, Germantown, N.Y.

EXHIBIT "B":
>   *LEDGER:*   A red leather bound notebook.
>   3–1/2 x 6 inches.
>   94 pages ruled in blue lines
>   Alphabetized index on right side.
>   Pages A and B missing.
>
>   DATE: 1913–1915 during novitiate in France.
>
>   MATERIAL: A collection of hymns, poems, and prayers written in Mother M. Angeline Teresa's own hand.
>
>   60 pages in French
>   34 pages in English
>
>   Possibly 2 or 3 are original compositions.
>
>   Document preserved in a plastic sleeve at the Motherhouse, Avila, Germantown, N.Y. (Archives)

EXHIBIT "C":

>   *"FOUNDATION" BOOK:*
>   A grey cloth bound notebook.
>   78 pages
>   7–1/2 x 4–3/4 inches
>   Alphabetized index on right side
>   Only first 8–1/4 pages were used.
>
>   DATE: Entry dated 1929–1930
>   St. Elizabeth's convent.
>   J.M.J.
>
>   MATERIAL: Mother M. Angeline Teresa's own account of the FOUNDATION of the Carmelite Sisters for the Aged and Infirm in her own hand.
>
>   The early days.
>   A list of the names of the first seven Sisters with Mother's own name last.

A list of the first four aged residents. This list erroneously changed to "seven" by another hand and blue pencil.

Document preserved in a plastic sleeve at the Motherhouse, Avila, Germantown, N.Y. (Archives)

EXHIBIT "D":

PERPETUAL YEAR BOOK: A Perennial diary:
    A brown leather bound diary.
    Gold stamped title
    Gold edges
    Brown silk ribbon marker.
    A calendar date book for year 1905

        6–1/2 x 4 inches.
        335 pages of which 322 are blank

    DATE: Begins January 31, 1905
            Pages Jan. 1–30th have been excised.

    MATERIAL: Printed Convenience Entries.
                Index of Information: Printed 13 pages.
                Altitudes, cities, U.S. and Foreign
                monies, Metric system, Postal
                information,time zones, thermometers,
                weights and measures.

                6 pages for Memoranda = unused.
                6 pages for Addresses = unused.

    CONTENTS:
                This book never used as a DIARY.
                13 pages written in Mother M.
                    Angeline's hand.
                Notes and instructions on the Spiritual Life;
                Degrees of Prayer, Ordinary Prayer.
                True Happiness attained by forgetfulness of self and self-denial.

Presence of God
Her preference for the reading of Holy
Scripture.
Silence and Solitude
Her intense love for Jesus in the
Blessed Sacrament.

This is an exquisite revelation of her own spirituality and her way to God.

Document preserved in a plastic sleeve at the Motherhouse, Avila, Germantown, N.Y. (Archives)

EXHIBIT "E":

MY TRIP ABROAD
A black leather bound note book. Pencil attached.
Copyright 1930, National Blank Book Co., Holyoke,
Mass.
Gold stamped cover, gold edges.
6–1/2 x 4 inches.
124 pages of which 56 are blank

Printed Introductory pages. 7 illustrated pages of
national and steamship flags. 1 alphabet
indexed pages. 10 pages of world maps at
back of book.

DATES: 1st trip to Europe: June 12, 1932 to August
5, 1932.
2nd trip to Europe: April–May 1938.

MATERIAL: 1st trip 17 pages in her own hand.
Eucharistic Congress Dublin 1932.
Scotland: Her Mother; Canon Taylor; Carfin
Grotto
England: London
France: Paris and Lisieux
Italy: Rome: Carmelite Fathers
"Blue Nuns" Little Company of
Mary.

First visit with Pope Pius XI who blessed the whole Congregation.

2nd trip: 21 pages in her own hand.
Italy: Rome: Carmelite Churches
Holy Thursday—St. Peter's
Good Friday—Holy Cross in Jerusalem and Scala Sancta
Holy Saturday—St. John Lateran
Easter Sunday—St. Peter's

Papal Audience—Saturday, April 21, 1938 at 1:30 p.m.
France: Lisieux—Relics, places of Little Flower.
Scotland and Ireland: Relatives

Dreadful disappointment that there was no Mass or priest on the return ship to New York.

Document preserved in a plastic sleeve at the Motherhouse, Avila, Germantown, N.Y. (Archives)

EXHIBIT "F"

CARMELITE INNOCENTS ABROAD:

A looseleaf binder.
8–1/2 X 7 inches
Grey cardboard cover
Linen binding
70 typewritten pages.
"I am Mother Angeline's Diary." p.4
DATE: Friday, August 27th–Tuesday, September 14, 1948
MATERIAL: "an account of how Mother Angeline, Mother Colette, sister Elizabeth* and old Father John** travelled into the land of France."

*sister Elizabeth is Elizabeth McCrory, Mother

Angeline's own sister.

**Old Father John is Canon John McCrory of Glasgow, Mother Angeline's cousin.

The original document here copied is described as having "gilt-edging of its leaves." p.7 "not a page had then been written on," p.4 Descriptions of Paris, Lourdes, Lisieux, Versailles and Chartres.

Style somewhat more elegant than Mother M. Angeline's usual writing

Document preserved in a plastic sleeve at the Motherhouse, Avila, Germantown, N.Y. (Archives)

EXHIBIT "G":

RECORD BOOK OF PROFESSIONS:

Covered in black cloth
10 x 8
Only 12 pages used
JMJ (Devotional Heading)
Page 1:

"The following Sisters made their perpetual vows in the Community of the Carmelite Sisters for the Aged and Infirm on the Feast of the Immaculate Conception December the eighth 1931.

These vows were made with the authorization of His Eminence Patrick Cardinal Hayes, Archbishop of New York according to the Rule of the Third Order of the Blessed Virgin Mary of Mount Carmel. Rev. Fr. Patrick Russell, O.Carm. gave the Retreat and received the Vows." Then follows the names of ten Sisters.

Page 2–11 contain the individual vow formulas signed by the Sisters. The formulas are signed:

Ego, Frater Patricius Russell Professionem
votum supra scripsit in manus meas recepi die
octava Decembris 1931.(sic)

IMPORTANCE: This is the official record of the canonical members
of the original Sisters in the new Community.

This book is preserved at the Motherhouse, Avila,
Germantown, N.Y. (Archives)

EXHIBIT "H":

RETREAT NOTES:

J.M.J. *Retraite 1925*

A La Tour St. Joseph

A small notebook
5–1/2 x 3–1/2
Not straight lined but scored for graphs
First 16 pages used only.
Written in French
A day to day (10 days) account of her retreat.
Contains reflections on the sermons of the Retreat
Master a certain "Father T.", S.J.
Also her resolutions and some prayers she selected.

IMPORTANCE: A glimpse into Mother M. Angeline Teresa's soul
as she begins her spiritual journey.

Conserved at the Motherhouse, Avila, New York
(Archives)

LETTERS

CIRCULAR LETTERS:

These are letters sent out to the Community during the years
1932–1978. They contain Mother M. Angeline Teresa's greetings,
Spiritual Counsels, Recommendations, Instructions, Admonitions,

and Community News items. There is a sum total of 169 such letters. They are contained in four loose binders as follows:

VOLUME ONE	1932–1954	62 Letters
VOLUME TWO	1955–1961	34 Letters
VOLUME THREE	1962–1968	36 Letters
VOLUME FOUR	1969–1978	37 Letters
TOTAL	1932–1978	169 Letters

This material is preserved at the Motherhouse
Avila, Germantown, N.Y. (Archives)

PERSONAL LETTERS:

These letters are of two kinds: Those in Mother M. Angeline Teresa's own handwriting and those typewritten but signed with Mother's personal signature. These were addressed to the Holy Father, members of the hierarchy, clergy, religious, her own Sisters, her family, friends and benefactors. Their enumeration and cataloguing has barely begun. Many are preserved at the Motherhouse, Avila, Germantown, New York, others may be found in the archives of the Congregation for Institutes of Consecrated Life, and Societies of Apostolic Life at Rome, in the Archives of the various Archdioceses in the United States, among the various houses of her Congregation, and her religious Sisters as well as in familial and personal collections.

UNPUBLISHED CONGREGATIONAL SOURCES

Carmelite Sisters for the Aged and Infirm.

CATEGORY BOOK:

Black leatherette loose leaf notebook.
11–1/2 x 10 inches.
Unpaginated.
1932–1989

Contains a record of 82 categories, i.e. novitiate groups. viz. dates of entrance, reception of the habit, first vows and perpetual profession.

Also contains a list of all the deceased members of the Carmelite Sisters from 1937 through 1989.

PUBLISHED SOURCES

1934   *Constitutions of the Congregation of the Carmelite Sisters for the Aged and Infirm.* Original text approved by Patrick Cardinal Hayes. January 12, 1934. Prefaced by the Rule of St. Albert

1957   *Constitutions of the Congregation of the Carmelite Sisters for the Aged and Infirm.* Mimeograph copy revised Constitutions presented for *Decretum Laudis.* Approved July 16, 1957. Rule of St. Albert omitted.

1969   *Revised Constitutions of the Carmelite Sisters for the Aged and Infirm.* Fifth General Chapter September 12, 1966. Approved by Rome (SCRIS) January 26, 1969. Presentation from Mother M. Angeline Teresa, O.Carm. A mimeo copy first, then a printed copy after Roman Approval. Rule of St. Albert omitted.

1972   Interim Directives, *Consuming Zeal*, Produced by Sixth General Chapter under date of October 15, 1972.

1978   *Constitutions of the Congregation of the Carmelite Sisters for the Aged and Infirm.* Retained title Consuming Zeal. Revised by Seventh General Chapter October 2, 1978. Approved by Rome (SCRIS) January 1979.

Pentelinear Workbook of Constitutions of 1978. Prepared to accompany above for presentation to Rome. In five parallel columns the disposition of material can be seen at once.

Column 1 = Votes
Column 2 = Text of 1978 constitutions
Column 3 = Text of 1966 constitutions
Column 4 = Text of 1972 Interim Directives
Column 5 = Disposition of Material, i.e. deleted, amended, or placed elsewhere.

1984 *Constitutions of the Congregation of the Carmelite Sisters for the Aged and Infirm.* Revised according to the New Code of Canon Law and presented for final approval September 1984.

1986 *Consuming Zeal*—Constitutions of the Congregation of the Carmelite Sisters for the Aged and Infirm. Definitive Approval on December 8, 1986 by the Congregation for Religious and Secular Institutes at Rome.

PRELIMINARY BIOGRAPHY

M. Bernadette de Lourdes (Wisely) O.Carm., *Woman of Faith/Foundress, Mother M. Angeline Teresa, O.Carm.* Carmelite Sisters for the Aged and Infirm/ 1984. xix, 512 p. Carmelite Sisters for the Aged and Infirm, Box 218, Rte 1, Germantown, New York, 12526. A preliminary biography, introductory history of Carmelite Sisters and personal reflections.

CONCILIAR AND PAPAL DOCUMENTS

A A   *Apostolicam Actuositatem*, On the Apostolate of the Laity, Vatican II, 18 November 1965

AGD   *Ad Gentes Divinitus*, On the Church's Missionary Activity. Vatican II, 7 December 1965

CD   *Christus Dominus*, On The Pastoral Office of Bishops in the Church. Vatican II, 28 October 1965

DPM   *Divinus Perfectionis Magister*, New Laws for the Causes of Saints 25 January 1983, Pope John Paul II. Congregation for the Causes of Saints, Rome. (Trans. Rev. Robert Sarno)

ES   *Ecclesiae Sanctae*, Norms for Implementing the Decree On The Up To Date Renewal of Religious Life. P.C. Pope Paul VI, 6 August 1966

ET   *Evangelica Testificatio*, Apostolic Exhortation of the Renewal of Religious Life Pope Paul VI, 29 June 1971 (SCRIS)

GS   *Gaudium et Spes*, Pastoral Constitution on the Church in the Modern World. Vatican II, 7 December 1965

LG   *Lumen Gentium*, Dogmatic Constitution on the Church. Vatican II, 21 November 1964

MR   *Mutuale Relationes*, Directions for the Mutual Relations Between Bishops and Religious in the Church. 1978

PC   *Perfectae Caritatis*, On The Renewal of Religious Life. Vatican II, 28 October 1965

SC   *Sacrosanctum Concilium*, On the Sacred Liturgy. Vatican II, 4 December 1963

CIC   *Code of Canon Law* Latin-English Edition, Washington, D.C. 1983.

ARCHDIOCESAN AND DIOCESAN SOURCES

AACH   Archives Archdiocese of Chicago
AADB   Archives Archdiocese of Dublin, Ireland
AADT   Archives Archdiocese of Detroit
AAMI   Archives Archdiocese of Miami
AANY   Archives Archdiocese of New York
AAPH   Archives Archdiocese of Philadelphia
AASE   Archives Archdiocese of Seattle
ADAL   Archives Diocese of Albany
ADCV   Archives Diocese of Covington
ADFR   Archives Diocese of Fall River
ADSA   Archives Diocese of St. Augustine
ADSP   Archives Diocese of St. Petersburg

ADYO   Archives Diocese of Youngstown

AVGA   Avila General Archives Carmelite Sisters
        1. Personal notes and memoirs
        2. Journals and Diaries
        3. Circular letters
        4. Personal correspondence
        5. Obituary files
        6. Acts of general chapters
        7. Newsletters
        8. Administrative records
        9. Civil documents
        10. Photos and memorabilia

GALSP   General Archives Little Sisters of the Poor

GENERAL BIBLIOGRAPHY

Appleton, Robert Co.,
"Ireland" article in *Catholic Encyclopedia* Vol. VIII, New York, N.Y.
1910 p. 114.

Bernadette de Lourdes (Wisely), O.Carm. Mother M.
Woman of Faith, Mother M. Angeline Teresa, O.Carm. Foundress published privately. Carmelite Sisters for the Aged and Infirm. St. Teresa's
Motherhouse, Avila on Hudson, Box 218 Rte 1, Germantown, N.Y.
1984.

Bradley, F.J.
Brief History of the Diocese of Fall River New York, NY 1931.

Burns, John S. & Sons.
St. Francis Xavier's Parish Carfin 1862–1962 *Centenary Book Glasgow,*
1962.

Holy Family Church, Mossend, 1884–1984. *November 16, 1984, 25 Fin-*
las Street, Glasgow, G22 5DS.

Carlen, Claudia, I.H.M.
Ed. *The Papal Encyclicals,* Consortium Books, McGrath Publishing Co.,
Vol. III 1903–1939, Raleigh, 1981.

Carmelite Sisters for the Aged and Infirm
Mission Statement and Philosophy of Care; Germantown, N.Y., St. Teresa's
Motherhouse; 1987

Statement on the Sanctity of Life; Germantown, N.Y., St. Teresa's Motherhouse; 1987

Catholic Book Publishing Co.
Preface for Christian Death I, p. 77 taken from *Sacramentary,* The
Roman Missal. New York, 1955, p. 527.
Thanksgiving Day Mass p. 747, 1974.

Congar, O.P., Y.M.J.
"The Theology of Religious" article in *Review for Religious* Vol.19 No.
1 Jan. 1960 p.15.

Cullen, T.F.
The Catholic Church in Rhode Island North Providence, R.I. 1936.

Dunleavy, Rev. Andrew, LL.D.
>The Catechism of Christian Doctrine. Published for the Royal Catholic College of St. Patrick, Maynooth. James Duffy, 10 Wellington Quay, 1848.

Evoy, S.J., John, J. and Christoph, S.J., Van F.
>*Maturity in Religious Life* Foreward; Leon-Joseph Cardinal Suenens. Sheed and Ward, New York 1963.

Gallen, S.J., Joseph F.
>*Canon Law for Religious* Alba House, New York, 1983, p. 62.

Gambari, S.M.M. Elio.
>*Religious Life.* Trans. & updated, II Italian Edition, Daughters of St. Paul, Boston 1986.

Gamble, A.D.
>*Notes on the History of Catholics in York County* Harrisburg, PA 1927.

Grady, Joseph.
>*From Ireland, Land of Pain and Sorrow.* A Historical Chronicle of Two Cultures. Phoenix—Erin, 1984.

Grollmes, S.J. Eugene E. Editor
>*Vows But No Walls*—an analysis of Religious Life, Foreward, Jospeh Cardinal Ritter. B. Herder Book Co. 1967. 2/3 Doughty News, London WCI.

Hammill, M.
>*Re-Expansion of the Catholic Church in Pennsylvania* Pittsburgh, PA 1960.

Hartley, J.J.
>*History of the Diocese of Columbus* 1918–1943 Columbus, Ohio 1943.

Hewitt, W.H.P.
>*History of the Diocese of Syracuse* Syracuse, New York 1909.

Huyghe, Gerald.
>*Tensions and Change: The Problems of Religious Orders Today.* Newman, Westminster 1965.

Kavanaugh, Kieran, O.C.D. and Rodriguez, Otilio, O.C.D.
>Translation of *Collected Works of St. Teresa of Avila,* Vol.I, I.C.S. Publications, Institute of Carmelite Studies, Washington, D.C. 1976.
>
>*Sketch of Mount Carmel, Collected writings of St. John of the Cross.* I.C.S. Publications, Institute of Carmelite Studies, Washington, D.C. 1973.

Knox, Ronald
>Trans. *Autobiography of St. Therese of Lisieux,* "L'histoire d'une Ame." P.J. Kenedy and Sons, New York 1958.

La Mott: J.H.
   History of the Archdiocese of Cincinnati 1821–1921 New York, New York 1921.

Lamberg, A.A.
   A History of the Catholic Church in the Diocese of Pittsburgh and Allegheny, New York 1880.

Leen, Kay.
   "Interview with Mother Angeline Teresa" article in *Catholic News* New York, October 27, 1956

Lord, R.H. et al
   History of the Archdiocese of Boston in the Various Stages of Its Development 1604–1943 *3 Vols. New York, NY 1944.*

McCaffrey, O.Carm. Rev. P.R.
   The White Friars, An outline of Carmelite History. Gill and Sons, Ltd. Dublin, 1926.

McGhee, Susan
   The Carfin Grotto, The First Sixty Years, Carfin, Motherwell, 1981.

Meltzer, Milton.
   Brother, Can You Spare A Dime? The Great Depression. 1929–1933. Knopf. New York 1926.

Milcent, Paul.
   Humble So As To Love More, trans. Alan Neame. Darton, Longman and Todd, London, 1980.

O'Reilly, Rev. Bernard, L.D. (Laval)
   The Mirror of True Womanhood. 17th Ed. P.J. Kennedy, 5 Barclay St., N.Y. 1892.

Orsy, Ladislaus M.,
   "The Decree of Religious Life". A Commentary. *America*, January 1, 1966 p.12.

Porter, David.
   Mother Teresa, The Early Years. Eerdmans Publishing Company, Grand Rapids, Ia. 1986.

Puhl, Louis, J., S.J.
   Translator, *The Spiritual Exercises of St. Ignatius.* Newman Press, Westminster, MD. 1963.

Purcell, W.P.
   Catholic Pittsburg's One Hundred Years. Chicago, IL 1943.

Ryan, John K., Trans. and Ed.
   History of the Diocese of Covington Kentucky. Covington, Kentucky, 1954.

Ryan, P.E.
History of the Diocese of Covington Kentucky Covington, Kentucky 1954.

St. Francis De Sales
Introduction to the Devout Life, Harper and Brothers, Publishers, New York, 1949.

Sarno, Rev. Msgr. Robert J.
Diocesan Inquiries Required by the Legislator in the New Legislation for the Causes of the Saints, Doctoral Dissertation, Pontificae Gregorian University, Rome, 1988.

Sharp, Rev. John K.
History of the Diocese of Brooklyn (1853–1953) II Vols. Fordham University Press, New York 1954.

Sister Rita Arlene, P.V.M.I.
Mother Mary Teresa Tallon. Marycrest. Monroe, N.Y. 1984.

Smet, Joachim, O.Carm.
The Carmelites. A History of the Brothers of Our Lady of Mount Carmel. IV Vols. Carmelite Spiritual Center, Darien, Ill. 1975–1985.

Tillard, O.P. J.M.R.
"Religious Life in the Mystery of the Church". Oct. *Review for Religious*. Vol 22, No. 6 Nov. 1963 p.613.

Werling, N.G.
The First Catholic Church in Joliet Illinois. Chicago, IL 1960.

NEWSPAPERS/MAGAZINES

Altoona Mirror, Altoona, PA. Sept. 27, 1973.

Carmelite Review, The Canadian-American Province, Barrington, IL. March 1, 1984.

Catholic Light, The Diocese of Scranton. November 21, 1974
February 12, 1976.

Catholic News The New York Archdiocese. December 26, 1931
October 3, 1936
October 27, 1956
March 7, 1959
September 22, 1966.

Catholic News-Register, The Diocese of Joliet. January 1, 1965
June 27, 1965.

Catholic Register, The (Altoona). July 2, 1965
February 4, 1986
July 31, 1989

Catholic Witness, The Harrisburg, PA April 5, 1973
                December 6, 1973.

Cincinnati Enquirer, The Cincinnati, Ohio. October 2, 1962.

Columbus Register, The Diocese of Columbus. January 23, 1948.

Daily Freeman, Rhinebeck, NY. January 20, 1971.

Evangelist, The Diocese of Albany. October 18, 1979.
                December 12 1985.

Florida Catholic, The December 27, 1978.

Joliet Herald-News, The Joliet, IL. February 13, 1964
                April 30, 1964
                June 28, 1965.

Manchester Union Leader Manchester, NH June 21, 1967.

Manor News, The (In house organ) St. Joseph Manor, Trumbull, CT
                Spring 1961
                Spring 1962
                November 1972
                March 1973.

Miami Voice, The Miami. November 19, 1960
                October 13, 1978
                March 16, 1984.

New York Times, Shipping and Arrivals, October 31, 1915.
                August 6, 1936
                March 20, 1964.

Palm Beacher, The Palm Beach, FL. February 8, 1979.

Paxton Herald, The Harrisburg, PA. April 11, 1973.

Post, The Miami, FL. A Complete Supplement, December 14, 1980.

Sunday Independent Dublin, Ireland. September 8, 1974.

Sunday News New York, NY. June 17, 1973.

Sword, The Joliet, IL. April, 1984.

Times-Leader, The Wilkes-Barre, PA. January 10, 1975.

Times Union Albany, NY. June 29, 1972
                August 11, 1989.

Vindicator, The Diocese of Youngstown, OH. June 27, 1952
                September 4, 1970.

CARMELITE REFERENCES

Adams, David, O.C.D. (ed), *Mount Carmel*, Oxford, Discalced Carmelite Fathers of the Anglo-Irish Province, Volume for Spring 1985

Albarran, A. DeCastro; Bernarda, Sr. Mary, B.V.M., (trans), *The Dust of Her Sandals*, New York, Cincinnati, Chicago, San Francisco, 1936

Alvarez, Tomas, CD., PP, and Domingo, Fernando, CD., O'Mahoney, Christopher (trans), *Saint Teresa of Avila, A Spiritual Adventure*, Burgos, Spain, Editorial Monte Carmelo; Washington, USA, ICS Publications, 1981

Alzin, Josse; Earl of Wicklow (trans), *A Dangerous Little Friar*, Dublin, Clonmore & Reynolds Ltd., 1957; London, Burns Oates & Washbourne Ltd., 1957

Anastasius of the Holy Rosary, General O.C.D., *The Praise of Glory*, Westminster, Newman Press, 1962

Anne of Saint Bartholemew, Blessed Mother; Carmelite (trans), *Autobiography of the Blessed Mother Anne of Saint Bartholemew*, Antwerp, Carmelites, 1916

Antonellis, Costanzo, J., C.SS.R., *A Saint of Ardent Desires*, Boston, Daughters of St. Paul, 1965

Arendrup, M. E. (trans), *A Carmelite of the Sacred Heart*, New York, Cincinnati, Chicago, Benziger Brothers, 1923

Auclair, Marcelle, *Saint Teresa of Avila*, New York, Pantheon, 1953

Auclair, Marcelle; Pond, Kathleen (trans), *Teresa of Avila*, Garden City, NY, Image Books, 1959

Bazar, Catherine Marie, O.P., *Teresa of Avila Valiant Woman*, San Jose, CA, Secular Order Discalced Carmelites, Western Jurisdiction (in cooperation with Teresian Centenary Commission), 1981

Beevers, John (trans), *The Autobiography of St. Therese of Lisieux*, Garden City, NY, Image Books, 1957

Beevers, John, *Storm of Glory*, New York, Sheed & Ward, 1950

Benedictines of Stanbrook (trans), *The Letters of Saint Teresa*, London, Thomas Baker, 1921

Benedictines of Stanbrook (trans), Zimmerman, O.C.D., Benedict (revised), *Minor Works of St. Teresa*, London, Thomas Baker, 1913

Borriello, Luigi, O.C.D., Aumann, Jordan, O.P. (trans), *Spiritual Doctrine of Blessed Elizabeth of the Trinity*, New York, Alba House, 1986

Boyle, Valentine L., O.Carm., *Mary and the Saints of Carmel*, Chicago, Carmelite Third Order Press, 1955

Brandsma, Titus, O.Carm. (Blessed 1985), *The Beauty of Carmel*, Dublin, Clonmore & Reynolds, Ltd. and London, Burns Oates & Washbourne Ltd., 1955

Brandsma, Titus, O.Carm. (Blessed 1985), *Carmelite Mysticism*, (Vols. 1–9), Kent, England, Carmelite Press, 1936 (Reprint 1980)

Brandsma, Titus, O.Carm. (Blessed 1985), *Carmelite Mysticism Historical Sketches*, Chicago, Carmelite Press, 1936

Brice, Father C. P., *Journey in the Night*, New York and Cincinnati, Frederick Pustet Co., Inc., 1945

Brice, Father C. P., *Spirit in Darkness*, New York and Cincinnati, Frederick Pustet Co., Inc., 1946

Brice, Father C. P., *Teresa, John, and Therese*, New York and Cincinnati, Frederick Pustet Co., Inc., 1946

Bruno, O.D.C., Fr; Zimmerman, Benedict, O.C.D. (ed), *St. John of the Cross*, New York, Cincinnati, Chicago, San Francisco, Benziger Brothers, 1932; New York, Sheed & Ward, 1932

Bruno de J. M., O.D.C., *Three Mystics*, New York, Sheed & Ward, 1949

Budnowski, Else; Eckhoff, Rev. Frederick C., (trans), *She Obeyed an Inner Voice*, Boston, Daughters of St. Paul, 1981

Bulger, James E., *Louis Martin's Daugher*, Milwaukee, Bruce Publishing 1952

Burton, Katherine, *With God and Two Ducats*, Chicago, Carmelite Press, 1958

Burrows, Ruth, *Fire Upon the Earth*, Denville, NJ, Dimension Books, 1981

Buzy, D., S.C.J., Finian, O.C.S.O. (trans), *Thoughts of Sister Mary of Jesus Crucified*, Carmel of Bethlehem, Jerusalem, 1974

Caravacci, Ariadne Katherine, *Loving Kindness*, Duarte, CA, Carmelite Sisters of the Most Sacred Heart of Los Angeles, 1983

Carroll, Eamon R., O.Carm., *The Mother of Christ* (Doctrinal Pamphlet Series), New York and Glen Rock NJ, Paulist Press, 1962

Catherine Thomas of Divine Providence, D.D., Mother, *My Beloved*, New York, Toronto, London, McGraw-Hill Book Co., 1955

Chesterton, Mrs. Cecil, *St. Teresa*, Garden City, NY, Doubleday, Doran, 1928

Clarke, John, O.C.D. (trans), *Saint Therese of Lisieux General Correspondence Volume 1*, Washington, DC, ICS Publications, 1982

Clarke, John, O.C.D. (trans), *St. Therese of Lisieux—Her Last Conversations*, Washington, DC, ICS Publications, 1977

Clarke, Rev. John P., *The Pilgrim's Path of Saint Therese of the Child Jesus*, Manchester NH, Magnificat Press, 1926

Clarkson, Tom, *Love is My Vocation*, London, Catholic Book Club, 1953; New York, Farrar, Straus and Young, 1953

Clissold, Stephen, *St. Teresa of Avila*, New York, Seabury Press, 1979; London, Sheldon Press, 1979

Clissold, Stephen, *The Wisdom of the Spanish Mystics*, New York, New Directions, 1977

Collins, Michael, A.M., (trans), *At the School of St. Therese of the Child Jesus*, London, Burns Oates & Washbourne, 1938

Colvill, Helen Hester, *Saint Teresa of Spain*, London, Methuen & Co., 1910

Combes, Abbe Andre, *The Heart of Saint Therese*, New York, P. J. Kenedy & Sons, 1951

Combes, Abbe Andre; Guinan, Alastair (trans), *Saint Therese and Her Mission*, New York, P. J. Kenedy & Sons, 1955

Combes, L'Abbe Andre, *The Spirituality of St. Therese*, New York, P. J. Kenedy & Sons, 1950

Carmel of Kilmacud (trans), *The Spirit of Saint Therese*, London, Burns Oates & Washbourne Ltd., 1925

Carmelite, An Irish, *A Modern Mystic*, London, Burns Oates & Washbourne Ltd., 1938

Carmelite Nun, *God and Rosanne*, London, Sands & Co., 1946

Combes, Abbe Andre; Hallett, Msgr. Philip E. (trans), *St. Therese and Suffering*, New York, P. J. Kenedy & Sons, 1951

Carmelite Nun, A, *Heartbreak Earth*, Westminster, MD, Newman Press, 1953

Carmelite Nun, *Mother Therese and the Carmel of Allentown*, Philadelphia, Jeffries and Manz, 1949

Carmelite Nun, *The Nun's Answer*, Chicago, Henry Regnery Co., 1958

Carmelite Nun, *Our Eternal Vocation*, Scotland, Sands & Co., 1948; Westminster, MD, Newman Press, 1949

Carmelite Nuns, Discalced (trans), *God's Word to His Church*, San Francisco, Ignatius Press, 1982 (translation from original by Discalced Carmelite Nuns of Noto, Italy)

Carmelite Nuns of Ancient Observance, *In Praise of His Glory*, Coopersburg, PA, Carmelite Monastery, 1981

Carmelite Nuns of New York (trans), *Novissima Verba*, New York, P. J. Kenedy & Sons, 1952

Carmelite Order, Discalced, *Pater Noster of Saint Teresa of Avila*, Detroit, Carmelite Monastery, 1982 (Centennial Edition)

Carmelite Sisters for the Aged and Infirm, *Silver Jubilee*, New York, New York 1954

Carmelite Tertiary, *Carmelite Devotions*, Milwaukee, Bruce Publishing, 1956

Carmelites, *Ascent—Review for Carmelite Sisters*, Rome, Carmelite College of St. Albert, Volumes 1968–1978

Carmelites, *Carmel 19521962*, Kansas City, Winnipeg, Inter-Collegiate Press, 1963

Carmelites, *The Carmelite Directory of the Spiritual Life*, Chicago, Carmelite Press, 1951

Carmelites, *The Marian*, (St. Albert's Preparatory Seminary), Middletown, New York

Carmelites, *Carmelite Writings—Reflections from the Hail Mary*, Newry, Ireland, Carmelite Monastery

Carmelites, *Carmelite Writings—Think of Your Soul as a Castle*, Newry, Ireland, Carmelite Monastery

Carmelites, *Carmelite Writings—Thoughts on the Glory Be to the Father*, Newry, Ireland, Carmelite Monastery

Carmelites, Corpus Christi, *A Great Adventure*, Trinidad, Trinidad Publishing Co., 1944

Carmelites, The Discalced of Boston and Santa Clara, *Carmel, Its History, Spirit, and Saints*, New York, P.J. Kenedy & Sons, 1927

Carmelites, Discalced, *Wholeness* (A Study Guide for Lay Carmelites), Brookline, MA, Discalced Carmelite Monastery, 1973

Carmelites of Lisieux, *Mother Agnes of Jesus*, Exeter, Catholic Records Press (printed)

Crisogono de Jesus, O.C.D., Pond, Kathleen (trans), *The Life of St. John of the Cross*, London, Longmans and New York, Harper & Brothers, 1958

Cugno, Alain; Wall, Barbara (trans), *Saint John of the Cross*, London and Tunbridge Wells, Burns & Oates, 1982

Curran, Thomas, O.C.D. (ed), *Living Flame Series*, Dublin, Carmelite Center of Spirituality, 1977–1983; Manchester, England, Koinonia Ltd., 1977–1982

Day, Dorothy, *Therese*, Notre Dame, Ind., Fides Publishers, 1960 de la Croix, Paul-Marie, O.C.D.; Donehy, Msgr. Wm. J., C.S.C., (revised), *The Biblical Spirituality of St. John*, Rome, Private Circulation, 1980

de la Vierge, R. P. Victor, O.C.D.; Carmelite Nuns, Discalced (trans), *Spiritual Realism of Saint Theresa of Lisieux*, Milwaukee, Bruce Publishing, 1961

Dent, Barbara, *The Cleansing of the Heart*, Denville, NJ, Dimension Books, 1973

de Puniet, P., O.S.B., Bernadot, M. V., O.P.; de la Mere de Dieu, Jerome, O.C.D., and Lajeunie, E.M., O.P., *Saint Teresa of the Child Jesus*, London, Burns Oates & Washbourne Ltd., 1926

Diefenbach, Gabriel, O.F.M. Cap., *Common Mystic Prayer*, Paterson, NJ, St. Anthony Guild Press, 1946

Diether, Lawrence C., O.Carm., *The Ascent of Carmel*, Chicago, Carmelite Press, 1935

Diether, Lawrence C., O.Carm., *Ave Maria*, Chicago, Carmelite Press, 1934

Diether, Lawrence C., O.Carm., *Rosa Mystica*, Chicago, Carmelite Press, 1936

Dolan, Albert H., O.Carm., *An Hour with the Little Flower*, Chicago, Carmelite Press, 1926

Dolan, Albert H., O.Carm., *Dare to Live!* 1941

Dolan, Albert H., O.Carm., *Enjoy the Mass*, Chicago, Carmelite Press, 1937

Dolan, Albert H., O.Carm., *God Made the Violet Too*, Chicago, Englewood, NJ, Carmelite Press, 1948

Dolan, Albert H., O.Carm., *The Living Sisters of the Little Flower*, Chicago, Carmelite Press, 1926

Dolan, Albert H., O.Carm., *Our Sister Is In Heaven*, Chicago, Carmelite Press, 1927

Dolan, Albert H., O.Carm., *Roses Fall Where Rivers Meet*, Englewood, NJ, and Chicago, Carmelite Press, 1937

Dolan, Albert H., O.Carm., *St. Therese Messenger of Mary*, Chicago, Englewood NJ, Carmelite Press, 1949

Dolan, Albert H., O.Carm., *St. Therese Returns*, Chicago, Carmelite Press, 1933 (Third Printing 1940)

Dolan, Albert H., O.Carm., *The Sisters of St. Therese Today*, Chicago and Englewood, NJ, Carmelite Press, 1948

Doheny, Msgr. Wm. J., C.S.C. (trans), *The Pater Noster of Saint Teresa*, New Pocket edition, 1949; Milwaukee, Bruce Publishing Co., 1942

Doheny, William J., C.S.C., *Selected Writings of St. Teresa of Avila*, Rome, Angelo Belardetti, 1950 (private distribution); Chicago, Franciscan Herald Press; Milwaukee, Bruce Publishing Company

Doheny, Wm. J., C.S.C., *Symposium on Mental Prayer*, Rome, private circulation. 1980 (Revised)

Dooley, L. M., S.V.D., *God's Guests of Tomorrow*, Sea Isle City, NJ, New York, Los Angeles, Scapular Press, 1943

Elliot, Edmund E. R., O.Carm., *Child of Calvary*, Melbourne, Carmelite Fathers, 1960

Elizabeth of the Trinity; Kane, Aletheia, O.C.D. (trans), *I Have Found God— Complete Works I*, Washington, D.C. ICS Publications, 1984

Emmanuel, Sr. M., O.S.B., *Life of Sister Marie de St. Pierre of the Holy Family*, London, Burns Oates and Washbourne Ltd., 1938

Esteve, Enrique, O.Carm., and Guarch, Joaquin M., O.Carm.; Pausback, Gabriel N., O.Carm. (trans), *Carmel—Mary's Own*, Chicago, Carmelite Third Order Press, 1955Francis, Mary Francis, P.C., *La Madre*, New York, Hollywood, London, Toronto, Samuel French, Inc., 1959

Friedman, Elias, O.C.D., *El-Muhraqa,—Here Elijah Raised His Altar*, Rome, Teresianum, 1985

Friedman, Elias, *The Mediaeval Abbey of St. Margaret of Mount Carmel*, Rome, Teresianum, 1971

Frost, Bede, *Saint John of the Cross*, New York and London, Harper and Brothers, 1937

Gabriel of St.Mary Magdalen, O.D.C., *St. Teresa of Jesus*, Westminster, MD, Newman Press, 1949

Garside, Charles B., M.A., *The Prophet of Carmel*, Wheeling W. Va., Discalced Carmelites, 1924

Genevieve of the Holy Face, Sister (Celine Martin); Carmelite Sisters of New York (trans), *A Memoir of My Sister St. Therese*, New York, P.J. Kenedy & Sons, 1959

Gorres, Ida Friederike, *The Hidden Face*, London, Burns & Oates, 1959; New York, Pantheon, 1959

Gheon, Henri; Attwater, Donald (trans), *The Secret of the Little Flower*, New York, Sheed & Ward, 1934

Grady, Laureen, O.C.D., *The Seasons of Carmel*, Reno, Carmelite Communities Associated, 1975

Graef, Hilda C., *The Scholar and the Cross*, Westminster, MD, Newman Press, 1955

Gray, Ronald, O.Carm., *Come to Lisieux*, Washington, DC, 1959

Groseclose, Elgin, *The Carmelite*, New York, MacMillan, 1955

Hamilton, Elizabeth, *Saint Teresa, A Journey to Spain*, New York, Charles Scribner's Sons, 1959

Haffert, John M., *The Brother and I* (formerly "From A Morning Prayer"), Washington, NJ, Ave Maria Institute, 1971 (reprint)

Haffert, John Mathias, *From A Morning Prayer*, New York, Los Angeles, Scapular Press, 1943

Haffert, John Mathias (trans), *A Letter from Lisieux*, Sea Isle City, NJ, Scapular Press, 1942

Haffert, John Matthias, *Mary in Her Scapular Promise*, Sea Isle City, NJ, Scapular Press, 1942; Washington, NJ, AMI Press, 1954

Heliodore of the Child Jesus, O.C.D., Miyares, Dr. Enrique H. (trans), *The Work of St. Teresa and Her First Monastery*, Buffalo, NY, Discalced Carmelite Nuns, 1967

Hamilton, Elizabeth, *The Voice of the Spirit*, Huntington, IN, Our Sunday Visitor, Inc., 1976 (First published in Great Britain, Darton, Longman, and Todd Ltd., 1976)

Haneman, Mary Alphonsetta, C.S.S.F., *The Spirituality of St. Teresa of Avila*, Boston, Daughters of St. Paul, 1983

Hardman, Anne, S.N.D., *English Carmelites in Penal Times*, London, Burns Oates & Washbourne, 1936

Hardman, Anne, S.N.D., *Two English Carmelites*, London, Burns Oates & Washbourne Ltd., 1939

Hardy, Richard P., *Search for Nothing*, New York, Crossroad, 1982

Heriz, Paschasius, O.C.D., *Saint John of the Cross*, Washington, DC, 1980 1919

Horgan, John, *Sweet Is The Echo*, Pittsburg, Echo House, 1953

Immaculata, Sr., O.C.D., *Communion With God*, Huntington, IN, Our Sunday Visitor, 1978

Isacsson, Alfred, O.Carm., *Carmel in New York, The Province of St. Elias 1906–1926*, Maspeth, New York, Vestigium Press, 1976

Isacsson, Alfred, O.Carm., *Carmel in New York, The Province of St. Elias 1927–1947*, Boca Raton, Fl., Vestigium Press, 1984

Isacsson, Alfred, O.Carm., *A History of Saint Albert's Jr. Seminary*, Maspeth, NY, Vestigium Press, 1976

Jamart, Francois, O.C.D., Van de Putte, Walter, C.S.SP., (trans), *Complete Spiritual Doctrine of St. Therese of Lisieux*, New York, Canfield, Derby and Boston, St. Paul Publications, 1961; New York, Alba House, 1977

John of the Cross; Lewis, David (trans), *The Ascent of Mount Carmel*, London, Thomas Baker, 1922

John of the Cross; Peers, E. Allison (trans), *Ascent of Mount Carmel*, Garden City, NY, Image Books, 1958

John of the Cross; Peers, E. Allison (trans), *The Complete Works of Saint John of the Cross*, Westminster, MD, Newman Press, 1953 (revised)

John of the Cross; Peers, E. Allison (trans), *Counsels of Light and Love*, Wheeling, WV, Carmelite Monastery (reprint), 1953; New York and Ramsey, NJ, Paulist Press, 1978

John of the Cross; Peers, E. Allison (trans), *Living Flame of Love*, Garden City, NY, Image Books, 1962

John of the Cross; Nims, John Frederick (trans), *The Poems of St. John of the Cross*, Chicago & London, University of Chicago Press, 1979

John of the Cross; Peers, E. Allison (trans), *Spiritual Canticle*, Garden City, NY, Image Books, 1961

Johnson, Msgr. Vernon, *Spiritual Childhood*, New York, Sheed and Ward, 1954

Johnston, William, S.J. (ed), *The Cloud of Unknowing*, Garden City, NY, Image Books, 1973

Kelly, Joseph P., *Meet Saint Teresa*, New York and Cincinnati, Frederick Pustet Co., 1958

Kavanaugh, Kiernan, O.C.D. (trans), and Rodriguez, O.C.D., Otilio (trans), *The Collected Works of St. John of the Cross*, Washington, DC, ICS Publications, 1973 and 1979

Kavanaugh, Kiernan, O.C.D. (trans), and Rodriguez, O.C.D., Otilio (trans), *The Collected Works of St. Teresa of Avila*, Washington, DC, ICS Publications, 1976 (Vol. 1), 1980 (Vol. 2), 1985 (Vol. 3)

Keyes, Francis Parkinson, *Written in Heaven*, N.Y., N.Y., Julian Messner, Inc., 1957

LaFrance, Jean; A nun of the Carmel du Pater Noster, Jerusalem (trans), *Elizabeth of the Trinity*, Jerusalem, Carmel of the Pater Noster, 1983

Lanshe, Sr. M. Elizabeth, O.Carm., *Echoes from Carmel in Saint Therese's Valley*, Coopersburg, PA, Carmelite Nuns of Allentown, 1986

Lanshe, Sr. M. Elizabeth, O.Carm., *God Will Provide*, Coopersburg, PA, Carmelite Nuns of Allentown, 1986

Lavielle, Msgr. August Pierre; Fitzsimmons, M., O.M.I., (trans), *Life of the Little Flower*, New York, McMullen Books, 1953

Lawrence of the Resurrection, Brother; David, Mary, S.S.N.D. (trans), *The Practice of the Presence of God*, Westminster, MD, Newman Book Shop, 1945

Lewis, David (trans); Zimmerman, Very Rev. Benedict (rev), *The Foundations of St. Teresa of Jesus*, New York, Cincinnati, Chicago, Benziger Brothers, 1913

Lewis, David (trans), *The Life of St. Teresa of Avila*, Westminster, MD, Newman Press, 1962

Lewis, David (trans); Zimmerman, Benedict, O.C.D. (re-ed), *The Life of St. Teresa of Jesus*, Westminster, MD, Newman Book Shop, 1944, 1951, and Newman Press, 1951

Lewis, David (trans); Zimmerman, Dom Benedict, O.C.D., (rev), *The Mystical Doctrine of St. John of the Cross*, New York, Sheed and Ward, 1944

Liagre, Pere, C.S.Sp., Owen, Dom P.J., O.S.B., (trans), *A Retreat With Saint Therese*, Westminster, MD, Newman Press, 1948

Lucas of St. Joseph, O.C.D.; Paschasius of Our Lady of Mount Carmel (trans), *Holiness in the Cloister*, Chicago, M. A. Donohue & Co., 1920

Luke of St. Joseph, Very Rev., *St. Teresa's Book Mark*, St. Louis, Discalced Carmelite Nuns, 1919

Lynch, E. K. (Kilian), O.Carm., *The Scapular of Carmel*, Washington, NJ, Blue Army of Our Lady of Fatima, 1955 and 1973 (revised 2nd edition)

Lynch, E. K. (Kilian), O.Carm., *Your Brown Scapular*, Westminster, MD, Newman Press, 1950

MacGalli, Rev. P. Aloysii, *Series et Effigies Priorum Gnalium Latinorum Totius Ordinis Fratrum B. Mariae Virginis de monte Carmelo*, Germany, M. Gladbach, Ex officina B. Kuhlen, typogr. Apost., 1893

Madeleine of St. Joseph, Sr., O.C.D.; Carmel of Pittsford (trans and abr), *Within the Castle with St. Teresa of Avila*, Chicago, Franciscan Herald Press, 1982

Magennis, P. E., Ord. Carm., *Elias the Prophet of Carmel*, Dublin, M. H. Gill & Son, 1925

Magennis, P. E., O.Carm., *The Life and Times of the Prophet of Carmel*, Dublin, M. H. Gill & Son, 1925

Magennis, P. E., O.Carm., *The Life of St. Simon Stock*, New York, Carmelite Press.

Magennis, P. E., Ord. Carm., *The Sabbatine Privilege of the Scapular*, New York, C. F. Connolly, 1923

Magennis, P. E., O.Carm., *The Scapular Devotion*, Dublin, M. H. Gill and Son, 1923

Marie-Eugene, P., O.C.D.; Clare, Sr. M. Verda, C.S.C., (trans), *I Want to See God* (Volume I), Chicago, Fides Publishers Assoc., 1953

Martin, Rev. G.; Maguire, Rev. Eugene A. (trans), *How to Love God as Saint Therese of the Child Jesus Loved Him*, London, Burns Oates & Washbourne Ltd., 1937

(Martin) Pauline; Murphy, Roland, O.Carm. (trans); Smet, Joachim, O.Carm. (trans); Dolan, Albert H., O.Carm. (ed), *Marie Sister of St. Therese*, Englewood, NJ, Chicago, Carmelite Press, 1943

Mary Minima, Sr.; Pausback, Gabriel, N., O.Carm. (trans and ed), *Seraph Among Angels*, Chicago, Carmelite Press, 1958

Mary of the Blessed Sacrament, Carmelite Nun, *A Retreat Under the Guidance of Saint John of the Cross*, New York, Cincinnati, Chicago, San Francisco, Benziger Brothers, 1930

Mary of the Blessed Sacrament, Carmelite Nun, *A Retreat Under the Guidance of Saint Teresa*, New York, Cincinnati, Chicago, Benziger Brothers, 1929

Mary of the Blessed Sacrament, Mother, *My Religious Life With Saint Therese*, Chicago, Carmelite Third Order Press, 1951

Mason, Sr. Agnes, C.H.F. (trans), *Saint Theresa—the History of Her Foundations*, Cambridge, University Press, 1909

McCaffrey, P. R., Ord. Carm., *The White Friars*, Dublin, M. H. Gill and Son, 1926

McCarthy, Alexis, O.Carm. (ed), Rafferty, Howard, O.Carm. (ed), *With Mary to the Mountain*, Darien, Il, Carmelite Press, 1981

McGinnis, Thomas, O.Carm., (trans and arr), *Life With Mary*, (A Treatise on the Marian Life by the Ven. Michaeal of St. Augustine, O.Carm.), New York, Scapular Press, 1953

McNamara, William, O.C.D., *The Human Adventure*, Garden City, NY, Image Books, 1976

Morales, Jose L., Ph.D., *Behold a Little Cloud Rising from the Sea*, New York, Brooklyn Carmel, 1972

Nevin, Winifred, *Heirs of St. Teresa of Avila*, Milwaukee, Bruce Publishing, 1959

Nevin, Winifred, *Teresa of Avila the Woman*, Milwaukee, Bruce Publishing, 1956

Notre Dame de Namur, a Sister of, *Life of the Venerable Anne of Jesus*, London, Sands & Co., 1932

Opdenaker, Theodore A., *White Flame*, New Brunswick, NJ, The Carmel of Mary Immaculate and Saint Mary Magdalen, 1952

O'Brien, Kate, *Teresa of Avila*, New York, Sheed & Ward, 1951

O'Mahonn, Christopher, O.C.D. (trans and ed), *St. Therese of Lisieux by Those Who Knew Her*, Huntington, IN, Our Sunday Visitor, 1976

Papasogli, Giorgio; Anzilotti, G. (trans), *St. Teresa of Avila*, New York, Canfield, Derby, Boston, Society of St. Paul, 1958

Paula, Mother, O.S.B. (trans), *The Rose Unpetaled*, Milwaukee, Bruce Publishing, 1942 and 1943

Pausback, Gabriel N., O.Carm. (trans), *The Complete Works of Saint Mary Magdalen DePazzi*, Fatima, Portugal; Aylesford (Maidstone), England; Aylesford (Westmont), Il; Carmelite Fathers—Distributors, (Vol I), 1974 (Vol II), 1975 (Vol III), 1971 (Vo. IV), 1973 (Vol V)

Peers, E. Allison (trans and ed), *The Life of Teresa of Jesus*, Garden City, NY, Image Books, 1960

Peers, E. Allison, *Mother of Carmel*, New York, Morehouse-Gorham Co., 1948; Wilton, CT, Morehouse-Barlow Co., 1979

Peers, E. Allison, *Spirit of Flame*, Wilton, CT, Morehouse-Barlow Co., 1946; New York, Morehouse-Gorham Co., 1944, 1945

Petitot, Henry, O.P., *Saint Teresa of Lisieux*, London, Burns Oates & Washbourne Ltd., 1927, 1941, 1948

Phelim, Fr., O.C.D., *Edith Stein in Her Writings*, Galway, Carmelite Publications,

Philip, Fr., O.C.D., *A Man of God*, Trivandrum, S. India, St. Joseph's Press, 1956

Philipon, M. M., O.P.; Ross, E. J. (trans), *The Message of Therese of Lisieux*, Westminster, MD, Newman Press, 1950

Philipon, M. M., O.P. (ed), *Sister Elizabeth of the Trinity*, Spiritual Writings, Rome, Private Circulation by Doheny, C.S.C., Wm. J., 1981

Philipon, M. M., O.P., *The Spiritual Doctrine of Sister Elizabeth of the Trinity*, Westminster, MD, Newman Bookshop, 1947

Piat, Stephane-Joseph, O.F.M., *The Story of a Family*, New York, P. J. Kenedy & Sons, 1946

Pierini, Pascal, O.C.D. (ed), *Carmelite Digest*, San Jose, CA, California-Arizona Province of Discalced Carmelites, Volumes 1986–1987

Poslusney, Venard, O.Carm., *Attaining Spiritual Maturity for Contemplation*, Locust Valley, NY, Living Flame Press, 1973

Poslusney, Venard, O.Carm. (trans and ed), *Prayer, Aspiration, and Contemplation*, New York, Alba House, 1975

Poslusney, Venard, O.Carm., *The Prayer of Love—The Art of Aspiration*, Locust Valley, NY, Living Flame Press, 1975

Power, Albert, S.J., M.A., *The Maid of Lisieux and Other Papers*, New York and Cincinnati, Frederick Pustet Co., 1932

Ramge, Sebastian V., O.C.D., *An Introduction to the Writings of Saint Teresa*, Chicago, Henry Regnery Co., 1963

Raymond-Barker, Mrs. F.; Sylvain, Abbe Charles (trans), *Life of the Reverend Father Herman*, New York, P. J. Kenedy & Sons, 1925

Rees, Joseph, *Titus Brandsma*, London, Sidgwick & Jackson, 1971

Religious of the Carmel of Pittsford (trans), *Anne of St. Bartholemew*, Madrid, Editorial de Espiritualidad, 1979

Rohrbach, Peter-Thomas, O.C.D., *The Photo Album of St. Therese of Lisieux*, New York, P. J. Kenedy & Sons, 1962

Rohrbach, Peter-Thomas, O.C.D., *The Search for Saint Therese*, Garden City, New York, Hanover House, 1961

Rubio, David, O.S.A., *The Mystic Soul of Spain*, New York, Cosmopolitan Science & Art Service Co., 1946

Sackville-West, V., *The Eagle and the Dove*, Garden City, NY, Doubleday, Doran & Co., 1944

Sancta Teresa de Jesus, *Camino de Perfeccion*, transcripcion, 1965, Tipografia Poliglotta Vaticana

Sanford, John and Paula, *The Elijah Task*, Plainfield, NJ, Logos International, 1977

Saggi, Louis, O.Carm. with Macca, Valentine, O.C.D.; Pausback, Gabriel N., O.Carm. (trans), *Saints of Carmel*, Rome, Carmelite Press, 1972

Sarmiento, Elvira (trans), *Depositions of the Process of St. Teresa of Jesus*, Flemington, NJ, Carmelites, 1969

Schryvers, Joseph, C.SS.R.; Carmel, A Religious of (trans), *The Gift of Oneself*, Bettendorf, Iowa, Carmelite Nuns, 1934; Westminster, MD, Newman Press, 1954, 1955 (reprint)

Sencourt, Robert, *Carmelite and Poet*, London, Hollis and Carter, 1943; New York, Macmillan Co., 1944

Shanley, Kevin, O.Carm. (ed), *The Sword*, Joliet Il., Carmelites of the Canadian-American Province of the Most Pure Heart of Mary, Volumes 1975–1987

Sheed, F. J. (trans), *Collected Letters of Saint Therese of Lisieux*, New York, Sheed & Ward, 1949

Sheppard, Lancelot C., *The English Carmelites*, London, Burns Oates, 1943

Sheppard, Lancelot C., *Barbe Acarie Wife and Mystic*, New York, David McKay Company Inc., 1953

Silverio de Sancta Teresa, R. P., O.D.C., *Saint Teresa of Jesus*, London and Glasgow, Sands & Co., 1947; Westminster, MD, Newman Bookshop, 1948

Sister of the Little Flower, *A Novice of Saint Therese*, Allentown, PA, Carmelite Monastery, 1946

Smet, Joachim, O.Carm. (trans), *A Passion Flower of Carmel*, Chicago, Carmelite Press, 1940

Smet, Joachim, O.Carm., *An Outline of Carmelite History*, Washington, DC, Carmelites, 1966

Smet, Joachim, O.Carm., *The Carmelites*, Rome, Carmelite Institute (private printing), 1975

Society for the Propagation of the Faith, *Shower of Roses Upon the Missions*, New York, Society for the Propagation of the Faith, 1924

Stanislaus of St. Theresa, O.D.C.; Newcomb, James F., P.A., J.C.D. (trans), *St. Theresa Margaret of the Sacred Heart of Jesus*, New York, Chicago, Cincinnati, San Francisco, Benziger Brothers, 1934

Sullivan, John, O.C.D., (ed), *Carmelite Studies Centenary of St. Teresa*, Washington, DC, ICS Publications, 1984

Sullivan, John, O.C.D., *Carmelite Studies—Contemporary Psychology and Carmel*, Washington, DC, ICS Publications, 1982

Sullivan, John, O.C.D., *Carmelite Studies—Spiritual Direction*, Washington, D.C, ICS Publications, 1980

Taylor, Rev. Thomas N. (trans), *Saint Therese of Lisieux, the Little Flower of Jesus*, New York, P. J. Kenedy & Sons, 1926

Taylor, T. N. (ed), *Soeur Therese of Lisieux, the Little Flower of Jesus*, New York, P. J. Kenedy & Sons, 1924

Teresa Margaret, D. C., *I Choose All*, Tenbury Wells, Worcestershire, England, Fowler Wright Books Ltd., 1964

Teresa of Avila; Lewis, David (trans), *The Life of St. Teresa of Jesus*, London, Thomas Baker, 1916 (re-impression)

Teresa of Jesus; Peers, E. Allison (trans), *The Complete Works of Saint Teresa of Jesus*, New York, Sheed & Ward, 1946 (Vol 1), London and New York, Sheed & Ward, 1946 (Vol 2), London, Sheed & Ward, 1949, (Vol 3)

Teresa of Jesus; Carmelite, Discalced (trans), *The Interior Castle*, London and Glasgow, Sands & Co., 1945; Westminster, MD, Newman Press,

Teresa of Jesus; Peers, E. Allison (trans), *Interior Castle*, Garden City, NY, Image Books, 1961

Teresa of Jesus; Peers, E. Allison (trans & ed), *The Letters of Saint Teresa of Jesus*, Westminster, MD, Newman Press, 1950

Teresa of Jesus; Carmelite, Discalced (trans), *The Way of Perfection*, Scotland, Carmelites, 1942

Teresa of Avila; Peers, E. Allison (trans), *The Way of Perfection*, Garden City NY, Image Books, 1964

Teresa of Jesus; Alexander, Alice (trans), *Way of Perfection*, Westminster, MD, Newman Bookshop, 1946

Teresia de Spiritu Sancto, O.C.D.; Hastings, Cecil (trans), Nicholl, Donald (trans), *Edith Stein*, New York, Sheed and Ward, 1952

Therese of Lisieux; Knox, Ronald (trans), *Autobiography of St. Therese of Lisieux*, New York, P. J. Kenedy & Sons, 1958

Therese of Lisieux, Clarke, John, O.C.D., (trans), *Story of a Soul*, Washington, DC, ICS Publications, 1976

Thor-Salviat, Salvator, A.A., S.T.D., *Secrets of a Seraph*, Fatima, Portugal and Downers Grove, Il, Carmelite Third Order Press, 1961

Thuis, Falco J., O.Carm., *In Wonder at the Mystery of God*, Rome, Letter of the Prior General to the Brothers and Sisters of the Carmelite Order, 1983

Valabek, Redemptus M., O.Carm. (ed), *Carmel in the World*, Rome, Institutum Carmelitanum, Volumes 1972 to 1989

Carmelite Daily Missal, Rome, Types Polyglottis Vaticanis, 1953

Prayer Life in Carmel, Rome, Institutem Carmelitanum, 1982

Proper Offices of the Saints of Mount Carmel, Boston, John Cashman & Co., 1896

Van der Kley, Francesca, O.Carm., *Marian Mystic*, Chicago, Carmelite Third Order Press, 1957

Von le Fort, Gertrude; Marx, Olga (trans), *The Song at the Scaffold*, New York, Sheed and Ward, 1933

Von Balthasar, Hans Urs; Nicholl, Donald (trans), *Therese of Lisieux*, London and New York, Sheed and Ward, 1953, 1954

Walsh, William Thomas, *Saint Teresa of Avila*, Milwaukee, Bruce Publishing, 1943

Walter, Leo J., O.Carm., (trans), *Life in Carmel*, Chicago, Carmelite Press, 1934

Williams, Michael, *The Little Flower of Carmel*, New York, P. J. Kenedy & Sons, 1925

Williamson, Benedict, *The Doctrinal Mission and Apostolate of St. Therese of Lisieux*, London, Alexander Ouseley, 1932

Williamson, Benedict, *The Sure Way*, London, Kegan Paul, Trench, Trubner & Co., and St. Louis, B. Herder, 1933

Williamson, Benedict, *The Victim State*, St. Louis, B. Herder, 1938

Williamson, Benedict (intro), *The World and the Cloister*, St. Louis, B. Herder Book Co., 1931

Windeatt, Mary Fabyan, *Little Queen*, St. Meinrad, IN, Grail Publication, 1950

Wojtyla, Karol, *Faith According to St. John of the Cross*, San Francisco, Ignatius Press, 1981 (translation of original doctoral theses presented at Pontifical University of St. Thomas Aquinas, Rome)

Wu, John C. H., *The Interior Carmel*, New York, Sheed & Ward, 1953

Wust, Louis and Marjorie, *Louis Martin an Ideal Father*, Boston, Daughters of St. Paul, 1953, 1957

Wust, Louis and Marjorie, *Zelie Martin Mother of St. Therese*, Boston, Daughters of St. Paul, 1969

GERONTOLOGICAL REFERENCES

Beauvoir, Simone de., (Trans. by O'Brian, Patrick), *The Coming of Age*, New York, G. P. Putnam's Sons, 1972

Becker, Arthur M., *Ministry with Older Persons*, Minneapolis, Augsburg Publishing House, 1986

Bianchi, Eugene C., *Aging as a Spiritual Journey*, New York, Crossroads Publishing Co., 1982

Botivinick, Jack, Ph.d., *Aging and Behavior*, New York, Springer Publishing Company Inc., 1973

Brickner, Philip W., M.D., F.A.C.P., *Care of the Nursing Home Patient*, New York, The Macmillan Company, 1971

Brungs, Robert A., S.J., *Towards a Theology of Health Care*, Art. Review for Religious, Vol. 45, Num. 1, Jan. Feb. 1986

Burgess, Ernest W., *Retirement Villages*, Michigan, Division of Gerontology 1961

Burnside, Irene, *Working with the Elderly*. Group Process and Techniques. Monterey, California. Wadsworth Health Sciences Division Publisher

Calhoun, Gerald J., *Pastoral Companionship, Ministry with Seriously Ill Persons and their Families*, Mahwah, N.J., Paulist Press, 1986

Campbell, Alastari V., *A Dictionary of Pastoral Care*, New York, Crossroad 1987

Carmody, John, *Holistic Spirituality*, New York, Paulist Press, 1983

Clements, William M., *Ministry with the Aging*, San Francisco, Harper and Row, 1981

Congregations for the Doctrine of the Faith, *Declaration on Euthanasia*, Origins, Aug. 14, 1980

Donahue, Wilma, and Tibbitts, Clark, *Politics of Age*, Michigan, Division of Gerontology 1961

Eyde, Donna R., Ph.D., Rich, Jay A., M.D., *Psychological Distress in Aging*, Rockville, Maryland. An Aspen Publication, 1983

Feder, Judith, and Hadley, Jack, *Cardinal Bernadin and the Survival of Catholic Hospitals, and Preferential Option for the Poor*, Georgetown university, Center of Health Policy Studies (Origins, June 30, 1985).

Fichter, Joseph H., S.J., *Healing Ministry Conversations on the Spiritual Dimensions of Health Care*, Mahwah, N.J., Paulist Press, 1986

Freeman, Joseph J., M.D., F.A.C.P., *Aging Its History and Literature*, New York, London, Human Sciences Press, 1979

Gusmer, Charles W., *And You Visited Me, Sacramental Ministry to the Sick and Dying*, New York, Pueblo Pub. Co., 1984

Haring, Bernhard, C.SS.R., *In Pursuit of Wholeness* Healing in Today's Church, MO., Liguori Press, 1987

Herold, Duchesne, SSM, MS., *New Life—Preparation of Religious for Retirement*, St. Louis, Missouri, The Catholic Hospital Association, 1973

Hogstel, Mildred O., *Nursing Care of the Older Adult*, New York, A. Wiley Medical Publication, 1981

Hooper, Celia R., and Dunkle, Ruth E., *The Older Aphasic Person*, Rockville, Md., Aspen Systems Corporation, 1984

Johnson, Colleen L., and Grant, Leslie A., *The Nursing Home in American Society*, Baltimore, Maryland, The John Hopkins University Press, 1985

Johnson, Richard, Ph.D., *Aging Parents—How to Understand and Help Them*, MO., Liguori Press, 1987

Kalish, Richard A., *The Later Years—Social Applications of Gerontology*, California, Brooks/Cole Publishing Company, 1977

Kastenbaum, Robert, Ph.D., *New Thoughts on Old Age*, New York, Springer Publishing Company, Inc., 1964

Kubler-Ross, Elizabeth, M.D., *On Death and Dying*, New York, MacMillan, Third Edition, 1972

Lawton, M. Powell and Newcomer, Robert J., Byerts, Thomas O., *Community Planning for an Aging Society*, Stroudsburg, Penn., Dowden, Hutchingen and Ross, Inc. 1976

Leeds, Morton, and Shore, Herbert, *Geriatric Institutional Management*, New York, G. P. Putnams Sons, 1964

Maxwell, Marjorie Eleanor, *The Blessing of Old Age—An Anthology*, London, Faber and Faber, 1939

Mendelson, Mary Adelaide, *Tender Loving Greed*, New York, Vintage Books, 1975

Miller, Dulcy B., and Barry, Jane T., *Nursing Home Organization and Operation*, Boston, Mass., CBI Publishing Company, Inc., 1979

Monk, Abraham, *The Age of Aging*, New York, Prometheus Books, 1979

Moss, Frank E., J.D., and Halamandaris, Val J., J.D., *Too Old Too Sick Too Bad*, Maryland, Aspen Systems Corporation, 1977

National Conference of Catholic Bishops, Committee for Pro-Life Activities, *Guidelines for Legislation on Life Sustaining Treatment*, Origins, Nov. 10, 1984

Nouwen, Henri J.M., Gaffney, Walter J., *Aging*, New York, Doubleday and Company, Inc., 1974

Osgood, Nancy J., Ph.D., *Suicide in the Elderly*, Maryland, An Aspen Publication, 1985

Pegelsl, C. Carl., *Health Care and the Elderly*, Rockville, Maryland, An Aspen Publication, 1981

Riley, Matilda White, Riley, John W., Jr., and Johnson, Marilyn E., *Aging and Society Vol. II*, New York, Russell Sage Foundation, 1969

Schlicht, R.W., *The Care of the Soul*, Nebraska, Interstate Printing Company, 1984

Smith, Bradford, *Dear Gift of Life, A Man's Encounter with Death*, Lebanon, Pa., Pendle Hill Publication, 1978

Somers, D. Sc., Anne R., and Fabian, Dorothy, R., Ed. D., *The Geriatric Imperative: An Introduction to Gerontology & Clinical Geriatrics*, New York, Appleton-Century-Crofts, 1981

Terreuive, Anna A., M.D., and Baars, Conrad W., M.D., *Psychic Wholeness and Healing*, New York, Alba House, 1981

Thorson, James A., and Cook, Thomas C., *Spiritual Well-Being of the Elderly*, Illinois, Charles C. Thomas Publishing, 1980

Today's English Version, *Good News for Modern Man*, New York, American Bible Society

Williams, Richard H., Tibbitts, Clark., Donahue, Wilma, *Process of Aging*, Social and Psychological Perspectives, Vol. II, New York, Atherton Press, 1963

Rarhbone-McCuan, Eloise, and Hashimi, Joan, *Isolated Elders*, Maryland, An Aspen Publication, 1982

INDEX

99